TheCowboy**Trail**

TheCowboy**Trail**
A Guide to Alberta's Historic Cowboy Country
(no horse required)

D. Larraine Andrews
illustrations by Janet Nash

BlueC O U C H**Books**

Library and Archives Canada Cataloguing in Publication
Andrews, Larraine, 1953–
The Cowboy Trail : a guide to Alberta's historic cowboy
country / D. Larraine Andrews.

Includes bibliographical references and index.
ISBN 1-894739-04-3

1. Highway 22 (Alta.)—Guidebooks. 2. Rocky Mountains,
Canadian (B.C. and Alta.)—Guidebooks. 3. Automobile travel—Rocky
Mountains, Canadian (B.C. and Alta.)—Guidebooks. I. Title.

FC3695.F66A52 2005   917.123'3   C2005-902170-5

Front cover photo: Great Bear Enterprises
Back cover photo: Walter Danylak
Interior photos: Credit is listed below each photo
Interior illustrations: Janet Nash

Blue Couch Books
an imprint of Brindle & Glass Publishing
www.bluecouchbooks.com

Brindle & Glass is committed to protecting the environment and to the
responsible use of natural resources. This book is printed on
100% post-consumer recycled and ancient-forest-friendly paper.
For more information please visit www.oldgrowthfree.com.

1   2   3   4   5   09   08   07   06

PRINTED AND BOUND IN CANADA

Cowboy — cowpoke, cowpuncher, buckaroo;
a person who herds and tends cattle.

CONTENTS

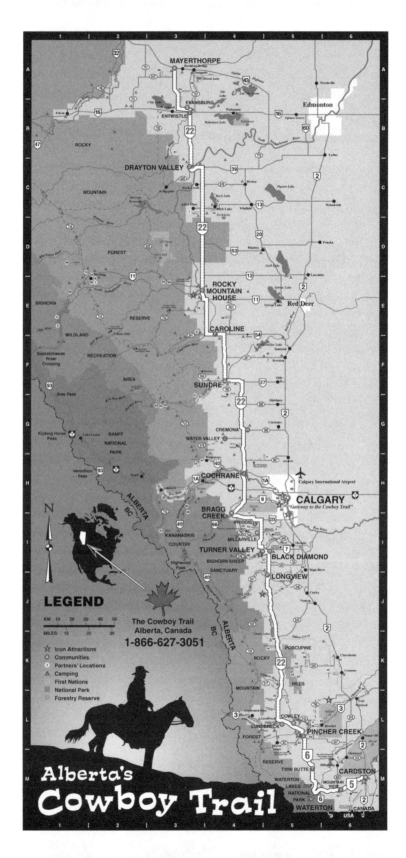

LEGEND

KM 10 20 30 40 50
MILES 10 20 30

The Cowboy Trail
Alberta, Canada
1-866-627-3051

★ Icon Attractions
○ Communities
❶ Partners' Locations
△ Camping
◻ First Nations
◼ National Park
◼ Forestry Reserve

N

ALBERTA
BC

Alberta's
Cowboy Trail

Accommodations

- Art on the Range Gallery Studio Bed & Breakfast & Bale MAP: E-3
- Aspen Village Inn MAP: M-5
- Aurum Lodge and Cottages MAP: E-1
- Big Springs Estate Bed and Breakfast Inn MAP: H-5
- Blue Sky Motel MAP: J-5
- Bow Rivers Edge Campground MAP: H-4
- Brewster's Kananaskis Guest Ranch MAP: H-3
- Camp 'n' Fun Adventures MAP: E-2
- Chain Lakes Provincial Park MAP: K-5
- Cheechako Cabins MAP: D-2
- Chimney Rock Bed and Breakfast MAP: K-5
- Crandell Mountain Lodge MAP: M-5
- Grandview Stage Resort MAP: E-3
- Hilltop Ranch Bed and Breakfast MAP: I-4
- Kramer Pond Lodge MAP: C-4
- Lone Pine Ranch Bed and Breakfast and Bale MAP: B-3
- Lyndon Creek Cottage MAP: K-5
- Mountain-Aire Lodge Motel and Campground MAP: G-3
- Mount Engadine Lodge MAP: I-3
- Mountain View Market and Motel MAP: M-6
- Myown River Ranch MAP: F-3
- Nordegg Resort Lodge MAP: D-2
- Parkway Motel and Hostel MAP: L-5
- Rockyview Hotel and Canyon Rose Steakhouse
- Rustic Ridge Ranch and Lodge MAP: A-3
- Rustlers Guest Lodge MAP: F-4
- South Country Inn and Yotee's Restaurant MAP: M-6
- Sundance Lodges MAP: H-3
- Sundre Hotel MAP: F-4
- Super 8 Motel Drayton Valley MAP: C-3
- The Barn on Whiskey Hill Bed and Breakfast MAP: I-4
- The Glenmore Inn and Convention Centre MAP: H-5
- Twin Cities Hotel MAP: J-5
- Two Country Inns MAP: M-6
- Walking Eagle Inn and Lodge MAP: E-3
- Welcome Acres Bed and Breakfast MAP: I-4

Attractions and Events

- Caroline Wheels of Time Museum MAP: E-3
- Carriage House Theatre MAP: M-6
- Em-Te-Town MAP: C-3
- Great Canadian Barn Dance and Family Campground MAP: M-6
- Heritage Acres MAP: L-5
- Icefield Helicopter Tours MAP: E-1
- Leighton Art Centre Museum and Gallery MAP: I-5
- Millarville Racing and Agricultural Society MAP: I-5
- Nordegg Heritage Centre and Industrial Museum MAP: D-2
- Rocky Mountain Acres Inc. MAP: M-5

FOREWORD

Ah! For the life of the cowboy! To be part of the romance and history of the Old West! Trailin' the great herds north, eatin' your grub 'round the campfire at night, and sleepin' under the stars on the vast open range.

Whoa there, pardner! You might want to take a reality check on that. The world of the real Canadian cowboy in the late 1800s was so far from our image, he would snort in disgust. Want to be a real cowboy? Get ready for lots of hard work and mind-numbing boredom mixed with the occasional terror of a stampede. Just signed on? Then no doubt you'll be eatin' dust at the back of the herd 'til you can prove yourself. You can look forward to ornery cows and half-broke broncos, and lots of beans for supper. And don't forget the night shifts, sometimes in the rain or snow – and you shivering in the cold, just hopin' a wolf or a streak of lightning won't set those dogies runnin' halfway 'cross the country. Got plans for retiring on your two-bit pay? Maybe the boys will dig you a hole deep enough to keep the varmints out.

Okay, so it wasn't as good as the movies and the pulp novels make it look. We know there's a big difference between the romance of a Hollywood western or a story by Louis L'Amour and the reality of the Old West, even if we don't want to admit it. Still, the mystique of the cowboy life continues to capture our imagination. Sure, the days of the open range are long gone. Today, most cowboys can count on a warm bed to sleep in and more than beans for supper (although the retirement fund may yet be an issue). But there are still plenty of cattle to be tended and horses to be broke, though there's probably a lot more fence fixin' than they would care to admit. In 1907, a *Calgary Daily News* reporter summed up his view of the cowboy life this way: "In spite of the long hours, the hard work, the inclement weather; in spite of the danger, the solitude; in spite of all these discomforts, men are fascinated by the life." And that hasn't changed. Maybe it's because, once we look beyond the trappings of fancy boots and tight-fitting jeans, we still admire the independent spirit, sheer grit, and determination it takes for today's real cowboys (and cowgirls) to stay doing what they do best – in the last best west, where the land is still wild and even now there's plenty of long hours, hard work, and solitude. The last best west – it still exists, you know. And you will find it as you drive the length of the Cowboy Trail. It's not a myth.

INTRODUCTION

Welcome to the Cowboy Trail, where you don't need a horse to find the "last best west." From Cardston to Mayerthorpe the trail snakes its way along Highways 5, 6, and 22, following the eastern slopes of Alberta's Rocky Mountains for a distance of over 700 kilometres. In the early 1880s, cowboys were drawn here by the moderate climate and the vast rangelands that were ideal for cattle. They trailed large herds north from Montana and Idaho to establish ranches along the foothills of the Rockies. It was the beginning of a ranching heritage that continues to thrive along the entire length of the Cowboy Trail. Now you can drive the trail in the comfort of your car. In the process, you will pass through a spectacular diversity of prairies, foothills, montane, mountains, aspen parkland, and boreal forest, not to mention some of the best ranching country in North America. Along the way, you will meet an extraordinary variety of people who take great pride in their western way of life and the culture that surrounds it. After all, they live it every day.

I found it first-hand on ranches where third- and fourth-generation families are working hard to preserve a way of life that has sustained this land for well over 100 years. I found it in the small towns and villages where western traditions are proudly preserved and celebrated in their rodeos, parades, and festivals. I found it in the restaurants and coffee shops where you can tie into some of the best beef in the world – probably raised just down the road – and where locals still come to meet their neighbours and commiserate on the price of cattle. I found it in the shops and galleries where talented local artisans are creating western art and crafts of exceptional quality, and in the museums and interpretive centres where you can learn the incredible story of the West.

Get out on the trail, and you can find it too. Expect to be overwhelmed with Western hospitality, good food, and the chance to ride a horse until your butt won't take any more. Help trail a cattle herd into the backcountry and eat your meals over a campfire. Get your hands dirty if you want to. Maybe you prefer to look at horses, not ride them. Maybe you prefer your beef on a plate served up with all the fixin's. No problem. With over 100 partners and over 20 small communities, the trail offers an incredible diversity of options for exploring our rich western heritage – everything from backcountry outfitters, farm and ranch vacations, cozy bed and breakfasts, attractions and events all celebrating the culture of the West – no horse required. Your only limit will be your time and your imagination.

How to Use This Book

Since the trail basically extends in a more or less straight line from south to north, you can choose to enter and leave it at whatever points fit your time, budget, and inclination. Take a day drive, take a week. There's plenty here to keep you coming back for many seasons, and while many Cowboy Trail partners do not operate during the winter, there are a number who are open year-round. (Dates of operation are included in each partner description.) Many offer winter activities such as cross-country skiing and snowshoeing, so you certainly aren't limited to summer excursions. This book is designed geographically and arbitrarily follows the course of the trail from its most southern point in Cardston to "Denny Hay Drive," the so-called end of the trail in Mayerthorpe. Each chapter provides a detailed map indexed to descriptions of the Cowboy Trail partners you will find along the way, mixed in with lots of local ranching and cowboy history, cowboy and native facts (and lore), recipes, and general information on each area to help you make the most of the time you have available. Look for "critter watch" notes on local wildlife, suggestions for drives off the beaten path, and a listing of books relating to the history of the area. A brief events list is also provided at the beginning of each chapter, but be sure to check out the Cowboy Trail website at www.thecowboytrail.com for a complete calendar. For cowboys with their own horses, there are a number of partners who offer horse-boarding facilities and the chance to ride in the backcountry on authentic cattle drives or trail rides using your own mount, without the worries of organizing meals and accommodations. Partners who supply these services are identified in the detailed index at the front of each chapter.

Icons

The following icons have been used throughout the book to help you quickly identify particular services and activities.

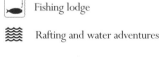

Abbreviations for Payment Options

A number of the partners accept credit cards, traveller's cheques, and personal cheques. The following abbreviations have been used to indicate the forms of payment taken at each establishment. Of course, it probably goes without saying, cold hard cash is always welcome too. (Please note that prices have not been included, since they tend to vary on a seasonal basis. Your best bet is to contact the partner directly for the most up-to-date fee schedule.)

>Debit – D
>Visa – V
>MasterCard – MC
>American Express – AMEX
>Diners Club – DC
>Discover – DIS
>EnRoute – ER
>Traveller's Cheques – TC
>Personal Cheques – PC
>Money Orders – MO
>Certified Cheque – CC

Other Abbreviations

>Bed and breakfast – B&B
>Range road – RR
>Township road – TWP

A Word About the Road System in Alberta

The original survey of the prairies, by the Dominion Land Survey, used the township system calculated in miles. Range roads run north–south every mile, and township roads run east–west every two miles. One mile equals 1.6 kilometres. You will usually find a sign at the intersections with township roads (identified as TWP) and range roads (identified as RR). As you travel north, the TWP road numbers increase. RR numbers increase as you go west. If you cross a meridian, the RR numbers begin repeating. The only place you will encounter this on the Cowboy Trail is in the very southern portion of the province, where you cross the Fifth Meridian just west of Pincher Creek. Some counties and municipal districts use a slightly different system to display the numbers on their signs. For example, you might see RR 3-2, RR 3.2 or RR 32, depending on which municipality you are in. To add to the possible confusion, the MD of Foothills, which borders Calgary to the south, uses a street/avenue system similar to that in a city, with the streets running north–south (like a RR) and avenues running east–west (like a TWP). The map at the beginning of each chapter, together with the partner descriptions, clearly indicate the directions and the distances, but you should always use the latest road map.

Back Road Driving

Many of the partners and attractions on the Cowboy Trail are located off the main highway on rural roads. Once you get on to the back roads, you are much more likely to encounter slow-moving farm vehicles or stray cattle. It can also mean driving on gravel for part of your journey. Dry gravel is not slippery, but excess gravel on the road can unexpectedly pull your vehicle off course. It's one of the reasons that rural residents have a habit of driving down the middle of the road, so keep your eye open for approaching dust and always take care when you are coming to the top of a hill or entering a curve. Remember that stopping times on gravel are generally longer than on pavement. Don't forget that flying gravel isn't just annoying – it can be dangerous for pedestrians and approaching traffic. Most rural drivers are careful to slow down when meeting an oncoming vehicle to avoid cracking your windshield with a stray rock – be sure to extend the same courtesy to them.

The main rule is to remain alert and slow down! Most of the railway crossings will be uncontrolled, so it's usually a good idea to come to a complete stop and have a good look before proceeding. Expect the unexpected. If you cross a cattle guard (otherwise known as a Texas gate, see page 57), there is a good chance you will encounter cattle or horses on the road, since you are probably driving in a grazing area. There will often be signs warning of cattle at large once you cross the guard.

You are also far more likely to come across cowboys moving cattle down a rural road. Many ranchers will place warning signs that a cattle drive is in progress, but this isn't always the case. Good cattle drive etiquette requires you to stop and wait for one of the riders to tell you what to do. Usually, one of them will ride in front of the vehicle and escort you through the herd. Don't get impatient! Slow down and enjoy the sight. This is the country, after all, and you should expect a few delays.

One last word on trespassing. You wouldn't do it in the city, so why do it here? Besides, you never know when you might come across an ornery bull that can outrun you.

Basic Rules for Watching Wildlife

It's important to remember that when you are watching wildlife, you are intruding on their territory. You are the spectator and it is up to you to make sure you don't cross the line from passive watching to the point where they perceive you as a threat. Different animals have different comfort zones. The main thing is to use some common sense. Always keep a safe distance and never feed wildlife. Even organic litter like fruit peels and apple cores should never be dumped on the ground, since it attracts wildlife and can help turn them into junk food junkies. Don't let an animal get into a situation where it feels trapped; it may become aggressive. Keep a close eye on children and dogs, which can startle or disturb animals.

When you are driving, pay close attention to the signs along the highway that warn of wildlife in the area – they are there for a reason. And slow down! It can be particularly dangerous at night when animals like deer and moose may be temporarily blinded by your headlights and step out in front of the vehicle. If you do spot an animal that you want to stop and watch, make sure you pull well off the road when it is safe for you, the animal, and other traffic on the highway. It is usually a good idea to stay in your car and take your photos from there.

Camping

Many of the partners offer camping facilities. There are also a number of provincial campgrounds along the way. Details about camping are provided in each chapter. If tenting doesn't appeal to you, but you would like the freedom offered by a recreation vehicle, check out CanaDream Campers at www.canadream.com (or toll-free at 1-800-461-7368). They offer a wide variety of campers and motorhomes for rent.

Associations Affiliated with the Cowboy Trail:

Alberta Country Vacations Association, www.albertacountryvacation.com, 1-866-217-2282; Brazeau Regional Tourism Association, www.brazeautourism.ca, 1-800-633-0899; Chinook Country Tourist Association, www.chinookcountry.com, 1-800-661-1222; Diamond Valley Chamber, www.diamondvalleychamber.com, 403-933-7890; Kananaskis Valley of Adventure, www.kananaskisvalley.com; Nordegg West Tourism Association, www.travelnordegg.com; The Cowboy Trail Tourism Association, www.thecowboytrail.com, 1-866-627-3051.

A number of partners offer packaged tours if you prefer the option of letting someone else make all the arrangements:

Creative Western Adventures Ltd., www.creativewestern.com, 1-866-333-7717; Home on the Range Adventure Tours Ltd., www.homeontherange.ca, 1-866-760-8334; Rocky Mountain Acres Inc., www.rockymountainacres.ca, 403-627-4335 (page 42); The Cowboy Trail Tourism Association Travel Packages, www.thecowboytrail.com, 1-866-627-3051; Trail of the Great Bear, www.trailofthegreatbear.com, 1-800-215-2395 (page 33).

What to Bring for Trail Riding in the Backcountry

The general rule with respect to weather in Alberta is that there is no rule about the weather in Alberta – measurable amounts of snow have been recorded in every month of the year here – and your chances of running into unseasonable weather are greatly increased in the mountain backcountry. Come prepared for all kinds of weather: rain, snow, and sun. You can count on cool evenings, especially at higher elevations.

Be sure to bring clothes you can put on and peel off in layers as the temperature changes through the day. A waterproof topcoat is a must, but make sure it is the proper length – long enough to keep you dry, but not so long that it will start flapping and annoying your horse. Shorts are definitely not a good idea. Bare legs and backcountry brush and bugs are not a good combination. It's worth it to invest in a good pair of heavy-duty jeans, with a flat inside seam to prevent chafing after several days in the saddle, to protect your legs from stray branches flipping back to whack you when you least expect it.

If you don't have a pair of cowboy boots, then bring something that is waterproof with a good heel to prevent your foot from slipping through the stirrup and getting caught – a potentially dangerous situation if you happen to fall off your horse. Since the stirrups are normally leather, it is a good idea to have footwear with ridged rubber soles, again to prevent your foot from slipping. Don't forget a good hat, some gloves, sunglasses (despite the above caution about snow, southern Alberta experiences some of the most hours of sunshine anywhere in Canada), and the ubiquitous bandana. (There's a reason it's called the "101" – there are supposed to be at least 101 uses for it out here in the Wild West.)

Riding Fitness

If you haven't been on a horse for a while, it is definitely worth your time to invest in some pre-vacation "limbering up" exercises before you hit the trail. Otherwise you will be sore in places you didn't even know existed, and this could ruin the first few days of your trip. It is well worth the effort to take some time in the weeks leading up to your vacation to include a simple regimen of stretching exercises in your daily routine. You will be glad you did when you can get off your horse and walk normally after six or seven hours in the saddle.

Information for Foreign and Out-of-Province Visitors

Booking Ahead: Many of the partners along the Cowboy Trail cater to foreign and out-of-province visitors and are easily accessible through email. Those that offer riding and ranch activities tend to book up quickly each summer, so make sure you start your planning well ahead of your arrival date to avoid disappointment. A few of them also offer services in other languages besides English, including Dutch and German.

Almost all the partners have well-developed websites that will often give you more detailed information than you will find in this book. Many of them offer vacation packages customized to the time you have available and the activities and events that are a priority for you. If you want to see a local rodeo or shop at a local western store, just ask. Chances are good that if a partner can't accommodate you, they will know someone who can. Some of the partners have teamed up with others along the trail to offer you a chance to sample different activities and at the same time to experience some of the broad ecological diversity that is such a highlight of what the trail has to offer.

Getting Here: The Cowboy Trail is readily accessible from either the Calgary or Edmonton International Airports. You can check the websites for detailed information on international airlines that use these airports at www.calgaryairport.com and www.edmontonairports.com. Many of the partners offer return airport transportation right from their ranches, so you won't even need to rent a car, but this must be booked in advance.

Money and Banking Facilities: Many partners and places along the trail accept traveller's cheques and some will even accept them in us dollars although you are probably better off to exchange these into Canadian cash at a bank in order to get the best rate. Automated teller machines (ATMs) are widely available, even in the smallest towns and villages along the trail, and many banks are open late on Thursdays and Fridays (but are closed on weekends).

Health and Emergency Services: Health care services are readily available in all the major cities. Towns along the trail that have hospitals include:

      Cardston: 403-653-4411
      Pincher Creek: 403-627-1234
      Black Diamond: 403-933-2222
      Sundre: 403-638-3033
      Rocky Mountain House: 403-845-3347
      Drayton Valley: 780-542-5321
      Mayerthorpe: 780-786-2261
      Emergency Services can be accessed by dialing 911.

It is important to have travel insurance before you leave home, since you will be billed for the services you use. Pharmacies are generally available in all but the smallest communities.

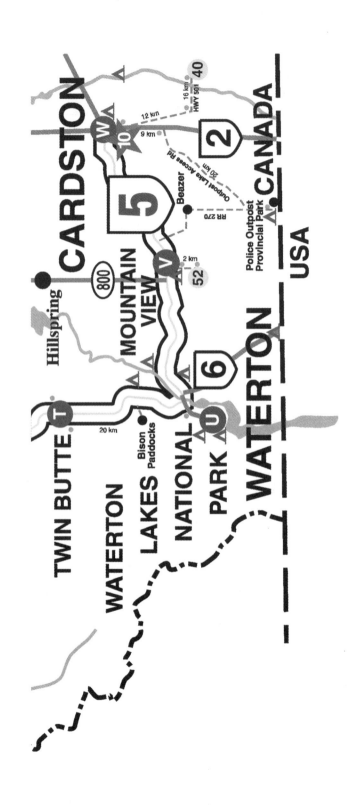

1 :   C A R D S T O N   T O   W A T E R T O N

"The only good thing you can say about tight boots is that they'll make you forget your other troubles."
—Ted Stone, *Cowboy Logic*

Communities

Ⓦ Cardston

Ⓤ Mountain View

Ⓥ Waterton Park

Accommodations

Ⓦ South Country Inn and Yotee's Restaurant

Ⓦ The Cobblestone Manor

Ⓥ Rocky Ridge Country Resort (Two Country Inns)

Ⓥ Mountain View Market and Motel

Ⓥ Mountain View Inn (Two Country Inns)

Ⓤ Aspen Village Inn

Ⓤ Crandell Mountain Lodge

Attractions & Events

Ⓦ Carriage House Theatre

Farm & Ranch Vacations

㊵ Rangeview Ranch

Outfitters

㊾ Mountain Meadow Trail Rides

Ⓤ Tamarack Village Square

Restaurants

Ⓦ Remington Carriage Museum Restaurant

Ⓦ South Country Inn and Yotee's Restaurant

Ⓦ The Cobblestone Manor

Shopping, Antiques & Artisans

Ⓦ Remington Carriage Museum

Ⓥ Mountain View Market and Motel

Ⓤ Tamarack Village Square

Ⓤ Trail of the Great Bear Gift Shop

Icon Attractions

 Remington Carriage Museum

MAJOR EVENTS ALONG THE TRAIL

(see www.thecowboytrail.com for a complete listing)

May
High Stakes Barrel Race, Cardston
South Country Derby, Cardston

June
Art Show, Cobblestone Manor
Waterton International French Film Festival, Waterton Park
Waterton Wild Flower Festival, Waterton Park

July
World Championship Miniature Chuckwagon Races, Remington Carriage Museum

August
Heritage Week Fair and Rodeo, Cardston
South Country Reining Futurity, Cardston

September
South Country Barrel Racing, Cardston

Belly-busters — one of many descriptive terms for baking-powder biscuits; also known as hot rocks or sinkers

(w) **Cardston**   www.town.cardston.ab.ca
     T: 1-888-434-3366

Blackfoot name – *akokimi*, meaning "many wives," because the early Mormon settlers practiced polygamy.

Cardston was named after Charles Ora Card, who was the son-in-law of
Mormon leader Brigham Young. In 1887 Card led a large group of Mormon settlers from Utah into southern Alberta on one of the last covered wagon migrations
of the century. They were fleeing harsh anti-polygamy laws in the US. The story is
that when cowboys from the nearby Cochrane Ranch (see sidebar page 171) told
William Cochrane that the Mormons were tearing up good grassland to farm,
Cochrane wasn't too worried, telling his men, "They'll winter kill." He was wrong.
The Mormons thrived, establishing the first irrigation projects in the south. In fact,
in 1905 the Mormon Church bought out the Cochrane Ranch, and opened the land
for settlement to their members.
Modern-day Cardston is a prosperous   Bang-tail — a wild horse
town of about 3,500, serving a mainly
rural trading area of 15,000. It boasts
several attractions that are definitely worth a look, but one you shouldn't miss is
the Remington Carriage Museum, voted Best Indoor Tourist Attraction in Canada
in 2002 by Attractions Canada.

OFF THE BEATEN PATH FROM CARDSTON

Police Outpost Provincial Park – From Cardston, take Hwy. 2 south for 9 KM, then turn
west on the Outpost Lake Access Road for about 20 KM. The park is located just north of the
international boundary and offers camping on a first-come, first-served basis, as well as
some of the finest fishing and hiking in the province. The NWMP established the Boundary
Creek Outpost here in 1891 to discourage whiskey runners from coming across the border.
The Outpost Wetlands are one of the most productive bird habitats in the region, and
panoramic views of Chief Mountain and the Rockies are stunning. You can head back to
Hwy. 5 via RR 270 and Secondary Hwy. 501 through the ghost town of Beazer.

Heavy horses strut their stuff.
REMINGTON CARRIAGE MUSEUM

Remington Carriage Museum   www.RemingtonCarriageMuseum.com
623 Main Street, P.O. Box 1649, Cardston, AB, T0K 0K0
T: 403-653-5139 (toll-free in Alberta by first dialing 310-0000)
E: info@RemingtonCarriageMuseum.com
ACCEPTS V, MC   ADMISSION CHARGED
Open daily, May 15 to September 14, 9:00 AM to 6:00 PM; September 15 to May 14, 10:00 AM to 5:00 PM; Restaurant open 10:00 AM to 5:00 PM daily, evening menu Thursday to Saturday, 5:00 PM to 9:00 PM, evening buffet Friday and Saturday.

Don Remington wasn't kidding when he said, "This hobby can drive you buggy." It all began in 1954 when the Cardston Rotary Club nominated Don to organize the annual Santa Claus parade. He thought Santa should arrive on a sleigh rather than in a truck as he had in the past. Don managed to hunt up an old sleigh near Marysville, BC, but it needed some work to make it usable. So began a lifelong hobby that eventually led to the 63,000-square-foot museum that sits just off Main Street in downtown Cardston.

Over the course of more than 35 years, Don and his wife, Afton, travelled all over North America and England collecting carriages and coaches, which Don then proceeded to restore. His painstaking attention to detail and extensive research helped ensure each piece was as authentic as he could make it.

TOM THREE PERSONS TAMES THE MIGHTY CYCLONE

Tom Three Persons was a Blood Indian born in 1886 at Standoff, just north of Cardston. At the first Calgary Stampede in 1912 he won the saddle bronc championship aboard the legendary black bronc called Cyclone. A *Calgary Daily Herald* reporter described his ride this way: "The horse thrown to the ground, Tom jumped across him, placed his feet in the stirrups, and with a wild 'whoop' the black demon was up and away with the Indian rider. Bucking, twisting, swapping ends and resorting to every artifice of the outlaw, Cyclone swept across the field. The Indian was jarred from one side of the saddle to the other, but as the crowds cheered themselves hoarse he settled every time into the saddle and waited for the next lurch or twist. His

Tom Three Persons during the 1912 Calgary Stampede.
GLENBOW ARCHIVES NA-335-79

bucking unable to dislodge the man, Cyclone stood at rest and reared straight up. Once it looked as though Tom was to follow the fate of his predecessors. He recovered rapidly and from that time forward, Cyclone bucked till he was tired. The Indian had mastered him." Tom became a wealthy rancher on the Blood Reserve and was inducted into the Canadian Rodeo Hall of Fame in 1983.

By 1985 he owned 49 fine carriages, most of which had been carefully restored in his own workshop. He offered to donate the entire collection to the Province of Alberta on the condition that the Province would build a museum to house and display it and that the building would be located in Cardston. The Glenbow Museum in Calgary, the Provincial Museum in Edmonton, and the Reynolds-Alberta Museum in Wetaskiwin all donated additional vehicles to make up the total of more than 250 vehicles now on display in the Remington Museum.

The museum sits on a 20-acre site adjacent to Lee Creek and is the largest collection of horse-drawn vehicles in North America. Visitors can begin their tour in the theatre, where the film *The Wheels of Change* introduces them to a bygone era when elegant horse-drawn carriages carried the rich in high style, and stagecoaches transported travellers across a continent. The main exhibit gallery houses 16 displays with over 50 vehicles arranged in a series of vignettes. Each portrays a scene from life as it was in the late 19th and early 20th century, before a newfangled contraption called a car sounded the death knell for horse-drawn vehicles. Interpretive panels and theatrical sets tell the stories behind the elegant landaus, broughams, and barouches, and the opening of the west with bull wagons, Red River carts, and chuckwagons. School vans and stagecoaches, fire wagons and elaborate hearses – each played a role on the frontier and each has a story that is well told here.

Belly-busters – one of many descriptive terms for baking-powder biscuits; also known as hot rocks or sinkers

Only a small portion of the collection is on display in the main gallery, but unlike most museums, visitors have viewing access to the vehicle storage room. The centre also maintains a fully operational shop where members of the public can watch technicians at work and ask questions about the restoration process. The Tack Room contains an outstanding collection of harnesses, including a fully harnessed life-size horse model.

Of course you can't have horse-drawn vehicles without horses. The centre keeps its own Clydesdale, quarter horse, and Canadian horses in a stable on the property. Carriage and wagon rides are offered on a seasonal basis, and the Great Lawn is an ideal place to relax and have a picnic after your tour.

In addition to the museum, you will find two other Cowboy Trail partners in town.

South Country Inn and Yotee's Restaurant   www.southcountryinn.ca
404 Main Street, P.O. Box 1710, Cardston, AB, T0K 0K0
T: 1-888-653-2615
ACCEPTS V, MC, AMEX, TC
Open all year; Restaurant open 6:00 AM to midnight in the summer; 6:00 AM to 10:00 PM in the winter

WHAT THE SOUTH COUNTRY INN OFFERS: 45 air-conditioned guest rooms (90 per cent non-smoking), including spa and executive suites with king-size beds, two-bedroom family suites with TV, some adjoining rooms, and a handicap room with adjoining companion room. Services include Internet access, cable TV, indoor pool and spa (open 24 hours in the summer season), 24-hour fitness centre one block away, guest laundry, tanning booth, fridge and microwave on request, room service from nearby Yotee's Restaurant. Popular packages include Romance, Golf, Theatre (at the Carriage House Theatre), and Raft and Ride.

WHAT YOTEE'S RESTAURANT OFFERS: A large menu with a good selection of appetizers (including coyote wings, rooster tails, and boneless ribs), salads and sandwiches (including the Roast Beef City and the Three-Storey Bunkhouse), dips, wraps, pasta, and a wide variety of entrees. The restaurant is well-known by the locals for its fresh soup and salad bar and specializes in steaks, chicken, and ribs. A popular roast beef buffet and salad bar is featured every Friday and a breakfast buffet on Saturday morning. Breakfasts offer a wide choice. You can even try a Grizzly Bear Waffle.

The Cobblestone Manor   www.thecobblestonemanor.com
Marsha and Ivan Negrych
173 – 7 Avenue West, P.O. Box 1327, Cardston, AB, T0K 0K0
T: 1-866-653-2701
E: ivannegrych@shaw.ca
ACCEPTS D, V, MC, AMEX
Open: B&B open all year. Restaurant offers breakfast, lunch, and dinner in the summer, lunch and dinner in the winter

Marsha and Ivan bought the famous Manor in 2004, but this Alberta Historic Resource has a history dating back to 1898 (see sidebar page 16). Over the years it has been known to the locals as the Rock House, the Wonder House, even the Ghost House. Now the Negrych family has transformed the Manor into a fine-dining establishment in one of the most unusual settings in southern Alberta.

WHAT THE RESTAURANT OFFERS: Fine dining in the Golden Oak Room and the Dark Oak Room, surrounded by the unsurpassed craftsmanship of Henry Hoet, a reclusive Belgian finishing carpenter who spent 15 years building the house (as the story goes) for his Belgian sweetheart. The Negrychs make everything on the premises from scratch, including dressings, marinades, sauces, soups, and horse-radish – they even cut their own steaks. Cinnamon buns and muffins are baked fresh daily, along with a selection of breads that include molasses, whole wheat, poppy seed, and focaccia (depending on the menu). Specialties include Alberta beef, but there is a full range of choices from chicken, pork, pastas, and fish to free-range buffalo steak. Take the "Big Steak" challenge – if you can eat the 36 oz. cut of Alberta beef, your next meal is free. Special theme nights and guest chefs offer

HENRY BUILDS A DREAM

Today the Cobblestone Manor is a fine dining establishment, but it had humble beginnings as a two-storey log home built in 1898 by Joseph Young. In 1913, Henry Hoet, a reclusive Belgian finishing carpenter, bought the structure for $200 and began building his dream home. Although the story was never verified, the home was supposedly for his Belgian sweetheart, who never did come to Canada. For 15 years, Henry laboured on the house, financing his project by working as a finisher on the Alberta Mormon Temple in Cardston and the Prince of Wales Hotel in Waterton. Henry covered the original log house with river rock, which he hauled from nearby Lee's Creek with the help of his faithful Newfoundland dog. Then he set to work on his mansion, using only the finest hardwoods and stained glass imported from Italy. One room, the Golden Oak Room, took eight years to construct. Henry's handmade Tiffany lights can still be seen at the Manor along with some pieces of his finely crafted furniture. In a time when most residents could boast a single light in the middle of the ceiling, Henry had more than 40 handmade lamps in the Dark Oak Room. Sadly, Hoet was committed to a mental institution in 1928 and the house and all its contents were sold at auction for $2,560 to help cover his medical bills. The building was designated an Alberta Historic Resource in 1983.

something different, but Friday is BBQ Rib Night and Saturday – Prime Rib. According to Marsha, ribs sell out fast to the locals, so get your order in early. The Manor is famous for its Cobblestone Apple Pie, with a coconut crust, Austrian filling, and whipped cream and caramel topping, while all the chocolate desserts use only the best world-famous Callebaut Belgian chocolate.

WHAT THE B&B OFFERS: A self-contained apartment over the carriage house sleeps five and includes a hot tub and barbecue on the deck as well as an exercise room complete with sauna.

Other Points of Interest in Cardston

Visitor Information Centre
Main Street by Remington Carriage Museum
T: 403-653-3787
Open daily May long weekend to September long weekend 8:30 AM to 6:30 PM

The Alberta Temple (348 – 3rd Street West) was completed in 1923 and was the first one to be built outside the US. The architects, Hyrum Pope and Harold Burton of Salt Lake City, were influenced by the designs of Frank Lloyd Wright. The result was a massive structure resembling the Mayan-Aztec temples of Central and South America.

Interpretive displays open to visitors May long weekend to September long weekend. Telephone: 403-653-1696.

The Mormon Temple in Cardston was the first to be built outside the US.
L. ANDREWS

The Card Pioneer Home (337 Main Street) is the log home built by Charles Ora Card when he first arrived in 1887. Known as Mother's Canton Flannel Palace, for the material used to paper the walls, it served as a community centre and stopping place for travellers until the first hotel was built in 1894. Open June through August, Monday to Saturday, 1:30 PM to 5:00 PM. Telephone: 403-653-3366.

The Museum of Miniatures (57 – 4th Avenue West) started out as a hobby for retired BC Ferries Captain Roy Wittman, but eventually expanded into a full-fledged museum complete with native villages, a pioneer fort, buffalo herd, western town, and forest with wild animals. Open May long weekend to September long weekend, Monday to Saturday, 9:00 AM to 9:00 PM, Sunday, Noon to 9:00 PM. Telephone: 403-653-1142. Their website is www.geocities.com/miniaturesmsm.

 Carriage House Theatre (353 Main Street). The old Mayfair Theatre was completely gutted and refurbished in an art deco motif that is worth a look even if you don't go to a show. They stage live productions in July and August and special productions throughout the year, and run the latest movies when live productions are not on. Telephone: 403-653-1000. Email: alonnaleavitt@hotmail.com. www.thecarriagehousetheatre.com.

The Courthouse Museum (89 – 3rd Avenue West) is housed in a beautiful sandstone structure that was used longer than any other courthouse in Alberta. The museum holds rooms of local pioneer artifacts as well as the judge's bench, witness stand, and original jail cells, complete with graffiti. Open June through August, Monday to Saturday, 9:00 AM to 12:30 PM. Telephone: 403-653-3366.

Courthouse Museum
L. ANDREWS

Fay Wray Fountain on Main Street just before the bridge. It's hard to imagine what King Kong is doing on a monument in the small prairie town of Cardston, but there is a connection. Starlet Fay Wray screamed her way to fame in the giant hand of the gorilla in the classic black and white movie. Wray was born on a ranch just west of town, and the fountain was erected in her honour.

Other Grub Stops in Cardston

Burgers and Bytes, 562 1st Avenue West, 403-653-2993; Carriage House, 623 Main Street, 403-653-1380; Dairy Queen, 385 Main Street, 403-653-1531; Grotto Pool and Pizza, 29 – 2nd Avenue West, 403-653-3231; Mandarin Gardens, 365 Main Street, 403-653-1288; Mings Garden, 262 Main Street, 403-653-1682; New Diamond, 263 Main Street, 403-653-3686; Our Place Café, 207 Main Street, 403-653-2585; Pizzas and Cream, 325 Main Street, 403-653-4143; Subway, 20 – 3rd Avenue West, 403-653-1585; The Smashed Tomato, 219 Main Street, 403-653-1195

Just southeast of Cardston is Rangeview Ranch.

Rangeview Ranch   www.rangeviewranch.com
Mel and Dianne Thomson; Roger and Lori Thomson
P.O. Box 28, Site 10, Cardston, AB, T0K 0K0
T: 403-653-2292
E: thomson@telusplanet.net
ACCEPTS V, MC, TC
Open mid-May to mid-September

The Thomson family has been raising cattle and purebred quarter horses on their ranch for over 30 years. The story is that "John Smith" started the original ranch after he fled Utah following an altercation that left a dead man in his wake. He holed up in a deep coulee where he was well hidden from prying eyes, and spent the rest of his life ranching in the area to avoid the long arm of the US law. Turns out he actually only wounded the man and could have gone home. But there is a good chance he got hooked on the country and didn't want to leave anyways.

WHAT THEY OFFER: Accommodations in eight one-bedroom cabins with modern amenities, three hearty home-cooked meals, and all the hands-on experience and riding time your butt can stand. Try your hand at fence mending, branding, or cattle driving, or just relax and enjoy the vista. The ranch sits on top of Milk River Ridge, with sweeping views of the prairies and the Rockies, and has access to over 150,000 acres on two of the largest ranches in Canada (the McIntyre and the

Knight). The land is filled with wildlife and wildflowers in a habitat that hasn't changed much in a thousand years.

GETTING THERE: From Cardston, head south on Hwy. 2 for 2.5 KM, then turn left (southeast) on Secondary Hwy. 501 for 12 KM. Cross the St. Mary's River and turn left (east) at the Jefferson turnoff, for 16 KM. The ranch is on the right-hand side.

Rangeview Ranch
MEL THOMSON

FAMOUS COWBOY GOT HIS
START AS "ALBERTA PEARL"

Herman Linder grew up in Cardston and eventu-ally built a large ranch from winnings earned during one of the most successful careers in Canadian rodeo history. But it took him some time to live down his initial debut as "Alberta Pearl" in the 1921 Cardston rodeo. As part of their promotion, the rodeo committee had advertised a special ride by a "girl bronc rider." For six dollars, Herman donned a wig and a dress and rode a bucking horse. By the time he retired in 1940 at the age of 32, he had managed to redeem himself, winning an unequalled 22 championships at the Calgary Stampede (including 12 All Around titles). The "King of Cowboys" went on to spend 30 years as a rodeo judge and successful rodeo producer, and was inducted into the Canadian Rodeo Hall of Fame in 1982.

MCINTYRE RANCH
ONE OF THE MOST DURABLE IN SOUTHERN ALBERTA

William McIntyre started out his life in 1848 in Grime County, Texas, where his father managed to acquire substantial land holdings after the Mexican War. In 1870 William and his brother sold their father's ranch and purchased a herd of almost 7000 Texas longhorns for $3.75 a head, trailing them north along the Chisholm Trail. Eight months later they arrived in Salt Lake City, fat and sleek, and the boys were able to sell them the next spring for $24 a head – not a bad profit for a first-time cattle venture. When sheep herders moved into the Utah cattle range, McIntyre headed north. In 1894 he bought 9,300 hectares (23,000 acres) of land east of Cardston on the Milk River Ridge, setting up his headquarters between two branches of Pot Hole Creek (so-called because it normally dried up to a few deep pot holes each summer). The ranch expanded to include about 26,000 hectares (64,000 acres) and became well-known for its purebred Herefords. Ralph Thrall Sr. purchased the ranch in 1947, and it is still operated by the Thrall family. It remains one of the largest and most successful ranches in southern Alberta, recognized for its long history of environmentally sensitive range management that was started by the McIntyres and has continued for over a century.

Mountain View

If you aren't headed to Rangeview Ranch, the trail heads west from Cardston on Hwy. 5. It won't take long for you to figure out why the tiny hamlet of Mountain View has this name. (The Blackfoot version is *enukukai-tapisko*, meaning "little town.") As you drive west, the prairie grasslands stop abruptly at the foot of the Rocky Mountains in one of the most spectacular scenes you are likely to see anywhere in the world.

The community began with the second migration of Mormon settlers in the late 1890s and became the site of a cheese-making factory and the famous Hang

HOME OF THUNDER

The Blackfoot regard Chief Mountain as a sacred place. Sacred places are sites where the ancient stories took place. The Blackfoot called Chief Mountain *Ninastako*, meaning "mountain that stands apart." It was the home of Thunder. When he stole the wife of a Blackfoot man, Thunder took her to his home inside the mountain. Raven came from his home at Crowsnest Mountain, fighting with Thunder on the slopes of Ninastako. Thunder shot lightning bolts at Raven, trying to kill him, but Raven flapped his wings and brought the cold north wind and snow, until Thunder gave up and returned the man's wife. Raven ordered Thunder to make peace with the man and to give the Blackfoot his pipe as a sign of agreement. Since then, the Blackfoot have opened their Thunder Medicine Pipe Bundles each spring at the first sound of thunder, when they ask for good weather, good crops, and good luck.

Chief Mountain is a sacred Blackfoot site.
DARREL SCHNEIDER

Sang Company, a general store that stocked everything imaginable. Operated by Leong Choy in the former hotel, the store became the town's most prominent landmark. It was torn down following Choy's death, and the town was in danger of becoming a ghost town like many of the other Mormon towns in the area. However, this trend has recently reversed, with more people moving to Mountain View to enjoy the slower pace of life.

Almost directly south of Mountain View, Chief Mountain, located on the us side of the border, rises on the horizon. It has taken on origin-myth significance because of its dominance. Blackfoot tradition holds that it was here that the three Blackfoot tribes (the Pikani or Peigan, the Kainai or Blood, and the Siksika or the Blackfoot) were created. The mountain was and continues to be an important site for vision quests (see sidebar page 59) by the Blackfoot.

Despite its tiny size, there are a number of partners located here.

Two Country Inns   www.twocountryinns.com

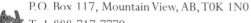
P.O. Box 117, Mountain View, AB, T0K 1N0
T: 1-888-717-7770
E: info@twocountryinns.com

ACCEPTS V, MC, AMEX
Open all year

As the name suggests, there are actually two inns located in the hamlet of Mountain View. They are located just off Hwy. 5 on opposite ends of town and are clearly

Rocky Ridge Country Resort.
TWO COUNTRY INNS

signed. Both offer 20 per cent rate reductions for the winter season from September 15 to May 15.

Rocky Ridge Country Resort

WHAT THEY OFFER: Six bedrooms — three with private bathroom and two with pine loft. Guests have access to large common rooms, a billiards room, sauna, and hot tub. Spacious grounds include picnic tables and a bonfire pit. As well, there are two fully self-contained luxury cabins. The two-bedroom cabin sleeps up to eight; the three-bedroom cottage sleeps up to six.

Mountain View Inn

WHAT THEY OFFER: Seven well-appointed rooms with private bath; honeymoon suite has gas fireplace, huge Jacuzzi tub, and king-size bed (you don't need to be a newlywed to enjoy these comforts). A stunning two-storey Great Room with mezzanine and panoramic view of the mountains, billiards room, and outdoor bonfire pit. The three-level A-frame cabin sleeps up to 17, with full kitchen, two bathrooms, TV, piano, fireplace, gas barbecue, and wrap-around deck. And, a full buffet breakfast is served for all guests at the Rocky Ridge Country Resort, just down the street.

Mountain View Market and Motel   www.mystic-spirit.com/mtnviewmarket
Nolan and Vicki Romeril; Trevor and Paula Virostek
P.O. Box 9, Mountain View, AB, T0K 1N0
T: 403-653-1992 or 403-653-2648
E: mvmarket@telusplanet.net
ACCEPTS V, MC
Market open 7:00 AM to 6:00 PM all year; **Motel open** all year

The Romerils run their family business together with their daughter Paula and son-in-law Trevor Virostek. Paula's great-grandfather William Payne, a former member of the North West Mounted Police, was one of the first settlers in the area. In fact, Payne Lake, a local fishing spot just west of town, was named after him. The store is known for its large ice cream cones in the summer and is one of the few places where you can still buy fireworks. According to Paula, you can often catch a good fireworks display down at Payne Lake on the weekends during the summer.

WHAT THEY OFFER: The market sells gasoline and diesel, fishing licenses, tackle and live bait, ice, film, hot snacks, and pop; there is also a well-stocked grocery section and a souvenir/gift shop. The motel offers very clean large rooms with queen beds and satellite TV at reasonable rates; kitchen suites are available that can accommodate up to 14 people; verandah at the back with barbecue has a magnificent view of Chief Mountain.

Mountain Meadow Trail Rides   www.mountainmeadowtrailrides.com
Dan and Terri Nelson

P.O. Box 38, Mountain View, AB, T0K 1N0
T: 1-866-653-2413 (Canada and US)
E: meadow1@telusplanet.net
ACCEPTS D, V, MC, TC, MO
Open May to October

Dan's grandfather homesteaded the historic Nelson Ranch over 100 years ago in 1898. By the 1920s, the ranch had one of the largest horse herds in the area. The family continues the traditions of Alberta ranching with fourth-generation guides and riders who work hard to maintain the integrity of their western lifestyle every single day. This is a 2,000 acre cattle and horse ranch with over 200 cows and 50 horses, where horses are trained in the "horse whisperer" (see sidebar page 203) tradition. And since the guides have been born and raised here, they are able to share some of the colourful legends and culture of the area, including stories about the infamous Joe Cosley (see sidebar page 25). Dan's grandfather knew the renegade trapper well. The family still has some of the traps Joe traded for supplies when he was on the run from US rangers for illegal hunting.

WHAT THEY OFFER: Trail rides, from one-and-a-half-hour to six- or seven-hour excursions; four-hour cookout rides with barbecued steak. As well, raft and

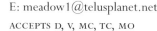
Bull-dogging —a rodeo event where the rider comes off his horse, grabs the horns and throws the steer flat on its side; also known as steer wrestling

ride combos offer half-day or full-day cookout options; the two-day deluxe combo includes riding, rafting, cookout, accommodations, and meals; two, three, and

Dan Nelson, mountain meadow trail rides
TERRI NELSON

four-day riding trips use a wilderness base camp with hot tub, sauna, hot shower, and accommodation in log-style cabins (bring your own sleeping bag); canoeing at nearby Little Beaver Lake; "Spirit of the West" cattle drive packages offer three- or four-day options for experienced riders.

GETTING THERE: As you head west out of Mountain View, watch for the sign on the left (south) side of the road. Turn left and go 2 KM to the gate, which is on the right (west).

Waterton Lakes National Park   www.explorewaterton.ca
T: 403-859-5133 (seasonal)

Blackfoot name — *pukto-na-sikimi*, meaning "inside lake," because the lakes are inside the first range of the Rocky Mountains. The Indians referred to the area as the Land of the Shining Mountains.

The park has been called the "Jewel of Chinook Country," yet it remains one of the province's best-kept secrets. Tucked away in the extreme southwest corner, the unique topography, including prairie, wetland, parkland, montane, subalpine forest, and alpine flora zones, makes it home to an astounding diversity of plants and wildlife. In less than one kilometre you will see dry rolling prairie give way to woodlands, glacial ice sheets, and mountains that rise to almost 3,000 metres (9,800 feet).

In 1895 Waterton was officially designated as the Waterton Lakes Forest Park, largely due to the efforts of local rancher Frederick Godsal (see sidebar page 26). Over the years, the size of the park has varied from 1095 square kilometres (423 square miles) in 1914, to its present size of about 525 square kilometres (203 square miles). In 1932 members of the Rotary Clubs on both sides of the border lobbied their respective governments to commemorate the cooperation and good-

WILL THE REAL JOE COSLEY PLEASE STAND UP?

Cosley was born in 1870 on the Seven Nations Reserve in Ontario. Somewhere along the road, he learned to shoot, ride, and tell a good story. When he arrived out west, he worked as a trapper and guide in the area that eventually became Glacier/Waterton International Peace Park. He rode a fancy alligator-hide saddle and thrilled tourists with his colourful tales. Joe was never one to let the truth interfere with a good story, and over the years he published and told tall tales of his adventures on both sides of the border. Although there is no record of a Cosley on the show's roster, he claimed to have been a famous marksman and fancy rider in Buffalo Bill's Wild West Show, travelling to London and Paris. Joe actually was a top sharpshooter during WWI, but when he returned he got into trouble with the law for illegal trapping in the parks. One night Joe paddled down the Waterton River and never returned. His bones were found in a trapper's log cabin 400 miles north of Prince Albert in October 1944. With a flair for the dramatic right to the finish, his diary told of a sinister curse, "creeping and deadly," closing with the words, "I have reached the end."

Joe Cosley in his army uniform.
ARLINE WEST COLLECTION

will that existed along the world's longest undefended border. The result was the establishment of the world's first International Peace Park. Both Glacier and Waterton have been designated as Biosphere Reserves. In 1995 the Waterton–Glacier International Peace Park became a UNESCO World Heritage Site in recognition of its scenic value; its significant climate, landforms, and ecological processes; and its enduring cultural importance. The area hosts the headwaters of rivers flowing to the Arctic, the Pacific, and the Gulf of Mexico. In the late 1800s, well-known naturalist and editor of *Field and Stream* George Bird Grinnell coined the term "Crown of the Continent" for the entire area.

Archaeological evidence indicates the presence of humans over 10,000 years ago, including the Upper Kootenay and the Blackfoot. It wasn't until 1858, when Lt. Thomas Blakiston, a member of the Palliser Expedition sent by the British to assess the area's agricultural value, became the first European to see Waterton Lakes. He named the three lakes after Sir Charles Waterton, a prominent English naturalist who never actually saw the lakes himself. In 1865 John George

Waterton Lakes National Park
L. ANDREWS

"Kootenai" Brown visited the area for the first time, vowing to return someday. Brown kept his promise, returning in the late 1870s to become one of the best-known early characters of the region and the park's first superintendent in 1911 (see sidebar page 27).

The meeting of the rolling prairie land with the mountains is unique to the Waterton area. Not only has it created some of the most dramatic scenery you are likely to see anywhere in the world, but it has also created one of the most diverse natural habitats for plants and animals in the province. Over 600 species of wild-

WATERTON'S UNSUNG HERO

In the history of Waterton Lakes National Park, the name Kootenai Brown is the one that is most often associated with the establishment of the park. But the foresight and efforts of Frederick Godsal, a respected local rancher, were also instrumental in saving this gem of pristine wilderness for the enjoyment of all. Godsal was a well-educated Englishman who came west to try his hand at ranching at the urging of his friend, the Marquis of Lorne. In 1883 he acquired an 8100-hectare (20,000-acre) grazing lease near the present-day site of Cowley. He used his connections and friendship with William Pearce, the Superintendent of Mines for Canada, to help establish the Waterton Lakes Forest Park in 1895. In a letter written to Pearce in 1893, Godsal spoke eloquently of the need to preserve this special area, saying, "I now only wish most earnestly to ask that this may be done and I am sure I have the feeling of the country with me." With the discovery of oil in 1902 at Oil City and the prospects of further development in the park, it was once again the words of Godsal to the Secretary of the Department of the Interior that began the long process of review that eventually led to the establishment of Waterton Lakes National Park.

"Sitting Bull ordered us to get off our horses and when we did he had us stripped as naked as the day we were born. They took everything, dispatches, mail, guns, horses, clothes ... Some of the young bucks began yelling 'Kash-ga, Kash-ga,' meaning kill them, kill them. Sitting Bull raised his hand and shouted, 'Don't be in a hurry, we'll make a fire and have some fun with them.' We understood every word they said, of course, and we knew that Sitting Bull meant some playful mode of torture." When a dispute arose over some horses, Brown and his friend Joe rolled into a coulee and sprinted for a nearby lake. "We were standing in water up to our necks, with Indians running up and down the shore firing at random into the weeds ... It was blowing a regular hurricane and pouring down torrents of rain and this is probably what saved us. Finally, half dead with cold, we stole quietly out in the pitch darkness and scrambling up the bank took to our heels."

John George "Kootenai" Brown.
GLENBOW ARCHIVES NA-678-1

For many men, it would have been the story of a lifetime. For John George "Kootenai" Brown, it was just one of many stories in a life filled with danger and adventure in the Wild West. Brown's life seemed to include every conceivable escapade that one person could possibly pack into one lifetime. From soldier in the British Army in India to gold seeker in the Cariboo to pony express rider in the Dakota Territory (when he was captured by Sioux warriors as recounted above), Brown's life was one of constant adventure. He even claimed to have known General George Custer and to have declined an invitation to act as guide for Custer on his ill-fated trek to the Little Bighorn.

Brown finally headed north to settle down on Kootenay (now Waterton) Lakes after his acquittal for a murder in Montana. He was one of the first settlers in the area and became known as a trapper and guide. When Oil City was established near Cameron Lake and game became scarce, Brown worked tirelessly for the establishment of the park. He was appointed Fishery Officer and Forest Ranger in 1895 and became the first Superintendent in 1911. He took his job seriously. At the age of 74 he was still making his rounds on snowshoes, travelling 20 miles in -36C weather. He is buried in the park on the west side of Knight's Lake.

RANCHERS AS CONSERVATIONISTS?

The small size of the park means that wildlife cannot confine itself to the artificial borders set by government bureaucrats. They need space to find mates and adequate food supplies. It is estimated that a single male grizzly needs about 800 square kilometres of undisturbed habitat to support itself. But the entire park is only 525 square kilometres and almost one-third of that area is rock and water. As a result, wildlife must depend on the good ecological sense of the park's neighbours to help maintain the fragile balance that ensures a healthy population of animals like bears, wolves, and cougars.

Bill Dolan, chief park warden, recalls his arrival in 1990: "I was coming from the east. The park boundary sign was down for repairs and I didn't even know I was in the park until I came to the main entrance two or three kilometres down the road. It says something about the landscape." He readily admits there is a close interdependence between the park and the ranching community that has existed on the surrounding grasslands for more than a century. He explains, "Waterton is a very small park, the smallest of the mountain parks. Its boundaries weren't necessarily set up to accommodate the wildlife species that populate the area." He believes the ranching community has played an integral role in preserving the natural wildlife corridors and scenic viewscapes that make this area unique.

Kevin Van Tighem spent seven years in Waterton as the park's conservation biologist. When he arrived in 1993 he shared a common perception that ranchers and conservationists couldn't peacefully co-exist. "After seven years, I realized that the reason the park is so viable is because of ranching. Many of the perceptions about ranchers are based on prejudice and assumptions that aren't valid. They have a 'live and let live' attitude. The ranchlands sustain the bears, the elk, the grasses, the hawks – they all need natural habitat, and ranching provides this. People say they love Waterton, but Waterton is the way it is because of the ranchland surrounding it."

In 2001 a decision by the County of Cardston to allow residential subdivision on prime ranchlands raised concerns about the disruption of this delicately balanced ecosystem. To date, the perceived threat has not materialized to the extent feared, perhaps partially due to the extremely harsh climate in the area. Persistent, howling winds, severe snowstorms, and winter temperatures that can vary between –40C and +15C in a matter of a day or two aren't for the timid. Only time will tell if the close interdependence that has existed between the ranching community and the park will continue in the future.

Bosal — a braided rawhide noseband

CRITTER WATCH: GRIZZLY BEAR (BROWN BEAR)

Grizzlies. Everyone wants to see one, but the only way to watch a wild grizzly is from a safe distance, preferably from inside your car. One of the best places to see grizzly bears in Canada is in Waterton Lakes National Park. You should be able to tell the difference between a black bear and a grizzly, since a black bear is generally more peaceful than a grizzly, often fleeing at the first sign of humans. But it's not as easy as saying a grizzly is brown and a black bear is black, since this isn't always the case. Confused yet? One of the main distinguishing characteristics of a grizzly is its large shoulder hump. It has a massive head with a dish-shaped – almost pig-like – face, while a black bear has a long face with a straight profile. Black bears will have a smoother-looking coat, and grizzlies look shaggier, often sporting a face ruff. Black bear males are much smaller, usually around 100 to 150 kilograms, with short, curved claws. Grizzly males will commonly weigh anywhere from 250 to 350 kilograms, and their long, straight claws are highly visible.

Grizzly bears are distinguished by a large shoulder hump.
JANET NASH

flowers are known to exist in this one little spot in the southwest corner of Alberta. Much of the diversity can be accounted for by the warm Chinook winds (see sidebar page 31) that alter the climate of the park.

In fact, Waterton is unique in many ways. It has some of the oldest exposed sedimentary rock in the Canadian Rockies. You can see it at Cameron Falls, located in the Waterton townsite, where 1.5-billion-year-old rock is clearly visible. Waterton receives Alberta's highest annual precipitation levels (at 1,072 millimetres) and is one of the windiest places in the province, with winds over 100 kilometres an hour a common occurrence. It is also one of the warmest areas in winter because of the frequency of Chinook winds that can cause temperatures to increase dramatically in a short period of time.

There are several Cowboy Trail partners located in Waterton.

Prince of Wales Hotel
L. ANDREWS

Aspen Village Inn   www.aspenvillageinn.com

Gerry and Leslie Muza

111 Windflower Avenue, P.O. Box 100, Waterton Park, AB, T0K 2M0

T: 1-888-859-8669

E: reservations@aspenvillageinn.com

ACCEPTS V, MC, AMEX, ER, DC, DIS, TC

Open May 1 to Thanksgiving weekend in October

Gerry and Leslie Muza started out as employees in Waterton Park almost 30 years ago. In 1980 they bought the Inn and over the years have extensively renovated and updated it. The bright-red pitched roofs and distinctive alpine exterior make the

Aspen an easy place to spot. It is well-known for its spectacular display of hanging baskets and flowers during the summer.

WHAT THEY OFFER: 51 immaculate units (the Inn has received 12 Good Housekeeping Awards), from large, well-appointed rooms to family units and deluxe two-bedroom suites with full kitchen and sitting room; honeymoon suite includes fireplace, two-person Jacuzzi tub, and private balcony with a magnificent view; cottages with full kitchens and fireplaces; access to Jacuzzi whirlpool, picnic area with barbecues, tables, on-site playground; barbecue packs include food and utensils; golf packages and Waterton Park Experience packages available.

Crandell Mountain Lodge
www.crandellmountainlodge.com

Darcy and Jocelyn Wright, Managers
102 Mountview Road, P.O. Box 114, Waterton Park, AB, T0K 2M0
T: 1-866-859-2288
E: crandell@telusplanet.net
ACCEPTS D, V, MC, DIS, TC
Open all year

The lodge has been a part of the park since Hilding Hagglund built it in 1939. In fact, the original telephone number was 11 – there were only 10 phones in Waterton before it came on line. Hilding and his father, Erik, were well-known and respected builders in the area who constructed many of the buildings in the park. In the early years, electricity and the water supply were only available in the summer. The lodge supplied coal oil lamps and even had its own water system in the off-season. But what the lodge lacked in luxury was made up with by a certain sense of elegance, with damask tablecloths in the dining room every day, candles on the mantels, live houseplants, and even a framed "Group of Seven" print in each unit.

WHAT THEY OFFER: 17 country-themed units, from standard rooms with shower and TV to three-room suites with full kitchen, microwave, gas fireplace, and TV; the Bear's Den has king-size bed, two-person Jacuzzi tub, wood-burning fire-

Crandell Mountain Lodge
DARCY WRIGHT

place, fridge, microwave, and bathroom; guests have access to shaded patio deck and gas barbecues. Off-season packages are available.

Tamarack Village Square   www.watertonvisitorservices.com
Brian Baker

214 Mount View Road, P.O. Box 67, Waterton Park, AB, T0K 2M0
T: 403-859-2378

E: wvsc@telusplanet.net

ACCEPTS ALL MAJOR CREDIT CARDS

Open Mid-May to Thanksgiving weekend in October; 8:00 AM to 8:00 PM daily in July and August; shoulder season hours vary

Brian is the fourth generation to run the Baker family business that was established by George Baker in the 1920s. It started as a nine-bay Esso gas station and truck depot for the Park Transport Company, but it also included the Alberta Government Telephone exchange and a General Motors car dealership. The original building has undergone a series of renovations over the years, expanding into Waterton's largest outdoor outfitter.

WHAT THEY OFFER: Besides gasoline, an amazing selection of outdoor gear, apparel, footwear, Tilley hats, camping and backpacking supplies, gifts, souvenirs, and high-quality nature prints; the hikers' market has fresh sandwiches, coffee, and snacks, plus books, maps, and trail information; hiker shuttle service runs daily; guided hikes and walks by reservation only; money exchange services, ATM on site.

Trail of the Great Bear Gift Shop   www.trailofthegreatbear.com
Marie Grant and Beth Russell-Towe
114 Waterton Avenue, P.O. Box 142, Waterton Park, AB, T0K 2M0
E: info@trailofthegreatbear.com
T: 403-859-2009
ACCEPTS D, V, MC, AMEX, TC
Open July to August, 9:00 AM to 9:00 PM daily; May to June, and September to October, 10:00 AM to 6:00 PM daily; most weekends in the winter (weather dependent)

This is the retail arm of the award-winning Trail of the Great Bear tour company. The shop focuses on a natural history theme in its gifts and books, with a particular emphasis on bears, birds, and wildflowers. They also organize the ten-day Wildflower Festival each June, with special events and guided excursions to view the extraordinary variety of wildflowers that call Waterton home.

WHAT THEY OFFER: An outstanding collection of local hiking, history, natural history, fiction, and children's books; a good selection of clothing, jewellery, framed art, souvenirs, and locally-made products. As well, there are day hikes (for groups, couples, or singles) or a "meet-and-greet walkabout" of the town (provides history and information about the area) with advance notice.

Other Points of Interest in the Park

Visitor Information Centre
Located on main entrance road into town.
T: 403-859-5133
Open daily, June to September long weekend, 8:00 AM to 7:00 PM; mid-May to June and mid-September to Canadian Thanksgiving in October, 9:00 AM to 5:00 PM

Waterton Heritage Centre
117 Waterton Avenue
T: 403-859-2267 or 403-859-2624
Open July and August, 9:00 AM to 9:00 PM; mid-May to end of June and mid-September to end of September, 10:00 AM to 6:00 PM

Good selection of local guidebooks and displays on the history of the area.

Cameron Falls
L.ANDREWS

Cameron Falls – Located in the townsite. The exposed rock is over 1.5 billion years old and is one of the oldest outcrops in the Rockies.

MV International – The vessel was built at the south end of Upper Waterton Lake and put into service in 1928. Every summer it runs daily interpretive excursions between Waterton and Goat Haunt on the Montana side of the lake.

Hikes and Interpretive Programs

Waterton offers some of the best hiking in the world; in fact, the Crypt Lake hike has been rated the number one hike in Canada. With over 200 kilometres of trails in the park, hikes range in difficulty from easy strolls to challenging treks of several days' duration. The trail system in Waterton connects to the system in Montana's Glacier National Park and British Columbia's Akamina-Kishinena Provincial Park.

Free International Peace Park hikes are held every Wednesday and Saturday in July and August. The 14-kilometre hikes are jointly led by Canadian and American park interpreters and begin at 10:00 AM from the Bertha Lake trailhead. They follow the lakeshore to Goat Haunt at the Montana end of Waterton Lake, returning via the MV International. Hikers must pre-register at the Visitor Information Centre. Advance boat reservations are recommended.

Interpretive programs are run in the evenings during the summer at the theatre adjacent to the campground, and the Waterton Natural History Association offers one- and two-day natural history courses led by internationally recognized experts on such topics as wildflowers, birds, butterflies, and bears. Telephone: 403-859-2624.

Scenic Drives

The entrance road provides eight kilometres of magnificent views that clearly illustrate why Waterton is called the place "where the mountains meet the prairies."

Akamina Parkway begins near the townsite and travels for 16 kilometres along Cameron Valley to Cameron Lake, past the Oil City (see sidebar page 35) site commemorating the first oil well drilled in Western Canada. Boat rentals and snacks are available at Cameron Lake.

OFF THE BEATEN PATH FROM WATERTON PARK

Red Rock Parkway – Turn off from the park entrance road at the sign and follow Blakiston Valley for 15 kilometres to Red Rock Canyon. The walls are streaked red and green by different minerals in the rock, and at over one billion years old, are some of the most colourful and oldest rock formations in the Rockies. The Blakiston Falls and Red Rock Canyon trails offer easy walking with spectacular scenery.

Chief Mountain Highway – Just outside the park entrance, Hwy. 6 turns south past Maskinonge Lake to a viewpoint with a breathtaking view of the Front Range of the Rockies and Waterton Valley.

Bison Paddock – Just outside the park entrance on Hwy. 6 north, the paddock features a small herd of plains bison. A road winds through the paddock for viewing, but do not leave your vehicle.

Grub Stop

Barley & Bean, Windflower Avenue, 403-859-2284; Beargrass Restaurant & Lounge, Clematis Avenue, 403-859-2150; Big Scoop Ice Cream Parlour, Waterton Avenue, 403-859-2346; Club House at Golf Course, Waterton Golf Course, 403-859-2601; Fireside Lounge, Bayshore Inn, 403-859-2211; Royal Stewart Dining Room, Prince of Wales Hotel, 403-859-2231; Gazebo Café, Kilmorey Lodge, 403-859-2334; Glacier Café, Bayshore Inn, 403-859-2211; Jugo Juice & Red Rock Burgers, Windflower Avenue, 403-859-2212; Lakeside Kootenai Brown Dining Room, Bayshore Inn, 403-859-2211; Lamp Post Dining Room, Kilmorey Lodge, 403-859-2334; New Frank's Restaurant, Waterton Avenue, 403-859-2240; Pat's of Waterton, Mountain View Road, 403-859-2266; Pizza of Waterton, Fountain Avenue, 403-859-2660; Ram's Head Lounge, Kilmorey Lodge, 403-859-2334; Subway, Windflower Avenue, 403-859-2121; Thirsty Bear Saloon, Bayshore Inn, 403-859-2211; Tuscana Ristorante, Waterton Avenue, 403-859-2236; Waterton Bagel and Coffee Co., In the Waterton Theatre, 403-859-2466; Welch's Chocolate Shop, Windflower Avenue, 403-859-2363; Windsor Lounge, Prince of Wales Hotel, 403-859-2231; Ye Olde Lick and Nibble Ice Cream, in the Waterton Theatre, 403-859-2466; Zum's Eatery, Waterton Avenue, 403-859-2388

BELIEVE IT OR NOT!
The greatest recorded series of snowstorms occurred from Claresholm south to the international border, where record snowfalls from 1.5 to 2 metres (5 to 6.5 feet) of snow fell in two storms, a week apart, between April 17 to 20 and April 27 to 29, 1967.

Cowboy Trail partner for this area added just prior to press time: Carriage House Theatre (featured on page 17).

Recommended Reading

Belly River's Famous Joe Cosley by Brian McClung
Ghost Towns of Southern Alberta by Harold Fryer
Grand Delusions: Henry Hoet and Cobblestone Manor by James Musson
High on a Windy Hill: The Story of the Prince of Wales Hotel by Ray Djuff
Kootenai Brown: His Life and Times by William Rodney
Vision Quest of the Plains Indians by Kathleen Dugan
Waterton and Northern Glacier Trails by Charles Russell, Beth Russell, John Russell, and Valerie Haig-Brown
Where the Mountains Meet the Prairies by Graham A. MacDonald

Buffaloed — bewildered or overcome with words

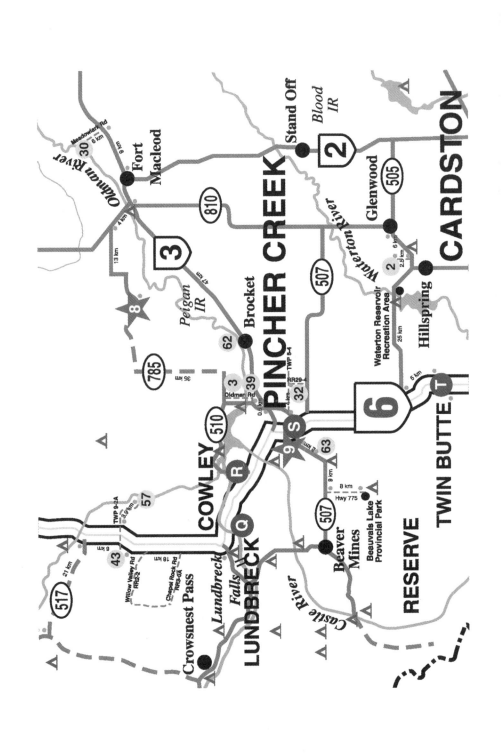

"Income tax has caused more ranchers to go out of business than low cattle prices. Before there was income tax, nobody kept track of how bad things really were."

—Ted Stone, *Cowboy Logic*

Communities

- Twin Butte
- Pincher Creek
- Cowley

Accommodations

- Great Canadian Barn Dance and Family Resort
- Parkway Motel and Hostel
- September Springs Ranch

Attractions & Events

- Rocky Mountain Acres
- Great Canadian Barn Dance and Family Resort
- Heritage Acres

Farm & Ranch Vacations

- Bloomin' Inn Bed and Breakfast (and Our Country Store)
- Misty Mountain Adventures
- Bent Creek Western Vacations Guest Ranch

Outfitters

- Misty Mountain Adventures

Camping

- Twin Butte Country General Store and Licensed Restaurant
- Great Canadian Barn Dance and Family Resort

- Heritage Acres
- Head-Smashed-In Buffalo Jump Interpretive Centre

Restaurants

- Twin Butte Country General Store and Licensed Restaurant
- September Springs Ranch
- Head-Smashed-In Buffalo Jump Interpretive Centre

Shopping, Antiques & Artisans

- Twin Butte Country General Store and Licensed Restaurant
- Rocky Mountain Acres
- Kootenai Brown Pioneer Village
- September Springs Ranch
- Our Country Store (and Bloomin' Inn Bed and Breakfast)
- Head-Smashed-In Buffalo Jump Interpretive Centre
- Peigan Crafts Ltd.

Icon Attractions

- Kootenai Brown Pioneer Village
- Head-Smashed-In Buffalo Jump Interpretive Centre

MAJOR EVENTS ALONG THE TRAIL
(see www.thecowboytrail.com for a complete listing)

June
Cowboy Poetry Gathering, Pincher Creek
Heritage Acres Chuckwagon Cookout, Heritage Acres
Iris Festival, September Springs Ranch
National Aboriginal Day, Head-Smashed-In Buffalo Jump

July
Annual Bluegrass and Classic Country Music Festival, Great Canadian Barn Dance
Barn Birthday, Great Canadian Barn Dance
Celebration of Drumming and Dancing, Head-Smashed-In Buffalo Jump
Iris Festival, September Springs Ranch
Kootenai Brown Tea, Kootenai Brown Pioneer Village
Wind Kite Festival, Pincher Creek

August
Annual Antique Fair, Bloomin' Inn
Annual Heritage Acres Show, Heritage Acres
Celebration of Drumming and Dancing, Head-Smashed-In Buffalo Jump
Cheese Festival, Glenwood
Fair and Pro Rodeo, Pincher Creek

September
Harvest Festival, Kootenai Brown Pioneer Village
Old Tyme Music and Dance Festival, Great Canadian Barn Dance

Twin Butte

The drive north from Waterton Park through the hamlet of Twin Butte to Pincher Creek is hard to top. From either direction, it is probably one of the most scenic drives in the province. To the west, rolling ranchlands meet majestic mountains, while open prairie stretches to the east. For a truly spectacular view, be sure to stop at the signed observation point just north of the park. It is on the left side of the road, so be careful turning across the traffic. As you approach Twin Butte, named *natsikapway-tomo* by the Blackfoot for the double hill, you will see the two buttes (now separated by Hwy. 6). Despite being barely more than a dot on the map, two Cowboy Trail partners call it home.

Twin Butte Country General Store and Licensed Restaurant

Jeny Davis and Clint Davis
P.O. Box 461, Twin Butte, AB, T0K 2J0
T: 403-627-4035
E: tbc1@telusplanet.net
ACCEPTS D, V, MC

Open 10:00 AM to 8:00 PM daily in the summer; 10:00 AM to 8:00 PM Wednesday to Sunday in the winter

WHAT THEY OFFER: Mexican and western fare (the steak fajitas and the Chorizo sausage meal are local favourites); a good selection of appetizers, salads, burritos, tacos, enchiladas and breakfast items like omelettes and steak and eggs; also plenty of beef, buffalo, and elk (burgers or steaks) or build your own pizza. On select days during the summer, live entertainment with musicians from as far away

WORLD'S LARGEST BIGHORN RAM

In 1911 local rancher Fred Weiller shot the world's largest Bighorn ram in Blind Canyon, 15 kilometres southwest of Twin Butte. The head, which Fred had mounted, weighed 32 kilograms. After Fred's death, the head came into the possession of Clarence Baird, who agreed to have it sent to the Boone and Crockett Club of New York to be officially measured. It established the new world's record at 208 1/8, beating out the previous record of 207 2/8 held by Martin Bovey. (In 1924 Bovey had bagged a ram on Oyster Creek while being guided by well-known Twin Butte hunting guide Bert Riggall.) Although the head was temporarily lost on its journey back from New York, it was eventually returned safely, only to be destroyed by fire when the Baird house burned to the ground in 1971.

as the North West Territories and Nova Scotia. The General Store sells basic grocery items, hard ice cream, and off-sale liquor; the gift shop has a good selection of local arts and crafts and jams made in the store; unserviced camping spots available.

Bull cook — the assistant or flunky cook

Twin Butte Country General Store
JENY DAVIS

Rocky Mountain Acres   www.rockymountainacres.ca
Liam Reid

P.O. Box 186, Twin Butte, AB, T0K 2J0
T: 403-627-4335
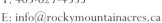
E: info@rockymountainacres.ca

ACCEPTS CC
Open by appointment

WHAT THEY OFFER: Handcrafted log furniture for every room of the house; packaged and customized tours.

Great Canadian Barn Dance and Family Resort

The Kunkel Family   www.greatcanadianbarndance.com

P.O. Box 163, Hill Spring, AB, T0K 1E0

T: 1-866-626-3407

E: barndanc@telusplanet.net

ACCEPTS D, V, MC

Resort open all year. Dinner and dance every Saturday, mid-May to October, and every Friday, July to September long weekend. Dinner show every Thursday, May to October.

The country barn dance was a true western tradition where neighbours met and made their own entertainment with good food and lively music. The Kunkels are a family of musicians whose weekly summer barn dances let you share some of that heritage in their wonderful old barn. You can tie into a home-cooked Alberta beef buffet dinner, then kick up your heels to some down-home country music.

The barn was built in 1913 by the widow Eliza Hurd on her farm north of Hill Spring. Eliza was left with five small children when her husband died suddenly in 1904, but she pioneered on, buying grassland on part of the former Cochrane Ranch (see sidebar page 44) in 1908 and living in an old granary until a house could be built. Eliza made sure

The historic barn was built in 1913.
GREAT CANADIAN BARN DANCE

the barn was solid and strong. It has withstood almost a century of wind and storm. Now it welcomes friends and neighbours to enjoy good food and lively music.

HAMLET OF GLENWOOD AND THE CHEESE FACTORY MUSEUM

Just north of Twin Butte you can turn east on Secondary Hwy. 505 and take the 31 KM drive to Glenwood. The village is home to a large cheese factory, the annual CheeseFest each August, and from the May long weekend to the September long weekend, the Cheese Factory Museum (403-626-3870) will tell you everything you ever wanted to know about cheese. The museum claims to serve the "biggest ice cream cones ever," so you may want to check that out. Along the road you'll find The Dam Art Gallery (403-627-5524), with handmade, one-of-a-kind gifts and fine woodworking. Further east, the Waterton Reservoir Provincial Recreation Area offers plenty of opportunity for swimming, boating, and fishing. Whether you choose to go west back to Hwy. 6 or south to Mountain View via Secondary Hwy. 800, the scenery – and sometimes the wind – will blow you away. Secondary Hwy. 505 is also the road to the Great Canadian Barn Dance.

WHAT THEY OFFER: At the barn — weekly barn dance, dinner, and show; barn birthday on the Saturday closest to July 1; Bluegrass Festival in July; Halloween dinner and dance in October; Cowboy Christmas Ball in December; Cowboy Christmas show runs Thursdays, November to mid-December, with live holiday music and dinner.

WHAT THEY OFFER: At the full-service resort — campground has 86 RV sites, most with water and power service; tent and group camping sites with modern bathrooms and hot showers, a portable pump out wagon, picnic tables, and fire pits. The accommodation options include four three-bedroom cottages with full kitchen and bathroom; B&B in lodge with three spacious country-themed rooms. Activities include fishing or canoeing on 15-acre pond, playground, snack concession, horseshoes; Granny's Gift Shop has local crafts and collectibles; covered outdoor pavilion has dining space for 80 people, a fully-equipped kitchen shelter, fire pit, and washrooms.

GETTING THERE: From Hwy. 22 take Secondary Hwy. 505 east for 25 KM. Just east of the turnoff for Secondary Hwy. 800 you will see the sign for GCBD. Head north for 2.5 KM to the entrance on the left (west) side of the road.

THE COCHRANE MOVES SOUTH

In 1881 Senator Matthew Cochrane established the Cochrane Ranch on the banks of the Bow River, near the site that would eventually become the town of Cochrane (see Chapter 6). In the summer of 1883, after two disastrous winters and the loss of almost 8,000 head of cattle, the herd was trailed south to 69,000 hectares (170,000 acres) of prime leases held by the ranch between the Belly and Waterton rivers. The first years on this part of the range weren't easy, but the ranch eventually became a profitable operation, with almost 13,000 head by 1891. Following the death of Senator Cochrane, the ranch was eventually sold to the Mormon Church. The story is that the Maunsell brothers of the Ivy Ranch purchased 12,000 head of the stock for $240,000 with a cheque that E.H. Maunsell wrote in pencil as he rode in the saddle.

As you head north on Hwy. 6 you will see a historical marker on the east side of the road. It is said that one of the biggest manhunts in the history of the North West Mounted Police (NWMP) took place to the east and south of the sign in the fall of 1896. An estimated 100 officers and men of the NWMP, cowboys, stockmen, farmers, and about 75 Indians from the Blood and Peigan reserves participated. They were in pursuit of a Blood Indian called Charcoal (alias Dried Meat), who was accused of murdering fellow tribesman Medicine Pipe Stem after he caught the young man with one of his two wives. When NWMP Sergeant William Wilde overtook the fugitive just a few miles east of where the sign is located, Charcoal shot him dead and stole his horse. Charcoal was eventually subdued by relatives, arrested, and found guilty of murder. According to NWMP journals, he died like a true warrior, chanting his death song as he walked to the gallows.

MOUNTAIN GUIDE EXTRAORDINARY

Bert Riggall started out life in a wealthy English family in 1884. He took his school holidays in Switzerland, where he developed a lifelong love of mountains. Bert was an excellent shot, but when he was accidentally shot in the thigh, the bullet lodged against a main artery and remained there for the rest of his life – the doctors didn't believe they could safely remove it. When he was recuperating, he saw an article with a mountain ram, and wrote in his diary, "I want to see what the ram sees. I've decided on Canada." It ended up being a good choice. Riggall went on to establish a guiding business just south of Twin Butte, with many wealthy Americans as frequent clients. According to his daughter Doris, "He carried a little vest pocket Kodak and he was so quick to size up a picture chance and snap it, it was uncanny." He coloured many of his own photos using paints distilled from leaves. After 40 years of guiding, he turned his business over to his son-in-law Andy Russell and oldest daughter, Kathleen. Andy would go on to become a legend himself, as a well-respected cowboy, trapper, author, and conservationist.

S **Pincher Creek** www.pincher-creek.com
T: 1-888-298-5855; 403-627-5199

Blackfoot name – *umpska-spitsi,* meaning "south tall trees." The name was descriptive of the area. The word "south" was added to distinguish it from High River, which was also called *spitsi* for its tall trees.

The English name Pincher Creek is said to have resulted from a pair of lost pincers. They were dropped by a group of prospectors in 1868 and finally found in the creek in 1874 by the North West Mounted Police. The creek became Pincher Creek, as did the detachment established by the NWMP in 1878 along its banks. Nearby, Colonel Macleod, the commander of the police force at Fort Macleod, had picked "a beautiful place about 25 miles west of the [fort] where the land is very good." Here they established a "Police Farm," growing feed and breeding horse remounts for the force. The operation was quite successful but was taking too much manpower away from law enforcement duties. In 1882 it became the foundation for the Stewart Ranch when it was privatized and taken over by Captain John Stewart.

DID YOU KNOW?

The Livingstone Range west of Pincher Creek was named after David Livingstone, the famous explorer of central Africa.

Chaw – a chew of tobacco

Wind turbines at Pincher Creek
L. ANDREWS

Even though it only operated four years, the NWMP ranch proved, without a doubt, that ranching would work here. Soon pioneers in search of land and the promise of the new frontier were settling along the Creek, and a thriving community began to flourish. By 1886 Stewart had about 2,500 cattle and 300 horses on his 20,200-hectare (50,000-acre) lease. Over the years, he was joined by a long list of Mounties who took their discharge after a compulsory three-year term and decided to settle – they knew a good thing when they saw it. During their patrols, they could see all the land had to offer. With (generally) mild winters, good water, nutritious grassland, and spectacular scenery, the country seemed ideal. Names like Kettles, Lynch-Staunton, Herron, Macleod, and Maunsell (to name a few) formed a big part of the ranching community in the area. Their reputation as fair dealers and their knowledge of the law helped ensure the peaceful development of the district. Ranching and farming remain cornerstone industries here, but oil and gas, and more recently, electrical power generation with wind turbines, are big contributors to the local economy.

To learn more about Pincher Creek's frontier history, don't miss the outstanding Kootenai Brown Pioneer Village. It's an absolute treasure, located on the banks of the creek right in the middle of town.

Kootenai Brown Pioneer Village
Visitor Information Centre in Pioneer Place

Farley Wuth, Curator   www.telusplanet.net/public/kootenai
1037 Bev McLachlin Drive, P.O. Box 1226, Pincher Creek, AB, T0K 1W0
T: 403-627-3684

E: kootenai@telusplanet.net

ACCEPTS V, MC   ADMISSION CHARGED

Open summer season, mid-May to mid-September, weekdays 8:00 AM to 8:00 PM; weekends and holidays 10:00 AM to 8:00 PM; winter season, weekdays 8:00 AM to 4:30 PM or by appointment.

If you have any interest in the history of the Canadian West circa 1890, the Pioneer

Village is a gem not to be missed. The size and quality of the exhibits here are unexpected in a town the size of Pincher Creek. The outstanding collection of historical buildings and over 15,000 artifacts speaks volumes about the community's pride in its western heritage.

The village includes a large collection of authentically restored and furnished turn-of-the-century buildings, which have been moved to the site from various locations in the Pincher Creek area, plus a CPR caboose, the original museum, and a magnificent new log structure called Pioneer Place. Built on land donated by the town, Pioneer Place forms the entrance to the village. Hundreds of volunteer hours, including a roof raising, helped to reduce construction costs, while many current and past residents of Pincher Creek and area sponsored the logs, floor tiles, windows, and doors. Two exhibition galleries feature rotating

Cavvy – a Spanish word for a herd of horses

artifact displays that highlight themes from local area history. There is a large well-stocked information centre, with an extremely helpful staff, a gift shop, and one of the best assortments of books on the history of Alberta's southwest ranching country that you will find anywhere.

The village takes its name from John George "Kootenai" Brown (see sidebar page 27), a colourful frontiersman who was instrumental in the establishment of Waterton Lakes National Park and who served as its first superintendent. His 1883 three-room log cabin has been preserved on the site, but there are a number of other buildings that are must-sees, like the Walrond ranch house (see sidebar page 82) that was built in 1894 and was the headquarters for the ranch. The ranch was

Kootenai Brown Historical Village is a gem not to be missed.
KOOTENAI BROWN HISTORICAL VILLAGE

established in 1883, north of Lundbreck along the road now called the Cowboy Trail. Between 15 and 20 men ate their meals and spent their evenings in the old ranch house, which is now the official home of the Alberta Cowboy Poetry Association.

The NWMP Outpost 1887 was used as an outpost by the North West Mounted Police from the 1880s to the beginning of World War I, and features historical NWMP uniforms along with histories of some of the officers who were stationed at the early Pincher Creek barracks. The Cox House came from the Mount View Ranch, five miles west of town. The house contains many original artifacts from the Cox family. It is hard to believe that the house accommodated the entire Cox family, which included eight daughters and three sons. Don't miss the handcrafted "Soddy," built to scale and decorated in the style similar to that of the early pioneer days.

Not only have the restorations been done by volunteers, but all of the flower gardens located throughout the village are maintained by a dedicated group of green thumbers who are responsible for the beautiful displays that showcase the entire site throughout the summer. Once you have had a wander through the exhibits, it's a good spot to sit and enjoy a picnic lunch by the creek and enjoy the blooms.

Other Points of Interest in Pincher Creek and Surrounding Area

Lebel Mansion on Kettles Street
L. ANDREWS

Lebel Mansion (696 Kettles Street) is a Provincial Historic Site built for the grand sum of $22,305.21 in 1910 by Timothe Lebel. In 1924 the house was sold to the Daughters of Jesus, and it operated as a hospital for nearly 60 years. The beautiful old mansion, with its ornate verandah, brick turrets, and bell-shaped roofs, was purchased by the town in 1985. The town's Allied Arts Council has worked to preserve and restore the building and promote the arts. A free public art gallery features new monthly exhibits, and a small gift shop offers local artwork. There are no guided tours, but you are welcome to have a look. The mansion is open all year from 1:00 PM to 5:00 PM Monday to Friday and on Saturdays in the summer.

Wall-sized murals are featured on several buildings in the downtown area. It is worth parking your car and taking a stroll around to have a look. There are currently five murals depicting various aspects of the history and culture of the area.

"The Pinchers" by Doug Drediger shows the finding of the famous pincers that gave the town its name.
L. ANDREWS

The Pincher Creek Hutterite Colony offers one-hour tours every day except Sunday. The colony is located three kilometres west of town on Hwy. 507, but tours must be pre-arranged. Contact Rosa Gross at 403-627-4021. (German spoken.)

DID YOU KNOW?

Hutterites take their name from Jakob Hutter, who preached a strict communal way of life and a rejection of the material world. He was arrested and burned at the stake in 1536 for his views. Hutterites fled religious persecution from many parts of Europe, eventually settling in South Dakota in the late 1870s, where their pacifist beliefs led to harassment by the US government. In an 1899 agreement, Canada promised to respect their pacifism and provide religious freedom in order to attract them as settlers to the west. Following WWI, about 2,000 Hutterites accepted the Canadian invitation and moved colonies north.

MARY ELLA AND HER "GREAT ADVENTURE"

Mary Ella Lees was one of the first white women to live in the district. Her father had threatened to cut off her inheritance if she didn't abandon her plans to join her half-brother William, who was managing a sawmill on Mill Creek. But Mary's attempted suicide finally convinced her father that she was serious, and she headed west, inheritance intact, in 1883.

Mary Ella (Lees) Inderwick c. 1880s
GLENBOW ARCHIVES NA-1365-2

Although Mary always called her time out west her "great adventure," like most women she endured her share of hardships, loneliness, and disappointments. Her diary describes the rough log shack that was her first home, "The floor had never been scrubbed, it had to be scraped with a spade before scrubbing," and weather that was "100,000 degrees below." To help fill the intense loneliness, she rode constantly, forgetting all her troubles "in this joyous air with the grand protecting mountains always standing on the western horizon." In 1884 she married local rancher Charlie Inderwick. At their North Fork Ranch, she described the cowboys as "a nice lot of men." She found she preferred their company to that of Charlie's snobby English friends. The adventure finished in 1888, when Charlie's financial mismanagement forced them to sell the ranch and return east. In the end, Mary may have agreed with a neighbour's comment that "99 per cent of the hardship [in the district] was suffered by the women."

Grub Stop

Antonio's Pizza, 695 Charlotte Street, 403-627-2898; Barry's Cookin', 942 Hyde Street, 403-627-1945; Bright Pearl, 745 Main Street, 403-627-4890; Daily Grind Coffee Shop, 823 Kettles Street, 403-627-2120; Denise's Bistro, 732 Kettles Street, 403-627-1875; Ginger Gardens, 757 Main Street, 403-627-3438; Heritage Inn Season's Café, 919 Waterton Avenue, 403-627-5000; Husky Junction, Junction of Hwy. 3 and Hwy. 6, 403-627-3188; Kentucky Fried Chicken, 970 Main Street, 403-627-4232; King's, 696 Main Street, 403-627-2079; Luigi's Steak and Pizza, 1315 Fairbarn Avenue, 403-627-2526; Mrs. P's Coffee Corner, Co-op Mall, 403-627-5558; Peking Palace, 729 Main Street, 403-627-5555; Subway, 878 Main Street, 403-627-4948; Swiss Alpine, 988 Main Street, 403-627-5079; The Royal Canadian Legion, 691 Main Street, 403-627-4024; The Windward, 1049 Waterton Avenue; 403-627-3011.

"OLD GLAD" LEFT HIS MARK

William and Harriett Gladstone were early Metis settlers who established the "Gladstone House," a stopping house along Pincher Creek. "Old Glad," as he was called, had a reputation as a top-notch carpenter, having constructed Fort Whoop-up near Lethbridge and the sawmill at Mill Creek. He built many homes in the area for settlers of means (including the Garnetts), which were generally regarded as some of the finest in the district. In 1958 his grandson James became Canada's first Native senator.

KEEPING UP APPEARANCES

The British-born Garnett brothers, who secured some 16,000 hectares (40,000 acres) of land in the Pincher Creek area, managed to keep up appearances by building one of the finest houses in the district, complete with carpet, wallpaper, and a piano. When J.R. Higinbotham visited one day for dinner, he was surprised to see them all appear in evening dress. "In answer to our looks of astonishment, Jack explained that this was not a display of swank, but a custom to which they had rigidly adhered since their arrival in the West . . . to keep them from reverting to savagery." It is said their sister, Miss Garnett, ruled supreme, to the point where she had her brothers wash the dishes after the meals – not a common occurrence in most ranching households, even now!

Parkway Motel and Hostel   www.parkwaymotel.ca

Bob Drouin

1070 Waterton Avenue, P.O. Box 130, Pincher Creek, AB, T0K 1W0

T: 1-888-209-9902

E: mogulty@telusplanet.net

ACCEPTS V, MC, AMEX

.**Open** all year

WHAT THEY OFFER: 41 units with a choice of kitchen apartments, one- and two-bedroom suites, kitchenettes and studio apartments; honeymoon suite has its own hot tub; rooms have colour cable TV, direct-dial phones, many with microwaves and VCRs; access to sauna, hot tub, steam shower, pool table, Internet service, and confectionary. A new five-unit bunkhouse hostel offers single-over-double bunk beds and separate, but private bathrooms. There are packages that combine accommodation and skiing at nearby Castle Mountain in the winter or golf at a local course in the summer.

There are also several Cowboy Trail partners and another Icon Attraction located in the Pincher Creek Area.

September Springs Ranch

Sheran and Maurice Carter

P.O. Box 216, Pincher Creek, AB, T0K 1W0

T: 1-877-686-4783

E: sheran@uniqueartantique.com

ACCEPTS D, V, MC, AMEX

www.uniqueartantique.com

Open May long weekend to Thanksgiving long weekend in October, 10:00 AM to 5:00 PM daily or by appointment.

Sheran and Maurice Carter originally built their barn to store extra furniture, but when it started to get too full, they decided to sell some of it instead. They converted the barn into an antique store and added a sunroom, where they serve lunches overlooking a spectacular view of the Rocky Mountains.

WHAT THEY OFFER: The tea room is famous for its Devonshire cream teas and homemade soups, but also offers salads, sandwiches, chili, fruit and veggie platters, and special desserts; there is live piano on Sunday afternoons. The main floor and barn loft are full of unexpected treasures, including an eclectic selection of antiques, collectibles, china, western artifacts, designer and vintage clothing, antique jewellery, and specialty foods. Don't miss the "Magic Dress" imported from New York. It can be converted into as many as thirty different designs. Sheran can show you four or five in the space of about thirty seconds. From mid-June to mid-July, the Iris Festival celebrates a riotous profusion of blooms with over 25 spectacular colours. Visitors are welcome to walk in the gardens or along the creek and enjoy the million-dollar view to the west. As well, there is a tipi and a rustic log cabin (with no power or running water) for rent on a self-catered basis.

GETTING THERE: From Hwy. 6 in Pincher Creek, head west on Secondary Hwy. 507 for 2 KM. The turnoff for the shop and tea room is on the left (south) side of the road. Follow the signs in.

Butte — a high isolated hill with steep sides and a flat top

Bloomin' Inn Bed and Breakfast and Our Country Store

Francis and Colleen Cyr   www.bloomin-inn.com

P.O. Box 1346, Pincher Creek, AB, T0K 1W0

T: 403-627-5829

E: bloominn@telusplanet.net

ACCEPTS D, V, MC

Bed and Breakfast open all year. **Our Country Store open** daily June to September from 10:00 AM to 4:00 PM; **High Country Meats open** daily year-round from 10:00 AM to 4:00 PM.

The Cyr family has been ranching in this spot just east of Pincher Creek since the early 1900s. Francis' grandfather headed west from New Brunswick and was part of a large French element that settled in the area. Signs of the early days are still in evidence on the property – an old wagon trail used by early settlers remains visible, as do buffalo wallows as deep as three feet.

PETE LAGRANDEUR, SADDLE BRONC CHAMPION, HAD A SPECIAL WAY WITH HORSES

It's said that no matter how rank the bronc or saddle horse was, Pete would have the patience to tame the animal and ride it as if it was a "Sunday pleasure horse." The animals seemed to sense he had no fear. He was born in 1890 on the family homestead near Pincher Creek. His father, Mose, was from Montreal, his mother, Julia, from Nebraska. Together they had come north through Montana in a covered wagon, trailing a string of horses to settle at the point where Pincher Creek flows into the Oldman River. It became known as LaGrandeur Crossing and a stopping place for stagecoaches. Pete grew up as a cowboy, working his entire life in the area on various ranches and as head stockman on the Peigan Indian Reservation. In 1924 he rode Yellow Fever to beat Pete Knight for the Calgary Stampede Bronc Championship and the All Round Cowboy title. He judged at the Stampede for ten years and was inducted into the Canadian Rodeo Hall of Fame in 1991.

For many years, the Cyrs ran a farm-based crafts industry, growing dried flowers that Colleen transformed into distinctive dried flower arrangements, wreaths, swags, and bunches, which she sold across Canada. When Colleen's artistic flair combined with Francis' talent for construction, the Bloomin' Inn was born. This place is a visual feast, inside and out. To the west, the entire horizon is filled with a breathtaking view of the mountains. Inside the ranch house, Colleen has translated her love of old general stores into the real thing. With high open-beam ceilings and a private library loft, there is plenty of space for her collection of antiques and pioneer memorabilia.

WHAT THEY OFFER: There are four themed rooms in the ranch house, with private bathroom, handmade linens and furniture, and spectacular views. (The former Governor General Adrienne

The Rocky Mountains fill the horizon to the west of the Bloomin' Inn.
BLOOMIN' INN

Clarkson actually stayed here during an official tour.) The Bunkhouse and Potting Shed cabins have lofts and handmade furniture straight out of the Old West; full breakfast is a culinary event, with fresh-baked breads, muffins, fruit, and a hot course; lunch or evening meals with advance notice feature homegrown veggies and ranch-raised meat or poultry; the separate workshop is an ideal spot for crafters and scrapbookers (don't miss the old-time town façade created by Francis on one of the interior walls). Our Country Store has a wide selection of dried flower creations, hand-woven baskets, handcrafted log furniture, and kitchen

BLOOMIN' INN MEATBALL STEW
(ONE OF THE MOST POPULAR DISHES AT THE RANCH)

Chop one medium turnip, six to eight large carrots, six to eight large potatoes, and six celery stalks into bite-size chunks. Sautee a large chopped onion in one Tbsp (15 ml) of canola oil, then combine all the vegetables in a Dutch oven and cover with four cups (1L) chicken or beef stock. Add up to two cups of water if needed. While the vegetables are cooking, brown meatballs (see below) in a large frying pan, drain on paper towels, then add the meatballs and one cup (250 ml) green beans to the pot. Simmer about 30 minutes and serve with dumplings or biscuits. For the meatballs, combine (but don't overmix) one pound (500 g) lean ground beef, ½ pound (250 g) ground pork, one envelope dry onion soup mix, 1 egg, two handfuls oatmeal, and salt and pepper. Shape into 1½ inch diameter meatballs for about five or six meatballs per serving. Serves six to eight.

antiques; High Country Meats sells consumer portions of ranch-raised meat, poultry, and eggs, as well as homemade lasagna.

DIRECTIONS: From Hwy. 6 (Waterton Avenue) in Pincher Creek, take Secondary Hwy. 785 northeast to Tower Road (TWP6-4). Turn right (east) and drive 4 KM to RR29-4. Turn right (south) for 1.6 KM. The ranch is on the right (west) side of the road.

39 **Misty Mountain Adventures**   www.mistymountainadventures.ca
Joe and Doreen Jacobson

P.O. Box 1655, Pincher Creek, AB, T0K 1W0
T: 403-627-1806

E: mistymtn@telusplanet.net
ACCEPTS PC

Open all year – pack trips and backcountry riding from July to September.

Joe and Doreen have been offering adventures in the mountain backcountry for over 25 years. Joe grew up in a rodeo family – his father owned the original Millar Ranch at Millarville – and took his first trip into the mountains in 1958. Since then, there isn't much of the Eastern Slopes country from Millarville south that he hasn't ridden into at some point in his life. According to Joe, at Misty Mountain you get "Ma and Pa Kettle" on every trip. They pride themselves on offering personalized service, Joe with over 40 years' experience as an outfitter and Doreen providing home-cooked gourmet meals after a hard day on the trail. In fact, some of their guests are actually the second generation of families that have been coming back to Misty Mountain for many years.

> **DID YOU KNOW?**
>
> Napi or Old Man appears in the ancient stories that tell how the Blackfoot tribes were given their traditions. Napi often got himself into hot water because he acted on impulse. He overdid things and caused chaos as a result. Stories about Napi teach the importance of balance in life – Napi always went to extremes and failed to maintain this balance.

WHAT THEY OFFER: Ranch packages have choice of accommodations in four guest rooms in main ranch house (sharing two bathrooms) or a tipi in private Cottonwood forest by the river (with outdoor hot tub, shower, and washroom facilities close by); the ranch house has a large great room, fireplace, indoor hot tub, and solarium, and a large concrete patio ideal for weddings; daily rate includes three hearty meals, a float trip on the river, and riding on the ranch; day rides in the mountains can be arranged.

The Kananaskis Adventure is a four-night, five-day wilderness trip from base

Ready for a Western wedding.
MISTY MOUNTAIN ADVENTURES

camp in the mountains; custom expeditions generally move camp from day to day with pack horses to access remote wilderness areas; weekender combines gourmet food and riding from base camp; overseas visitors can get airport pickup, sleeping gear for the camping trips, and pre-and/or post-B&B; custom guided fishing wade or float trips can be arranged, as well as pack trips that access remote trout streams.

Rocky Mountain Ranch Adventure teams up with Lucasia Ranch Vacations in the Porcupine Hills (see page 84), where you will spend time riding with the cowboys, checking the herd, or moving cattle; then transfer to the trailhead, where Misty Mountain will take you on a scenic pack trip into the Rocky Mountains. Eight- or ten-day options include all accommodations, meals, and trailhead transfers.

GETTING THERE: From the junction of Hwy. 6 and Hwy. 3, head east on Hwy. 3 to the sign marked Old Man Road. Turn left (north) and drive 0.5 KM to the Texas gate. Turn right (east) into the ranch.

> **DID YOU KNOW?**
> A Texas gate isn't an entry into Texas, but a cattle guard. It is a steel grid, with spaces large enough for a hoof to pass through, placed over a ditch at the entrance to a fenced-off area. Vehicles can drive over it, but it will contain horses or cattle because they refuse to step on it. The gates originated in the oilfields of Texas, where they were made from drill stem. They allowed easy access to a well site in a pasture without the inconvenience of opening and closing gates.

Heritage Acres

www.pincher-creek.com

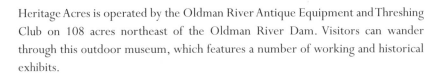

Pat Watson (resident caretaker)

P.O. Box 2496, Pincher Creek, AB, T0K 1W0

T: 403-627-2082

! Open daily May 1 to September 30

Admission by donation

Heritage Acres is operated by the Oldman River Antique Equipment and Threshing Club on 108 acres northeast of the Oldman River Dam. Visitors can wander through this outdoor museum, which features a number of working and historical exhibits.

WHAT THEY OFFER: A variety of restored machinery and buildings from the area, including the 1917 Presbyterian Church from Jumbo Valley, east of Granum (still used for Christmas and Easter services) and the Brocket elevator, acquired in 1999; Crystal Village is a complete village of buildings handmade by "Boss" Zoeteman entirely from glass telephone insulators; the historic Doukhobor Barn was built in 1917–18 and moved over two days and 53 miles to its present site. The huge loft is used for dances and group functions; the main floor houses an outstanding collection of miniature farming equipment and mini hand-carved horse teams complete with harnesses.

The restored Brocket elevator at Heritage Acres.
L. ANDREWS

There is a chuckwagon cook-off the last weekend of June. The Annual Show on the August long weekend has working demonstrations of restored antique horse and tractor equipment, including a 1920s wooden threshing machine; the day includes breakfast, barbecue, and barn dance. Unserviced camping all summer.

GETTING THERE: From Hwy. 3, head north on Secondary Hwy. 785 until you see the sign for Heritage Acres on the right (east) side of the road.

THE VISION QUEST

Although the specifics of the rituals varied, the vision quest was a fundamental element in the spiritual life of practically every native North American tribe. For the Plains Indians, it was usually the mature person (almost always a man) who sought the vision. A person could seek a vision on numerous occasions throughout his life when he faced a big challenge or felt compelled to find spiritual guidance. It was a solitary experience, in which the person isolated himself from his community in an attempt to gain wisdom and direction in his life choices. Before the quest began, the seeker would undergo a process of purification with the assistance of a holy man. Depending on the tribe, this could involve participating in a sweat lodge and the smoking of the sacred pipe to the Great Spirit. He would then strip off most of his clothing and make his way to a sacred spot, often at the top of a mountain. The spot had to be as rugged and lonely as possible to intensify a feeling of isolation and nearness to the Great Mystery. One of the most sacred places for the vision quest of the Blackfoot was (and continues to be) Chief Mountain (south of Cardston). (See sidebar page 20). The person would fast and pray for a number of days, waiting for guidance to come in the form of a vision. The vision could come in the form of anything that breathed, or from an inanimate thing like a rock. Although the experience was intensely personal, the vision itself was submitted to the elders for scrutiny and interpretation to ensure its integrity. The vision was not considered just an individual matter, but was viewed as belonging to the entire people.

BEFORE THE HORSE

It is estimated the Alberta Plains Indians did not have access to horses until around 1730. As a result, they depended on other methods of hunting bison long before they harnessed the speed and flexibility that the horse brought. To be successful, these hunting methods required an intimate understanding of the environment in which they lived and the development of sophisticated communal hunting techniques. Everyone had to work together to ensure the success of the hunt – survival depended on it. Buffalo were driven along drive lines where rows of rock piles known as "dead men" acted as a funnel to bring the animals to the edge of the jump. Hunters behind the "dead men" would keep the buffalo moving forward by waving robes to frighten them, until they plunged to their deaths over the precipice of the jump, or were driven into specially built pounds or corrals, where they were surrounded and killed.

Head-Smashed-In Buffalo Jump Interpretive Centre

P.O. Box 1977, Fort Macleod, AB, T0L 0Z0 www.head-smashed-in.com

 T: 403-553-2731 (toll-free in Alberta by first dialing 310-0000)

E: info@head-smashed-in.com

 ACCEPTS V, MC, TC, CC ADMISSION CHARGED

Open daily May 15 to September 14, 9:00 AM to 6:00 PM; September 15 to May 14, 10:00 AM to 5:00 PM

Contrary to popular belief, the name of the jump does not refer to the smashed heads of the buffalo. According to legend, "About 150 years ago, a young brave wanted to witness the plunge of countless buffalo as his people drove them to their deaths over the sandstone cliffs. Standing under the shelter of a ledge like a man behind a waterfall, he watched the great beasts fall past him. The hunt was unusually good that day. As the bodies mounted, he became trapped between the animals and the cliffs. When his people came to do the butchering, they found him with his skull crushed by the weight of the buffalo carcasses. Thus they named the place Head-Smashed-In."

This buffalo jump is one of the oldest, largest, and best-preserved sites in North America. It is estimated that it was first used for killing bison at least 5,700

Viewing point at the top of Head-Smashed-In Buffalo Jump.
HEAD-SMASHED-IN BUFFALO JUMP

years ago and perhaps as early as 10,000 years ago. In 1981 UNESCO recognized its outstanding archaeological, historical, and ethnological significance by naming it a World Heritage Site. Archaeologists believe that 150,000 buffalo were killed here before the introduction of the horse to the Plains Indians ended the need to conduct large-scale communal hunts.

A visit to the jump can easily take half a day, but if you don't have that much time to spend, be prepared to take at least a couple of hours. Guided interpretive tours, which can take up to three hours depending on your level of interest, are also available. The interpretive centre has been built right into the rock next to the main part of the jump; in fact, it blends in so well with the surrounding terrain that you might not even notice it when you first drive up.

The centre features five levels, each level documenting a different aspect of the buffalo hunting culture of the Plains people,

> **WHAT'S IN A NAME?**
> The Blackfoot call the peaks of the Livingstone Range "tipi liners" because they rise above the prairies in a solid wall resembling liners inside a tipi. They use these "tipi liners" to predict the weather – atmospheric conditions actually make the range appear closer or farther away, almost like a mirage.

from ancient times to the arrival of the Europeans. You can watch a short film that describes the planning and rituals that went into ensuring a successful hunt, then start your explorations from the top or the bottom. Exhibits explain the process and significance of the buffalo hunt and give insight into the lifestyles, legends, religion, and history of the Blackfoot people.

Don't miss the short walk outside to the viewpoint overlooking the jump area. On a clear day you can almost see to forever from here. A vast panorama of prairies and mountains will take your breath away with its stark windswept beauty. Once you have explored the centre, you can take the buffalo jump trail to the lower kill site, where you will be able to view a tipi ring and the site of the archaeological dig, as well as an incredible variety of trees, shrubs, and small animals that call this place home.

If you are looking for a more in-depth understanding of the Blackfoot culture and the importance of the buffalo, the centre offers one- and two-night camping adventures at their tipi site just below the main entrance. Packages include meals and accommodation in tipis equipped with air mattresses, water, camping wood stove, wood, and flashlights. Meals are served at the cafeteria in the centre (where you can dine on buffalo stew and bannock). Guided tours of the centre are included, as well as interpretive learning programs led by knowledgeable Blackfoot guides. Overnight tipi camping is also available without all the other services.

GETTING THERE: Head east of the Pincher Creek turnoff on Hwy. 3 to Secondary Hwy. 785. Turn left (north) and follow the signs for 35 KM to the site. This is a gravel road and can be hard to navigate after a heavy rain. It is a beautiful drive if the road is good. Otherwise, head east of Pincher Creek on Hwy. 3 for 51 KM to Fort Macleod. Take Hwy. 2 north for 4 KM and then turn left (west) on Secondary Hwy. 785 and go 13 KM to the site.

Two additional Cowboy Trail partners are located east of the Pincher Creek turnoff on Hwy. 3.

Peigan Crafts Ltd.   www.peigancrafts.com
P.O. Box 100, Brocket, AB, T0K 0H0

T: 1-800-800-1478
E: peigancrafts@telus.net

WHAT THEY OFFER: The Piikani Blackfoot Nation (or Peigan) is one of the original tribes of the Blackfoot Confederacy that once dominated the northern Great Plains. Located midway between Pincher Creek and Fort Macleod, the Peigan-owned factory at Brocket has been making authentic handmade moccasins, mukluks, and mittens for almost thirty years, using only the best leather and furs,

PLAINS BISON (BUFFALO) (BLACKFOOT IINIIKSI)

There is no such thing as a North American buffalo, but the name stuck after early explorers began using it. The animals found here have a unique shoulder hump that distinguishes them from the buffalo that are native to Africa and Asia. Their proper name is bison, and the animals you will see along the Cowboy Trail are called plains bison. The bison hunted at Head-Smashed-In Buffalo Jump for 6,000 years probably ranged over a territory extending from Alaska to Mexico, and from the Rocky Mountains to the Appalachians in the east.

It is estimated that as many as 60 million of these magnificent beasts ranged through most of the central region of North America at the time of the first European contact. Evidence of the huge herds can still be found in southern Alberta, where large isolated boulders are often smoothly polished because itchy bison used them as back rubs for thousands of years. Despite the staggering numbers of bison that once existed, they were reduced to virtual extinction by a wholesale slaughter that saw their numbers dwindle to less than 1,000 by the late 1880s. The Canadian government played a key role in saving them when it purchased 709 bison from Montana rancher Don Michel Pablo. A herd was eventually established at Elk Island and Wood Buffalo National Parks. Along the trail you can view them at the bison paddocks in Waterton Lakes National Park and at the Rocky Mountain House National Historic Site. But keep a look out along the road, where you will often see private herds on bison ranches.

More than 60 million of these magnificent beasts once ranged the great plains.
JANET NASH

and glass beadwork that reflects traditional Piikani Blackfoot designs. There is a small storefront at the factory, but products are available at many fine stores across Canada, including Ten Thousand Villages. In Alberta you will find them at the Glenbow Museum shop in Calgary and the Kootenai Brown Pioneer Village shop in Pincher Creek (to name just two). Phone orders are welcome, and tours can be arranged with prior notice.

GETTING THERE: Head east of the Pincher Creek turnoff on Hwy. 3 for 14 KM to the hamlet of Brocket.

Bent Creek Western Vacations Guest Ranch   www.bentcreek.ca

Gerry and Kathy Karchuk
P.O. Box 542, Fort Macleod, AB, T0L 0Z0
T: 1-866-553-3974 (in North America)
E: cowboss@bentcreek.ca
ACCEPTS MC, V, TC
Open June to September

Kathy and Gerry raise Black Angus cattle and horses on their ranch in Meadowlark Valley on the banks of the Oldman River. Gerry is a retired teacher with an extensive background in native studies – in fact, he has been honoured with a native name, "Mountain Horse," by the nearby Blood Tribe. Gerry combines over 25 years of professional teaching expertise with *Equine Canada* National Coaching training to help guests gain a deeper appreciation of horses and horsemanship during their visit. He takes his time matching horse to rider, giving you some practice time with your mount so you get the best riding experience possible. Then at the end of a day in the saddle, you can relax and tuck into one of Kathy's hearty, home-cooked meals.

Your home away from home at Bent Creek Western Vacations Guest Ranch.
L. ANDREWS

WHAT THEY OFFER: There are accommodations for up to eight in the main ranch-style home; one queen room with private bath, remainder with shared facilities; private sitting room with access to ping-pong; riverbank and firepit right outside the door offer a great place for fishing, walking, birding, and photography, or just pull up a chair and read a good book.

Packages include one-, three- and five-day stays with three substantial meals a day; (Kathy will accommodate dietary requirements with advance notice); the Weekender offers a two-night stay, five meals and one and a half days of riding; Cowgirl Getaway can include any combination that works for your group; ranch clinics offer three-day options focusing on horsemanship, ranch horses, and cattle handling, or pack horses and trail riding; there is even a six day Cowboy 101 Boot Camp, aimed at cowboys looking for a job on a ranch or guest ranch, or wannabes who just want to learn; riding lessons, full-day trips with barbecue, or half-day rides also offered; customized packages available. Just let them know what you need.

With the Open Range Cowboy Adventure Package, spend a week at Bent Creek learning the basics of Western riding theory and practice, then transfer to Willow Lane Ranch (see page 87) for the chance to practice everything you have learned on a working cattle ranch. Includes an evening at the famous Ranchman's (see page 152) for some foot-stompin' Western music and dancing

GETTING THERE: From the town of Fort Macleod, head east on Hwy. 3 for 9 KM to Meadowlark Road. Turn left (north) and follow the gravel road for 6 KM to a wrought iron sign on the left (west) side of the road. Follow the trail into the valley to the ranch.

Once you are finished exploring the territory east of Pincher Creek, you can resume your journey west on Hwy. 3 past the village of Cowley.

Cowley is called *akai-sow kaas* in Blackfoot, meaning "many prairie turnips," after the edible wild turnips found in the area. It was originally called French Flats because of the large number of French settlers in the area. The name "Cowley" (an English term for "pasture for cows") is said to have been suggested by local rancher Frederick Godsal, for the excellent grazing close by.

The village is located three kilometres north of Pincher Creek on Hwy. 6 and 10

BENT CREEK'S FAMOUS DRUMSTICK CAKE "A LITTLE TASTE OF YOUR CHILDHOOD"

Mix 1½ cups (375 ml) crushed vanilla wafers, ½ cup (125 ml) chopped peanuts, ¼ cup (63 ml) melted butter, and 3 Tbsp (45 ml) peanut butter. Mix and press into a 9 x 13 pan. Keep some aside for topping. Cream ½ pound (250 g) package cream cheese, ½ cup (125 ml) sugar, ½ cup (125 ml) peanut butter in a large bowl. Add 2 Tsp (10 ml) vanilla and 4 eggs, one at a time. Fold in one large bowl of Cool Whip and pour mixture over base. Drizzle ½ cup (125 ml) chocolate sauce over top and cut through diagonally with knife. Sprinkle remaining crumbs on top. Freeze, but remember to take it out ½ hour before serving.

kilometres west on Hwy. 3. The view of the Livingstone Range as you travel west is breathtaking. Locals recommend the Savory Suite Café (403-627-9177) as a good place to eat. About half a kilometre past Cowley, a highway marker commemorates the early Doukhobor settlers in the area. Formerly known as the Christian Community of Universal Brotherhood, the Doukhobors fled religious persecution in Russia in 1899, only to find it again when they settled in BC and Saskatchewan. In 1915, about 300 moved to an area near Cowley, determined to follow their motto of "toil and a peaceful life." A large Doukhobor barn from the area is now preserved at Heritage Acres near Pincher Creek.

Massacre Butte: Just north of the hamlet of Cowley, Massacre Butte marks the site where a group of a dozen American settlers were killed by a war party of Blood Indians in 1867. The settlers had travelled west from Minnesota in a wagon train led by Captain James L. Fisk, but somewhere along the Missouri River in what is now Montana, they decided to head north to investigate claims of gold fields on the North Saskatchewan River. They travelled at night, believing this to be safer, but were surrounded near the Butte by Medicine Calf and his warriors. Once their ammunition ran out, they were all killed. Stories about a blond scalp from one of the victims persisted for many years. When the train still stopped at Cowley, passengers would often walk up to the Butte in search of souvenirs.

Recommended Reading

60 Years in an Old Cow Town by A.L. Freebairn

Bert Riggall: Mountain Guide Extraordinary by Doris Burton

Charcoal's World by Hugh Dempsey

Grizzly Country by Andy Russell

Head-Smashed-In Buffalo Jump by Gordon Reid

Leaning on the Wind by Sid Marty

The People: A Historical Guide to the First Nations of Alberta, Saskatchewan and Manitoba by Donald Ward

Rocky Mountain Rangers: Southern Alberta's Cowboy Cavalry in the North West Rebellion—1885 by Gordon E. Tolton (occasional paper no. 28 by the Lethbridge Historical Society)

Trails of a Wilderness Wanderer by Andy Russell

Where the Rivers Meet: A History of the Upper Oldman River by Barry Potyondi

The Waldron Range
By A.L. Freebairn

Gee, but the city's a lonesome place
      For a man who has lived in the hills,
Has rode on the range in the old cattle days,
      And known all its romance and thrills.
I'm crowded to death in its canyon-like streets,
      I'm sick of its jazz and its noise —
You can take it from me that I'd far sooner be
      On the range with the old Waldron boys.

I'm tired of the sights and the city's bright lights,
      I long for the peace of the range,
The spell of the mountains, majestic and grand,
      The nights that are awesome and strange;
The men who will smile as they cuss you the while
      In a language no preacher employs —
You can take if from me, that I'd sure like to be
      On the range with the old Waldron boys.

I sit here and dream of that far away scene,
      And I live it all over again;
The round-up, the branding, the heat and the dust,
      The free open life on the plain;
The lure of the past that forever will last,
      For distance ne'er dims or destroys —
You can take it from me, it's worth while to be
      On the range with the old Waldron boys.

So I'm hitting the trail for the Porcupine Hills,
      Going back to the rangeland once more,
Where I'll straddle a horse for the W.R.,
      Perhaps sleep on the old bunkhouse floor.
It's a helluva life, as I've often times said,
      With none of the pleasures or joys —
But take it from me, I'm soon going to be
      On the range with the old Waldron boys.

REPRINTED WITH THE PERMISSION OF AGNES FREEBAIRN MITCHELL AND L. FREEBAIRN FARLEY

3 : LUNDBRECK TO BAR U RANCH NATIONAL HISTORIC SITE OF CANADA

"A good horse goes until he can't go anymore, and then he goes some more."

—Ted Stone, *Cowboy Logic*

Communities

 Lundbreck

Accommodations

19 Lyndon Creek Cottage

14 Chimney Rock Bed and Breakfast

Farm & Ranch Vacations

43 Sierra West Cabins and Ranch Vacations

44 Skyline Ranching and Outfitting

33 Brown Creek Ranch Vacations

34 Circle 6 Ranch Getaway

38 Lucasia Ranch Vacations

45 Willow Lane Ranch

Fishing Lodge

57 Anchor B Ranch Fly-Fishing Lodge

Bring Your Own Horse

43 Sierra West Cabins and Ranch Vacations

33 Brown Creek Ranch Vacations

34 Circle 6 Ranch Getaway

19 Lyndon Creek Cottage

Outfitters

50 Highlandview Guest Ranch

Camping

29 Chain Lakes Provincial Park

Restaurants

29 Chain Lakes Provincial Park

☆ Bar U Ranch National Historic Site of Canada

Shopping, Antiques & Artisans

61 Frontier Western Shop

☆ Bar U Ranch National Historic Site of Canada

Icon Attractions

☆ Bar U Ranch National Historic Site of Canada

MAJOR EVENTS ALONG THE TRAIL

(check www.thecowboytrail.com for a complete listing)

May
Blacksmith Competition, Bar U Ranch National Historic Site of Canada
Peddlers' Market, Sierra West Cabins and Ranch Vacations

June
Ranch Horse Competition, Bar U Ranch National Historic Site of Canada

August
Old Time Ranch Rodeo, Bar U Ranch National Historic Site of Canada
Polo at the Bar U, Bar U Ranch National Historic Site of Canada

September
Bar U Chore Horse Competition, Bar U Ranch National Historic Site of Canada

October
Peddlers' Market, Sierra West Cabins and Ranch Vacations
Sundays are Special – all summer, Bar U Ranch National Historic Site of Canada

Crick – a creek

3 : LUNDBRECK TO BAR U RANCH
NATIONAL HISTORIC SITE OF CANADA

Lundbreck

Blackfoot name – *ahk-takoyi,* meaning "waterfall," for the nearby falls. The English version is a combination cobbled together from the names of Peter Lund and John Breckenridge, who formed the Breckenridge and Lund Coal Company in 1903 to develop a coal mine west of Cowley. The town that grew up near the site was called Lundbreck.

You can stop for an ice cream at O'bies General Mercantile in town, then head west towards the junction of Hwy. 3 and Hwy. 22. On the left (south) side of the road you will see a sign for Lundbreck Falls Provincial Park, a good spot to picnic or camp by the river. Take the pathway leading down to the falls (or drive if you must) to see the Crowsnest River as it plunges 17 metres over a sandstone cliff.

The junction for Hwy. 3 and Hwy. 22 is just west of the falls, but you may want to take a short detour and stay on Hwy. 3 for another five or six kilometres. Just before the ghost town of Burmis, on the right (north) side of the road is the Burmis Tree, supposedly the most photographed tree in the country. Vandals recently damaged one of the branches, but the tree is a superb example of a limber pine that has been shaped by a lifetime of standing in strong chinook winds.

Return to the junction of Hwy. 3 and Hwy. 22 and head north. As you travel up the highway, the Livingstone Range dominates the horizon to the west, but the country starts to change as open prairies give way to foothills. On the right (east) side of the road, the distinctive Porcupine Hills run for a length of approxi-

Lundbreck Falls
L. ANDREWS

DID YOU KNOW?

In 1982 "Black Beauty" was discovered about 5.5 KM east of Lundbreck on the Crowsnest River. No, it wasn't a horse, but a well-preserved rich-black Tyrannosaurus rex that is now on display at the Royal Tyrell Museum of Palaeontology in Drumheller.

Burmis Tree — shaped by a lifetime of wind.
GINNY DONAHUE

mately 90 kilometres, from Cowley in the south to Willow Creek in the north. The Blackfoot named the hills after the distinctive forested ridges of Douglas fir and limber pine that resemble the quills on a porcupine. The native word *Ky-es-kaghp-ogh-suy-is* actually means *porcupine tails*. Because the lower parts of the hills supported extensive grasslands of fescue (see sidebar below) and wheat grass, coulees for shelter, and many natural springs, early ranchers were drawn to the area. The hills sustain an extraordinary diversity of wildflowers, birds, and wildlife since they encompass montane and subalpine forest, aspen parkland, and prairie grassland, all within a relatively small area.

THE QUEEN OF THE GRASSES

Rough fescue has been called the "queen of the grasses." It is Alberta's official grass and was instrumental in the establishment of the ranching industry in southern Alberta. A large, tufted bunchgrass, it throws down roots that can be over a metre in depth and is extremely nutritious. Early cattlemen relied on the chinooks (see sidebar page 36) to uncover the fescue and sustain their herds each winter, a gamble that didn't always pay off if chinooks were scarce. The grass is vulnerable to overgrazing and has been replaced in many areas by more grazing-tolerant species or by cultivated crops. Alberta has the largest area of rough fescue grassland in the world and is the only place in North America that hosts the plains, foothills, and northern types of rough fescue.

OFF THE BEATEN PATH:
WHERE THE PRAIRIES MEET THE MOUNTAINS

From Hwy. 22 turn left (west) on Willow Valley Road (signed gravel road RR2-2 just before Sierra West Cabins). It curves around to the north, then west, then south, offering superb views of the prairies meeting the mountains. Loop back to Hwy. 22 by taking Chapel Rock Road (RR3-0A) east for a total distance of about 25 km.

The view on Willow Valley Road — where the prairies meet the mountains.
GINNY DONAHUE

43 **Sierra West Cabins and Ranch Vacations** www.sierrawest-777.com

Randy and Ginny Donahue

P.O. Box 153, Lundbreck, AB, T0K 1H0

T: 403-628-2431

E: sierra_west_777@hotmail.com

ACCEPTS D, V

Open all year

Randy and Ginny have been ranching on their Lonesome Pine Ranch for close to 30 years. The ranch was named for a large tree growing behind the main ranch house. It was packed out of the Gap (see page 76) in the 1940s in a saddle bag and now towers over the house. Ginny admits that the tree is actually a spruce, but she liked

You can't miss the sign to Sierra West.
SIERRA WEST CABINS AND RANCH VACATIONS

the ring of Lonesome Pine. Randy and Ginny's most recent claim to fame is starring as extras in Kevin Costner's western movie *Open Range*, which was filmed west of Cochrane. Well, maybe they weren't stars, but they are in the movie.

WHAT THEY OFFER: Two private self-contained log cabins by Todd Creek (good rainbow trout): The Homesteader (sleeps eight) was the first building erected on the ranch in 1905; the Sundowner (sleeps seven) with spiral staircase to loft and breathtaking view from the porch. Linens and stocked fridge supplied for an extra fee. Board your own horse, or hourly riding and trail rides with advance notice; access to roping and riding arena, horseshoe pits, and nearby fishing, skiing,

Cow chips — dried droppings or manure that were used as fuel on the open range when wood was scarce (also buffalo chips)

boating, hiking, and biking. Seven-day Rocky Mountain Getaway combines time at Sierra West, learning basic riding and roping, with meals self-catered from daily stocked fridge; then head to Brown Creek Ranch (see page 82) in Porcupine Hills to the north, to ride and work with cattle; meals and accommodations in a pine log cabin included at Brown Creek; also includes two daytrips to nearby attractions.

Sierra West Ranch Roping and Peddlers' Market, each May and October, features pancake breakfast, live music, face painting, horse demos, shootouts, and much more.

GETTING THERE: The ranch is located 18 KM north of Hwy. 3 on Hwy. 22. Look for the chuckwagon sign on the left (west) side of the road.

Anchor B Ranch Fly-Fishing Lodge   www.anchorbranch.com; www.orvis.com
Max Muselius
P.O. Box 185, Cowley, AB, T0K 0P0
T: 403-627-7967
E: max403@telus.net
ACCEPTS V
Open mid-May to mid-September

The Lodge is one of ten *Orvis*-endorsed fly-fishing lodges in Canada, with two miles of exclusive river access in the Oldman River valley. "Catch and release" fly-fishing is the focus, but you may find yourself just sitting on one of the secluded decks, watching the incredible variety of wildlife that calls the valley home.

WHAT THEY OFFER: One-week all-inclusive fishing packages (for a maximum of eight fishing guests) with four full-time fishing guides can be customized to include fishing in many nearby rivers and creeks, including the Crowsnest, Livingstone, and Elk; additional packages can be developed to suit specific requests; fly-fishing schools led by a well-known Alberta fishing expert; corporate retreats take up to 12 participants; a private casting pond gives you a chance for some practice before you hit the trail; accommodations in one of two comfortable cabins with private facilities or in the bunkhouse above the saloon; guests can relax in the wood-fired sauna and the 1850s western-style saloon, complete with well-stocked bar, piano, and poker table; the dining hall features a comfortable leather seating lounge with wood stove and substantial home-cooked meals served "family style" at the huge dining table; don't miss the outhouse, complete with flush toilet and a magnificent view of the river valley.

GETTING THERE: Head north of Hwy. 3 on Hwy. 22 for 18 KM to the sign for Sierra West Cabins and Ranch Vacations. Turn right (east) on TWP 9-2A for 2.3 KM. The road swings right (south) on RR2-0 past a dugout. Turn left (east) on TWP 9-2 and follow it for 1.6 KM to a T-intersection with RR1-5. The Anchor B sign is in front of you (looking east). Follow the trail in for about 3.6 KM to the lodge.

OFF THE BEATEN PATH:
"THE GAP" AND "THE HUMP"

From Hwy. 22, turn west on Secondary Hwy. 517 just before the bridge over the Oldman

"The Gap" in the Livingstone Range
GINNY DONAHUE

River. There is a gas station and store on the corner. You will drive past the spot where the community of Maycroft once included a store and post office (operated by May and A.C. Raper) that served the large ranching community in the area. In 1885 Richard Lynch-Staunton (father of Frank, one of Alberta's lieutenant-governors) settled near here. Other early comers included Barbed Wire Johnny Speers (see sidebar below) and Post Hole Smith. In the 1920s, Frank McDonald arrived and put Maycroft on the map in the 1940s when he became World Champion cowboy. You can continue west through "The Gap" (see page 77) to Secondary Hwy. 734 (21 KM from Hwy. 22). Turn right (north) and complete a loop that will take you about 40 kilometres to Secondary Hwy. 532, then right (east) for 27 kilometres to hook up again with Hwy. 22. Secondary Hwy. 532 is known locally as "The Hump" road since it goes over a high spot that overlooks the vast prairies to the east. On a clear day you can literally almost see forever. Along this loop you will find several good picnic, fishing, and camping spots, including picturesque Livingstone Falls, located on Secondary Hwy. 734 and Indian Graves Campground on Secondary Hwy. 532.

WHAT'S IN A NAME?

According to George Zarn in his book *Above the Forks*, there were several versions of how Barbed Wire Johnny got his name, but Zarn liked this version best. "When I asked him, he said when he was young he couldn't afford spurs, so he wrapped barbwire around his boot heels." Zarn, who owned a small general store near present-day Chain Lakes, recalls, "I asked Johnny how he made out trapping one spring and he said, 'I got a grizzly bear and two mice.'" Zarn notes, "Barbed Wire's diet would hardly be approved of by today's dieticians. One fall he took six hundred pounds of oatmeal and one case of raw grapefruit to his cabin – of course, it was supplemented by an odd deer or elk, of which he always kept a quarter hanging on the leg of his kitchen table."

As you head north past the turn-off for Secondary Hwy. 517 and across the bridge that straddles the Oldman River, the distinctive Whaleback Ridge will soon come into sight on the left (west) side of Hwy. 22. According to Bob Blaxley in *The Whaleback*, his excellent walking guide to the area, this rare montane landscape is "the largest relatively undisturbed representative landscape of the montane section of the Rocky Mountain natural region in Alberta." The Whaleback is treasured for its incredible diversity, including grasslands, limber pine, Douglas fir, and lodgepole pine forests. The climate is strongly influenced by "The Gap," a steep valley cut through the wall of the Livingstones by the Oldman River, allowing chinooks to blow over the area, keeping it warmer and drier in the winter.

THE COMING OF THE "PATRIARCHS"

When Treaty Seven was signed with the Blackfoot in 1877, the great rangelands of the west became Crown lands, available for development. The virtual annihilation of the great buffalo herds in Canada by 1879 meant these vast lands were practically empty. The Canadian government was anxious to attract British capital that was financing US beef interests and to encourage a ranching industry in the west to supply the needs of the North West Mounted Police and the Indians, who were now confined to reservations.

In 1881 the Government of Canada passed an order-in-council that allowed a person or company to lease up to a maximum of 100,000 acres (40,000 hectares) for 21 years at a rate of $10 per thousand acres (400 hectares) – or one cent per acre per year. The only requirement was that there be one cow on every ten acres under lease. So if an investor leased the maximum 100,000 acres, he needed 10,000 cattle to stock it.

Eastern and British investors liked the terms and they liked what they saw. So began the era of the big corporate ranches. Four of them dominated Alberta's ranching frontier. Historian David Breen called them the "patriarchs." At their peak they controlled 40 per cent of the leased land in southern Alberta and owned about the same percentage of cattle. They were the Oxley (see sidebar page 84), the Walrond (see sidebar page 82), the North West Cattle Company (or the Bar U, see page 93), and the Cochrane (see sidebar page 171). American cowboys trailed in huge herds of cattle from Montana and Idaho to the open rangelands of southern Alberta to stock these ranches.

The cowboys also liked what they saw, and many of them stayed to put down roots. It was the beginning of Alberta's cowboy culture.

As you drive the Cowboy Trail from south of Pincher Creek to Cochrane, you are passing through the area where the "patriarchs" of Alberta's ranching frontier (see sidebar above) established their huge spreads in the foothills and rangelands of some of the finest ranching country in North America. Not only did the patriarchs set up shop here, by 1884 there were estimated to be over 40 small ranches established in the region – and no fences! It meant that each spring a general roundup was held to brand the new calves, and another one each fall to cut out the stock that was ready for market. As you follow the road north in your air-conditioned vehicle, try to imagine the perspective from the top of a horse in 1884.

LET THE "OP'RA" BEGIN . . .

In 1884 Fred Ings, who had established his Rio Alto ranch (see sidebar page 109) the year before, rode in the first general roundup that took place on the open range country of southern Alberta. In his book *Before the Fences*, he recalls, "On that trail . . . we passed through an absolutely unsettled land: no towns, no farms, no fences, just one big grass-covered range." One of the main purposes of such roundups was to prevent some ranchers from having first claim to all the new unbranded calves running free. In the US, ranchers who began working their own cattle – and maybe other ranchers' cattle as well – were called "sooners."

The 1884 spring roundup covered an area of almost 10,000 square miles. On the 1884 roundup there were 15 chuckwagons, 100 cowboys, and 500 saddle horses. Each of the major ranches participating in the roundup sent an outfit with a chuckwagon and cook-driver, a bed wagon, and a number of cowboys with their string of horses. Each cowboy would have five or six horses.

The roundups gave the cowboys a chance to display their skills as the giant herds were gathered and the "op'ra" – the big branding show – began. As usual, cowboys put their own distinctive twist on the lingo. "Hook 'em cow!" became the battle cry of the branding corral. "Ironing the calf crop" referred to the branding of the calves, and the cry for "more straw" was the call of the branders for more calves. The "iron tender" heated and tended the branding irons, while the "iron man" or "rawhide artist" would actually do the branding because of his skill with the irons. The "ketch hand" roped or "heeled" the calves by the hind legs and dragged them to the fire, where two "rasslers" held the calf down as the brand was applied.

Overseeing the whole process was the "tally man," who was appointed by the captain of the roundup to record the calves branded for each outfit. He was generally regarded as a man of scrupulous honesty, since he had the opportunity to alter records that could determine a rancher's profits for the entire season. Hot iron branding was, and remains, the method of choice for most ranchers. If done properly, it provides a clearly readable brand that is generally tamperproof and no worse than a bad sunburn.

Cold-jawed — a horse that doesn't respond to the bridle

Charlie Lehr's cook tent.
GLENBOW ARCHIVES NA-466-22

RULE #1 – DON'T ARGUE WITH THE COOK

When the cook yelled, "Grub pile!" it was time to eat. Not surprisingly, one of the most important people on the roundup, or the ranch for that matter, was the cook. A good cook was a big part of keeping the men happy, so ranchers tended to go out of their way to hire the best cooks they could find. Everyone wanted to keep the cook happy; a common expression was "only a fool argues with a skunk, a mule, or a cook." Some cooks, like Charlie Lehr, who handled the Bar U wagon, were almost legendary. Ed Larkin was said to make the best raisin pies, and Cookie Green prompted fond recollections of his "duff and dip" (a boiled pudding with sauce) long after the end of the roundup.

As you continue north on Hwy. 22, you will pass Secondary Hwy. 520. The drive east on this road is quite spectacular as you emerge from the Porcupine Hills on to the open prairie. You can go as far east as you want and then head back to Hwy. 22 for a totally different perspective going west back into the hills. Or you might want to take the 46 kilometre drive to Claresholm to visit one of the most authentic western lifestyle stores you are likely to find anywhere in the country (see page 89). While you are in Claresholm, don't miss the Appaloosa Horse Club of Canada Museum and Archives (open weekdays from 8:30 AM to 4:30 PM year-round). It is the centre for the breed in Canada (see sidebar page 107). There are also a number of partners located on your way to Claresholm, each offering something a little different.

IF IT'S "SLICK" IT'S FINDERS KEEPERS

In the early days of ranching in the United States, unbranded or "slick" animals were called "mavericks." They were motherless calves whose ownership could not be proven, so the rule became "finders keepers." In the early days of the open-range roundups in southern Alberta, the legal status of mavericks was vague to say the least, and it was customary to kill them for the camp food supply. In later years, as stock associations became more established, it became common to sell any animals whose ownership could not be verified and to turn the money over to a general fund.

The term "maverick" is said to have originated from the name of Samuel Maverick. Contrary to popular belief, he was not a thief, but a prominent Texas lawyer and one of the signers of the Texas Declaration of Independence. Before the Civil War, he received a herd of cattle in payment of a debt. He hired a family to tend them, but they failed to brand the offspring and let the animals wander free. In 1855, Maverick sold his outfit to a neighbour, Toutant de Beauregard. It was agreed that he could have all the branded and unbranded cattle found on Maverick's former range. Beauregard's riders began claiming that every unbranded animal they found was one of Maverick's. The term eventually came to be applied to all unbranded range cattle.

 Skyline Ranching and Outfitting   www.skylineranching.com

Bill and Reid Moynihan

  P.O. Box 2065, Claresholm, AB, T0L 0T0

T: 1-888-621-2398

E: skylineoutfitters@hotmail.com

ACCEPTS V, MC, AMEX, TC

Open all year by reservation and viewed by appointment only

Cowboys relax after a hard day.
SKYLINE RANCH

Skyline is located in a secluded valley on East Sharples Creek in the Porcupine Hills. Portions of the ranch were originally part of the famous Walrond Ranch (see sidebar page 82). Just over on West Sharples Creek, the eccentric King brothers, Maurice and Harold, were neighbours of the Moynihans for many years (see sidebar page 81).

WHAT THEY OFFER: B&B in refurbished 1918 homestead house furnished with antiques; self-catered rustic cabin equipped with fridge, propane stove, wood stove, barbecue, and fire pit on secluded 125 acres. Also, an abundance of wildlife and bird species, with trails for walking or riding. There are riding lessons, half-day, full-day and one-, four- and seven-day mountain rides, and pack trips into the backcountry just west of the ranch; pack horse and horseshoeing clinics; Alberta fly-fishing college includes instruction and access to stocked ponds; ranch/mountain combo has three days of instructions, then head for the hills to practice what you learned.

Packages include Calgary Stampede Stay: four nights, riding and ranch activities, and tickets to rodeo, chuckwagons, and evening show; Branding Special on the first weekend in June features three nights, cattle roundup, branding, campfires, and music at the Bar M7 Saloon (a restored wrangler's shack); Cattle Drive in the first week of July trails cattle into a nearby forestry reserve; two-, three-, and seven-day packages include accommodations, meals, riding, and ranch activities, and touring options; Gunfighter Package combines a two-night stay at the cabin with entertainment at the Bar M7 Saloon in the evening.

GETTING THERE: From Hwy. 22, head east on Secondary Hwy. 520 for 12.5 KM. At RR300A (East Sharples Creek Rd.), turn right (south) and go 5 KM to the white house on the right side of the road.

THE ECCENTRIC MILLIONAIRE KING BROTHERS OF SHARPLES CREEK

Maurice and Harold lived like paupers in a log cabin on the banks of Sharples Creek for over 60 years, with no electricity and no running water. After Maurice died in 1996, a year after Harold and just short of his 99th birthday, his estate was sold at a High River auction in 1997 for $6.325 million. Over the years, wild tales about them abounded, such as serving mice meat sandwiches to their guests and burying their wealth in tomato cans. Mary-Jo Burles, who knew the brothers and called them friends for over fifty years, sets the record straight in her book *First and Second Kings*. She was a frequent guest at their home, where they welcomed visitors and were always ready to talk about politics, religion, or sex. Burles recalls, "I often thought their attitudes a bit naïve but always genuine – they had no guile." Still, there is no doubt the brothers fit the definition of eccentric. They sported long shaggy hair, and their worn-out pants were often held up with binder twine.

Although the brothers never went to school (Maurice quit in grade one), they did learn how to read. Burles remembers, "Wheeling and dealing kept Maurice going. He enjoyed doing the math in his head. I rarely saw him use a pencil and paper – he was an expert at mental arithmetic." Although they lived together all their lives, Maurice claimed they didn't get along: "Can't remember two things in our life we ever agreed upon." Burles remembers, "Maurice was known for his lunches, or lack of them." He would trail cattle into Lundbreck –a two-day trip on horseback – then pick up his cheque and ride home without lunch. He wouldn't pay the $1 for the full meal offered by the local church ladies, complete with homemade pie.

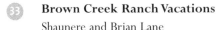

Brown Creek Ranch Vacations

www.browncreekranchvacations.com

Shaunere and Brian Lane
P.O. Box 2203, Claresholm, AB, T0L 0T0
T: 403-625-4032

E: shaunere@telus.net
ACCEPTS V, MC

Open all year

"Where the Lone Star meets the Alberta Rose." At Brown Creek Ranch, you will find a unique blend of two famous cowboy cultures. Shaunere is a cowgirl from San Antonio who met Brian when he was vacationing in Texas. Brian is a team roper who comes from a long-time ranching family in the Claresholm area. Together they run a cow–calf operation in the Porcupine Hills.

WALROND LIVES ON AS THE WALDRON

Extending from north of Hwy. 3 almost to Secondary Hwy. 520 is the Waldron Grazing Co-op. (Signs along Hwy. 22 indicate its boundaries.) It is all that remains of the Walrond Ranch, established by Dr. Duncan McEachran in 1883. McEachran was the Dominion veterinarian and became the general manager of the giant operation (with leases totalling 260,000 acres or 105,000 hectares). One of the big corporate ranches, it was financed mainly by British investors, the primary one being Sir John Walrond-Walrond. McEachran was well-known for his abrasive personality and on-going feuds with homesteaders in the area. The disastrous chinook-free winter of 1906–7 wiped out over 5,000 head of its cattle, and in 1908 the ranch disposed of the remaining herd to Pat Burns at $26.50 a head. Some of the original range has been reassembled as the Waldron Grazing Co-op used by local ranchers.

WHAT THEY OFFER: Private self-contained pine log cabin complete with fireplace on the banks of Brown Creek; cabin rental, B&B, or daily room and board with three meals.

As well, hourly riding or bring your own horse; Cowboy Weekend offers a two-night stay, meals, riding, and ranch activities; the four-night Ranch Holiday adds a day trip of your choice; Cowhand's Week adds extra days to the Ranch Holiday, trailing cattle in the Rockies; the Country Honeymoon package includes meals, ranch activities, and extras like fresh flowers, chocolates, champagne, and candlelight dinners; four- and five-day packages in June or September trail cattle to and from summer pasture; Leather and Lace is a four-night adventure for up to four cowgirls that combines ranch activities with some real pampering; the seven-day Rocky Mountain Getaway starts at Sierra West Cabins & Ranch Vacations (see page 73), learning basic riding and roping; stay in a self-contained historic log cabin with meals self-catered from a daily stocked fridge. Then head to Brown Creek to practice what you've learned. Includes meals, accommodations, and two day-trips to local attractions.

GETTING THERE: From Hwy. 22, head east on Secondary Hwy. 520 for 15 KM. Look for the Cowboy Trail sign on the left (north) side of the road.

Circle 6 Ranch Getaway   www.circle6ranchgetaway.com

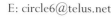
Sherry and Charlie Ewing

P.O. Box 430, Claresholm, AB, T0L 0T0

T: 403-625-2157

E: circle6@telus.net

ACCEPTS V, MC, AMEX, TC, PC

Open all year

Sherry and Charlie Ewing are seedstock producers for a cattle breeding program they run on their working SN Ranch. They chose the Circle 6 name for the "ranch vacation" part of their business, to honour a long-standing local horse brand that was registered to the Box X, now a part of the SN. The SN had its origins as part of the famous Oxley Ranch (see sidebar page 84).

Noah Sitton started his ranch on the site in 1912. Rumour has it he was a horse thief on both sides of the border. Although he applied for the NS brand, he had to settle for SN since NS was already taken.

Charlie claims to have been a rancher since the age of two – he has lived on the SN since that age. When he's not busy doing cowboy things, Charlie is a bit of a crooner, playing his guitar and writing and composing songs for his musical group, "The Dirty Hat Band."

WHAT THEY OFFER: Two self-catered cabins (breakfast with prior notice): the Coop (sleeps up to six) and the Silverspring House (sleeps up to nine) are completely private and self-contained, both recently refurbished with distinctive country and cowboy themes that make them extremely homey.

The two- and four-night packages include branding and various cattle drives during the spring and summer; you must supply your own horse and timing is weather-dependent; the two-night romantic getaway includes treats like champagne and chocolate-covered strawberries; a three-night Calgary Stampede package includes tickets to the famous rodeo, chuckwagons, and grandstand show, one day at a local attraction, and one day at the ranch; the Antique Tour heads to "Antique Road" in Nanton; the Christmas Tree Holiday helps you find the perfect Christmas tree. (The Ewings know all the good spots.)

GETTING THERE: From Hwy. 22, head east on Secondary Hwy. 520 for 19.5 KM. At RR291A turn south and go 9.5 KM. The ranch is on the right (west) side of the road.

Trailing cattle in the Porcupine Hills on Lucasia Ranch.
LUCASIA RANCH VACATIONS

 Lucasia Ranch Vacations www.lucasiaranch.com

 Judy and Wayne Lucas

P.O. Box 1206, Claresholm, AB, T0L 0T0

T: 1-877-477-2624 (toll-free in North America)

 E: lucasia@telusplanet.net

 ACCEPTS V, MC, TC

Open May to October

Judy and Wayne invite their guests to "come live with us." Their aim is to make you feel like one of the family by the time you leave. This is a working ranch that covers 4,000 acres of land in the heart of the Porcupine Hills. With 600 head of Texas longhorns and crossbred cattle, and 80 head of horses (including purebred Percherons, quarter horses, and Appaloosas), there is plenty of real cowboying to be done. Herds of wild elk and deer are common, and the incredible variety of birds and wildflowers make it a paradise for hikers and photographers.

The ranch is actually a designated historic site. Formerly known as the Circle L Ranch, it was one of the first established in the district by Captain Charles Augustus Lyndon and his wife, Margaret, in July 1881. (See sidebar). The Lucas family has owned the property since 1974. Although they have made many changes since then, several of the old log buildings are still in use, and the spring has never gone dry. It feeds a pond in the yard that is full of colourful ducks and geese.

WHAT THEY OFFER: B&B plus several packages; accommodations in two double rooms with a shared bath and sitting room on a private floor in the main ranch house, a newly refurbished turn-of-the-century log bunkhouse with wood-burning stove and outhouse (and access to washroom in the ranch house), or a new self-contained log cabin.

There is hourly trail riding and lessons; packages include all meals; Family Getaways geared for non-riders include a two-night stay and a chance to play with and learn about ranch animals; the Ranch Weekend adds riding/ranch activities; five- and seven-day Ranch Vacations feature additional tours to Head-Smashed-In Buffalo Jump and/or Historic Fort Macleod; the Calgary Stampede Rodeo/Ranch Stay combines a five-night stay and riding/ranch activities with tickets to the rodeo, chuckwagon races, and evening stage show; Branding Week in June includes a four-night stay, cattle roundup, branding, and neighbourhood social; June in the Porcupines includes eight nights, riding, and a day trip to Head-Smashed-In Buffalo Jump; Hiking in the High Country allows you to roam the hills with a biologist guide from Destination Outdoors during a five-day stay; add a Walk and Wade option onto any package; or

DOODNEY MAKES A DEAL

Captain Charles Lyndon had served in the British navy during the Crimean War then immigrated to the US, settling in Salt Lake City. Here he met and married Margaret Erwin from Kentucky. The Lyndons had heard many stories of the fabulous grass country and the large buffalo herds to the north. In 1881 they headed to Fort Macleod. Here the Captain enlisted the help of an Indian named Doodney who took a fancy to his pinto horse. They struck a deal. If Doodney could find some land with plenty of grass, shelter and water he could have the pony. After several days, Lyndon found a site that fit the bill perfectly (now Lucasia Ranch) and Doodney got his horse. The Lyndon ranch was one of the first in the district, and Margaret was the second white woman to settle in Alberta. Following her death, the local paper described her as "one of the best known and most highly respected pioneer women of Alberta."

join in one of three authentic cattle drives — in the first part of June, mid-July, and mid-October—moving cattle to or from the forest reserve.

Rocky Mountain Ranch Adventure teams up with Misty Mountain Adventures (see page 56) near Pincher Creek. Spend time at Lucasia Ranch, riding with the cowboys, checking the herd, or moving cattle; then transfer to the trailhead, where Misty Mountain will take you on a scenic pack trip into the Rocky Mountains. Eight- or ten-day options include all accommodations, meals, and trailhead transfers.

GETTING THERE: From Hwy. 22, head 23.5 KM east on Secondary Hwy. 520 to RR290A (Lyndon Creek Road). Turn left (north) and go 8 KM. The ranch is on the west (left) side of the road.

Coulee — a deep ravine with steep sides

RECIPE FOR BUTTERFLIED PRAIRIE OYSTERS FROM RUSTY LUCAS OF LUCASIA RANCH

You need a supply of raw prairie oysters, cleaned and butterflied (i.e., cut open to resemble a butterfly shape). Then arrange ½ cup (125 ml) of milk, 2 beaten eggs, and a package of soda crackers, finely crushed and ready for dipping. Dip each prairie oyster in the milk, then in the eggs, then coat them with the crushed crackers. Fry them up in melted butter until they are golden brown, and enjoy! (For the uninitiated, prairie oysters are what's left over after the little bull calves become steers.)

 **Lyndon Creek Cottage**   www.lyndoncreekcottage.com
Rob and Robin Chisholm
 P.O. Box 1660, Claresholm, AB, T0L 0T0
T: 403-625-2394
 ACCEPTS D, V, MC, AMEX
Open all year

WHAT THEY OFFER: A self-catered, private cottage (sleeps eight) and barn with three box stalls and four rail pens for your horses; cottage includes fully equipped kitchen with dishwasher and microwave, games room with wood stove, two full bathrooms, washer and dryer for extended stays, and hot tub on wrap-around deck. As well, riding can be arranged with advance notice; bring your mountain bikes (no ATVs or motorbikes), try trout fishing in one of the stocked spring-fed ponds, or just walk along the trails.

GETTING THERE: From Hwy. 22, head east for 23.5 KM to RR290A (Lyndon Creek Road). Turn left (north) and go 12.6 KM. The cottage and barn are on the left (west) side of the road.

Lyndon Creek Cottage, tucked away in the Porcupine Hills.
ROBIN CHISHOLM

 Willow Lane Ranch Vacations   www.willowlaneranch.com
Keith and LeAnne Lane
 P.O. Box 114, Granum, AB, T0L 1A0
T: 1-800-665-0284
E: LeAnne@willowlaneranch.com
ACCEPTS V, MC
Open May to October

"The cowboy way" isn't just an expression at Willow Lane. Keith's family has been ranching in the area for several generations, while LeAnne's family has provided stock to rodeos, including the world-famous Calgary Stampede, for more than 50 years. Keith and LeAnne make it their business to preserve cowboy traditions and to give people the genuine experience. This working cattle ranch runs 1,100 head of cattle, so "real west" is what you are going to find here.

WHAT THEY OFFER: Weekender, five- and seven-day all-inclusive packages with

Taking a break at Willow Lane Ranch.
LEANNE LANE

accommodations, in one of three rooms on a private floor in the main ranch house (two with shared bathroom, one with ensuite) or cozy log cabin with private bath, meals, riding, and ranch activities. (Riders must be over the age of 16 years.) The four-night Calgary Stampede/Ranch Stay combines a four-night all-inclusive ranch stay with one day at the Calgary Stampede with tickets for rodeo, chuckwagon races, evening grandstand show, and return transportation to Calgary; the Porcupine Hills western cow camp combines comfortable tent camp, plenty of cattle work, and wildlife viewing (package includes one night at ranch and five under canvas); shorter camps are available plus a "City Slickers" cattle drive with three-night stay, two-day roundup, cattle drive, and all meals; Porcupine Hills scenic riding tours include five nights at a tent camp with real beds and shower house, four days of riding, and round-trip airport transfers; hourly riding or day rides available; non-riders can book rooms and meals at a special rate; B&B with maximum one-night stay.

The Great Canadian Cowboy package combines 10, 13, or 14 nights at two different ranches, with all accommodations, meals, lessons, ranch activities, and transfers. Spend time at Lazy M Ranch, near Caroline (see page 202), learning western horsemanship, then transfer to Willow Lane to put your expertise to work on a cattle drive.

On the Open Range Cowboy Adventure Package, spend a week at Bent Creek Western Vacations Guest Ranch (see page 64) learning the basics of Western riding theory and practice, then transfer to Willow Lane Ranch for the chance to practice everything you have learned. Includes an evening at the famous Ranchman's (see page 152) for some foot-stompin' Western music and dancing.

GETTING THERE: From Hwy. 22, head east on Secondary Hwy. 520 for 46 KM to Claresholm. Take Hwy. 2 south for 17 KM and turn right (west) at TWP 110 (watch for the sign). Follow TWP 110 for 10 KM. Turn right (north) at RR275 and go 1 KM. The ranch is on the left (west) side of the road.

WILLOW LANE RANCH BAKED BEANS
(FROM *COOKIN' FOR THE BOSS* BY LEANNE LANE)

Soak four pounds (1820 g) white pea beans overnight in cold water and drain. Then cover beans with water and boil with two chopped onions, a meaty ham bone, and salt and pepper for two hours. Remove the bone and cut the meat off, then put meat back with the beans. Add two cups (500 ml) ketchup, one cup (250 ml) brown sugar, one cup (250 ml) vinegar, ½ cup (125 ml) molasses, one Tbsp (15 ml) dry mustard, ½ cup (125 ml) barbecue sauce, two Tbsp (30 ml) Worcestershire sauce, and four to five drops of Tabasco sauce. Mix gently until well blended, then bake for four to five hours at 250F (120 C) with the lid off. Serves 15 to 20 people.

Frontier Western Shop   www.westernshop.com
Brenda and Stuart Derochie
Main Street, P.O. Box 1450, Claresholm, AB, T0L 0T0
T: 1-800-661-7939 (toll-free in North America)
E: frontier@telusplanet.net
ACCEPTS V, MC, AMEX
Open Monday to Saturday 9:00 AM to 6:00 PM, Sunday 11:00 AM to 4:00 PM

Brenda and Stuart started out 25 years ago in a small store in Claresholm. Over the years they have expanded to 10,000 square feet of space, jam-packed with every conceivable accoutrement of the western lifestyle. Real cowboys shop here. So do wannabes from every corner of the world. Brenda's motto is, "If we don't have it, you don't need it." Even if you aren't buying, it is worth a stop to have a look at the extraordinary selection of saddles and western gear.

WHAT THEY OFFER: All types of tack and western gear, including (but not limited to) saddles, ropes, spurs, bridles, chaps, clothing, hats, boots, furniture, western home décor, books, magazines, clocks, dishes, linens, silver jewellery, purses, and much more. Mail order catalogue and online store make shopping easy no matter where you are.

Once you are finished your explorations on Secondary Hwy. 520 and in Claresholm, continue north on Hwy. 22 to the Bar U National Historic Site of Canada. Every mile delivers a new vista of extraordinary beauty, as foothills meet the Rocky Mountains in some of the best ranching country in North America. Along the road, two more partners sit tucked away at the foot of the Rockies.

Chimney Rock Bed and Breakfast

Debbie and Tony Webster
P.O. Box 419, Nanton, AB, T0L 1R0
T: 403-646-0151
E: chimneyrockbandb@telus.net
ACCEPTS V, MC, TC
Open all year

How loud can quiet be? Debbie and Tony challenge you to find the answer at the Webster Ranch, where they run a working cow/calf operation. Tony grew up spending his summers on this family ranch in Breeding Valley, named after homesteader William Patterson Breeding, on Chaffen Creek near Chimney Rock. Tony's father, Art, purchased the ranch when he returned to Canada at the end of World War II. Tony's mother, Betty, came out as a war bride from England, with no idea of what the Wild West would throw at her (see sidebar page 92). It was a world away

Chimeny Rock bed and breakfast in the solitude of Breeding Valley.
L. ANDREWS

from the chaos of the London blitz, but Betty welcomed the silence.

That part hasn't changed much. Tucked away in its own private valley, the ranch is surrounded by the peaks of the Livingstone Range to the west and the spruce-studded heights of the Porcupine Hills to the east. Chimney Rock is clearly visible to the southwest. The rock was regarded as a sacred spot by Native tribes in the area who used it for vision quests (see sidebar page 59). It is believed the Chimney Rock was considered special because there is an unobstructed view in all directions and on a clear day, it is possible to view Chief Mountain (see sidebar page 20) to the south.

WHAT THEY OFFER: B&B in two bedrooms, each with private bathroom, queen-sized beds, and a separate, keyed entrance and sitting room; additional meals with advance notice; guests can help with the chores (Tony claims there is always plenty of fencing to be done) or just sit on the verandah and watch the panoramic view unfold; check out Debbie's pressed flower/weed collection, the bear, beaver, bobcat, and lynx skulls in the sitting room, and the stunning framed photographs of past cattle drives on the ranch.

GETTING THERE: On Hwy. 22, look for the green "Chimney Rock Road" highway sign. (The sign is about 65 KM north of Hwy. 3 or 10 KM south of Chain Lakes Provincial Park.) Turn left (west) and go 3.2 KM. The ranch is on the left (south) side of the road.

29 Chain Lakes Provincial Park
www.cd.gov.ab.ca

Twyla Cyr, MD of Ranchland #66
P.O. Box 1060, Nanton, AB, T0L 1R0

T: 403-646-5887
E: mdranch@telusplanet.net
ACCEPTS PC OR CASH
SELF-REGISTRATION IN EFFECT; NO RESERVATIONS
Open all year

During the summer months, the lakes are a haven for an impressive variety of waterfowl and shore birds, including white pelicans, eagles, and osprey. Abundant wildlife inhabits the park's willow shrub and grassland habitat, and there are over 200 types of plants.

WHAT THEY OFFER: 127 campsites (some with power), tables, drinking water,

"I REMEMBER IT WELL"

Betty Webster was a young war bride when she boarded the R.M.S. Samaria on June 6, 1945 to sail from England to her new home in western Canada. Art, her husband of nine months would remain in England until December to complete his job as a medical administrator closing hospitals that had been used by the Canadian military. Betty spent a good part of that first summer living with Art's cousin Jean and a friend, Jake Caron, in a remote area west of Stavely called Happy Valley. Eventually, Hwy. 22 would snake along a portion of this valley, but when Betty arrived there were little more than dirt trails. Betty's personal memoir captures the excitement of her arrival in the West. As a young girl she remembered reading Zane Grey novels and daydreaming "about how wonderful it would be to ride a horse all day and sleep in a log house in the pines at night." She lived it for real that summer, catching her first trout, packing into Livingstone Falls on a three-day trip and riding in her first cattle drive. When Jake shot a bear that had been lurking just outside the garden, Betty helped him skin it, remarking, "So we ate well for the next little while, bear steaks, a roast, etc. and it was all delicious." On Art's return from England, they bought the Webster Ranch in Breeding Valley close to Chimney Rock. They lived in the old house on the place while they started building a small four-room cabin. Betty recalls, "Our bed stood covered with a tarpaulin to keep the rain off. The mice played on the steps and the mosquitoes came in through cracked and broken windows." Now, almost 60 years later, their son Tony continues the ranching tradition.

cooking shelters, horseshoe pits, and boat launch; canoeing, kayaking, sailing, windsurfing, and power boating allowed; lakes are stocked with bull trout and are popular for winter ice fishing; Chain Lakes Taste of Country Cookhouse is open May long weekend to September long weekend, daily in July and August, Thursday to Sunday and holidays in May, June, and September; Ranchers' Special Buffet Supper on Thursday from 6:00 to 8:00 PM, reservations recommended at 403-336-2625.

Chain Lakes Provincial Park is a haven for waterfowl and shore birds.
MD RANCHLANDS

GETTING THERE: The park is 74 KM north of Hwy. 33 or 39 KM south of Longview on Hwy. 22, on the west side of the road.

Just down the road from the park, a piece of ranching heritage has been preserved at the Bar U National Historic Site of Canada.

Bar U Ranch National Historic Site of Canada   www.pc.gc.ca

P.O. Box 168, Longview, AB, T0L 1H0
T: 1-800-568-4996
E: BarU.info@pc.gc.ca

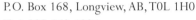

ACCEPTS D, V, MC, AMEX, TC   ADMISSION CHARGED

Open daily 9:00 AM to 5:00 PM, late May to Canadian Thanksgiving in October

This is the real thing. From its beginnings in 1881 until the Bar U's original holdings were split up and sold in 1950, this ranch epitomized the ranching culture in the Alberta foothills. But it also had close ties to the "mythic west," having hosted Prince Edward, the Prince of Wales (who later abdicated the British throne to marry Wallace Warfield Simpson), Charlie Russell, the famed western artist from Montana, and the infamous outlaw Harry Longabaugh, better known as the Sundance Kid.

The ranch was the most successful of the large corporate ranches that started up in the 1880s when the Government of Canada offered leases on large tracts of western land for the bargain-basement price of one cent an acre (see sidebar page 77). Fred Stimson, an experienced Quebec stockman, was able to convince the wealthy Allan family of Montreal to invest in a ranching venture called the North West Cattle Company (see sidebar page 146). Stimson became the resident manager, and in 1882 he had 3,000 Durham shorthorn stocker cattle and 21 purebred bulls trailed north from the US. By 1890 the ranch reported 10,410 cattle and 832 horses ranging over 157,960 acres (63,700 hectares) of leased land. Over the years, the Bar U brand would become one of the most recognizable symbols in the opening of the west.

The *Calgary Herald* summed it up well in an article in 1902, the same year that former manager George Lane took over the ranch.

Historic buildings of the "Might Bar U."
BAR U RANCH

"The Bar U Ranche is undoubtedly one of the most desirable in Alberta. The outfit came in among the very first, and had their pick of the whole country, and that
they made a wise selection is indicated by the fact that the ranch is recognized by
cattlemen as one of the very best locations in Alberta, and that means on the entire
continent, for there is no finer ranching country anywhere than right here."

In 1991 Parks Canada purchased 367 acres (148 hectares) of the original Bar U
headquarters to create and preserve a living celebration of the ranching industry in
Canada. Thirty-five historic buildings still remain on the site. It's a good idea to
begin your visit at the Visitor Orientation Centre, where you can watch a short
video entitled "The Mighty Bar U" and have a look
at the historical exhibits. Then hop on a horse-
drawn wagon shuttle or walk down to the main
site where self-guided tours let you take your
time wandering through many of the restored
buildings.

Wandering interpreters are available to
answer your questions and show you how the
real cowboys lived in the Bar U's heyday.

DID YOU KNOW?

The Prince of Wales became so enam-
oured of the western way of life typified by
the Bar U that he bought a ranch (called
the EP for Edward Prince) adjacent to the
famous Bar U. He owned it for a total of 43
years until it was sold in 1962 to local
rancher Jim Cartwright.

GEORGE LANE PUT BAR U PERCHERONS ON THE WORLD MAP

When George Lane first arrived from Montana to work as foreman at the Bar U in 1883, he was impressed by what he called "the absence of horses such as we had been accustomed to ... by this I mean horses that were able to do ordinary hauling and farm work, and that also had the endurance and speed necessary for making long trips to the railroad ... I came to the conclusion that it was Percheron blood that was lacking in the horses of western Canada." He began by importing breeding stock from Montana and North Dakota, and in 1909 made his first purchase of 72 mares and two stallions from le Perche, France, the recognized breeding centre at the time. Lane had realized he could turn the threat of incoming settlers into an advantage by breeding and selling the horses they would need to farm and open up the country. He would go on to establish the largest Percheron stud in the world. Bruce Roy is a champion Percheron breeder near Cremona. According to Roy, "The Bar U made the Percheron to Alberta, what the thoroughbred was to Kentucky." Alberta Percherons continue to be synonymous with quality worldwide, largely due to the efforts of Lane and the breeding program he established at the Bar U.

Three famous Bar U Percheron stallions, left to right, Garou, Halifax, and Americain.
PARKS CANADA

(One-hour guided tours are also available for a fee.) You can stop and watch the "smithy" demonstrating his craft at the forge or head over to the cookhouse, the "belly of the Bar U," where the Chinese cook served up enormous meals and the cowboys slept upstairs in a dormitory. The ranch office performed triple duty as office and residence of the ranch bookkeeper, the Pekisko Post Office, and a meeting place for the Pekisko Polo Club. It's not hard to imagine the steady stream of neighbours stopping by on mail day to collect their parcels and letters and catch up on the latest gossip. Don't miss the roundup camp where you can sit around the campfire, sample some heavy-duty cowboy coffee, and listen to some of the stories, songs, and poems of real old-time cowboys.

If you time your visit right, you might be lucky enough to get in on one of the special-event Sundays held throughout the season. They include blacksmith, ranch horse, and chore horse competitions, as well as a polo day and an old-time ranch rodeo.

When you are done your tour, the Bar U Ranch Café at the Visitor Centre is a good place for some cow camp stew and biscuits or a hearty beef burger. The Pekisko Creek General Store features a good selection of local crafts, books, homemade soaps, and preserves. Whatever you do, make sure you take a few minutes to admire the view. You won't see much better on the whole Eastern Slopes of the Rocky Mountains. The Prince of Wales summed it up with typical British understatement when he wrote "Some Ranch" in the Bar U visitors' book in the fall of 1919.

GETTING THERE: The ranch is 99 KM north of Hwy. 3 and 14 KM south of Longview on Hwy. 22.

EVERYONE LIKED HARRY

In 1890 Harry Longabaugh (AKA the Sundance Kid) worked as a horse breaker at the Bar U Ranch and became a partner in a saloon at the Grand Central Hotel in Calgary during the winter of 1891–92. By all reports, he was well liked. He was even the best man at the wedding of the Bar U's foreman, Everett Johnson. Frederick Ings of the Midway Ranch recalled, "While here for a few years, likely evading the US law, no one could have been better behaved or more decent. A thoroughly likeable fellow was Harry, a general favourite with everyone, a splendid rider and a top-notch cowhand. We all felt sorry when he left and got in bad again across the line."

CRITTER WATCH: COYOTE

Coyotes can be seen in virtually every part of Alberta, despite concerted human efforts to eradicate them over the last 150 years. The increase in their numbers is due in part to the reduction of the wolf populations, but also because of their willingness to eat just about anything and to adapt to a variety of habitats as agriculture and forestry change the land-scape around them. Coyotes will eat rodents, hares, insects, frogs, berries, grass, fruits, and vegetables (to name a few). If you spot a wild dog, chances are that it is a coy-ote, since wolves are very reclusive and rarely seen. Coyotes are usually tawny-coloured, with pointed ears and a bushy tail, often with a black tip at the end. They have a pointed muzzle that forms an almost straight, continuous line with the forehead. Their distinctive

Wily coyote will eat almost anything.
JANET NASH

yapping and howling is a common sound in the evenings in many parts of rural Alberta. Often started by one animal, the howling soon becomes a chorus that fills the night air with a cackling, almost maniacal noise.

WHICH WAS THE WORST?

Ask five ranchers which was the worst winter in history and you're likely to get five different answers. But there is little doubt that the killer of 1906–7 has seen few equals. Historian L.V. Kelly described it this way: "One day in January the citizens of [Fort] Macleod saw what appeared to be a low, black cloud above the snow to the north, which drew slowly nearer until it was seen that a herd of thousands of suffering range cattle were coming from the north ... in search of open places to feed. There were Bar U and other cattle and their numbers were so great that it took over half an hour for them to pass a given point. Right through the town they dragged themselves ... the route being marked with a string of carcasses ... out into the blackness of the prairie beyond, where they were swallowed up and never heard of again." The Bar U lost a staggering 16,000 head that winter, but the ranch survived. For many ranchers, who had relied on chinooks to keep the range free for grazing, it was the end of the road.

Cowboy Trail partner for this area added just prior to press time:

Highlandview Guest Ranch
High River, Alberta

T: 403-395-3945

Recommended Reading

Above the Forks by George Zarn
The Bar U and Canadian Ranching History by Simon M. Evans
Before the Fences (Tales from the Midway Ranch) by Frederick William Ings
Braehead: Three Founding Families in Nineteenth Century Canada by Sherrill MacLaren
Cattle Kingdom: Early Ranching in Alberta by Edward Brado
Cowboys, Gentlemen and Cattle Thieves by Warren M. Elofson
First and Second Kings, Maurice and Harold by Mary-Jo Burles
Golden Age of the Canadian Cowboy by Hugh A. Dempsey
Peter Fidler: Canada's Forgotten Explorer 1769–1822 by J.G. MacGregor
Ranching: Ranching in Western Canada by Ed Gould
The Range Men by L.V. Kelly
The Whaleback: A Walking Guide by Bob Blaxley

Digger — a great bucking horse

Lost Love

Noel Burles

Molly was a great one
One I shoulda' kept
But to say that now is easy
As I sit here on the steps.

I wish I'd done things different
Shoulda' had her stay
But that was long ago
What else is there to say?

Sometimes I recall her
See her face in my mind's eye
She really wasn't pretty
But then, neither nor am I.

Just another love gone lost
It happens all the time
But Molly was a work horse
And she really turned out fine.

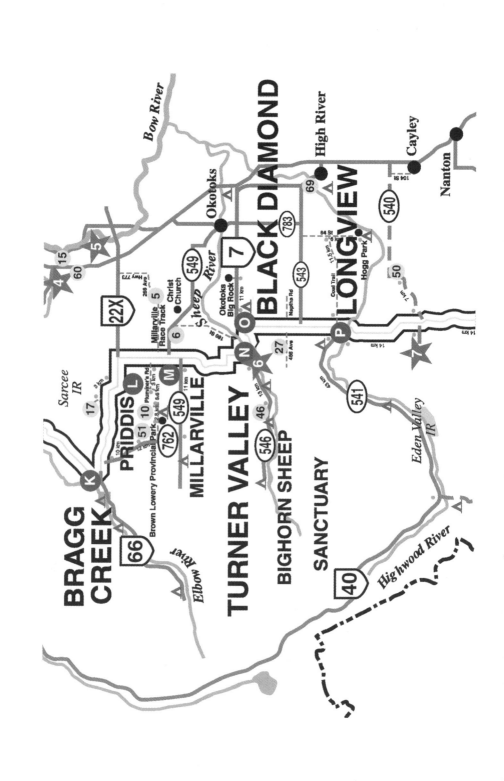

4 : L O N G V I E W   T O   P R I D D I S

"It don't matter how big a ranch you own, or how many cows you brand, or how much money you make, the size of your funeral is still going to depend on the weather."

—Ted Stone, *Cowboy Logic*

Communities

- (P) Longview
- (O) Black Diamond
- (N) Turner Valley
- (M) Millarville
- (L) Priddis

Accommodations

- (P) Blue Sky Motel
- (P) Twin Cities Hotel
- (27) Welcome Acres Bed and Breakfast
- (46) Anchor D Guiding and Outfitting
- (10) The Barn on Whiskey Hill Bed and Breakfast
- (17) Hilltop Ranch Bed and Breakfast

Attractions & Events

- (5) Leighton Art Centre Museum and Gallery
- (6) Millarville Racing and Agricultural Society

Outfitters

- (46) Anchor D Guiding and Outfitting

Bring Your Own Horse

- (17) Hilltop Ranch Bed and Breakfast

Restaurants

- (P) Twin Cities Café
- (P) Memories Inn Restaurant
- (P) Heidi's Food Saloon
- (P) Black Cat: The Swiss Restaurant
- (O) Black Diamond Bakery and Coffee Shop
- (O) Marv's Classic Soda Shop and Diner
- (N) Chuckwagon Café and Grill
- (O) Wonders Coffee House and Gift Shop

Shopping, Antiques & Artisans

- (O) Marv's Classic Soda Shop and Diner
- (O) Tumbleweed Mercantile and Design
- (O) Wonders Coffee House and Gift Shop

Icon Attractions

- (6) Turner Valley Gas Plant National and Provincial Historic Site

MAJOR EVENTS ALONG THE TRAIL

(check www.thecowboytrail.com for a complete listing)

June

Diamond Valley Discovery Days, Black Diamond/Turner Valley
Millarville Rodeo, Millarville

July

Little New York Daze, Longview
Millarville Races, Millarville

August

Priddis/Millarville Fair, Millarville

September

Cowboy Trail Chili Cook-off, Diamond Valley
Mountains, Music, and Memories Fall Harvest Festival, Turner Valley

Hackamore — a bridle that has a loop that tightens over the nose and replaces a mouth bit

4 : L O N G V I E W   T O   P R I D D I S

Longview   www.village.longview.ab.ca
T: 403-558-3922

Stoney name – *ba-ha-a-humbi*, meaning "long view"; descriptive of a hill northeast of Longview, once used as a village.

"Longview" is a combination of the family name of Thomas Long, who homesteaded at Big Hill, and the view from the original post office, which was actually about five miles east of the present village site. When it closed in 1937, Guy Weadick, who lived at nearby Stampede Ranch (see sidebar page 109), started a petition to apply the name to the new post office opening in "Little New York." The ramshackle town with such a grand name (the locals actually dubbed it that because of the density of the settlement) was really a

Main Street, Little New York c. 1938–39
GLENBOW ARCHIVES NA-4386-1

collection of tents and tarpaper shacks. They had sprouted up virtually overnight when the British American Oil Company began construction of a natural gas processing plant on the south slope of Big Hill as a result of the discovery of oil at Turner Valley in 1936. In the early years, the town boomed, boasting four restaurants, three general stores, a theatre, and the new Twin Cities hotel – the name referred to the "cities" of "Little New York" and "Little Chicago."

"Little Chicago" popped up out of nowhere when crude oil was discovered in the area just north of Longview. Its colourful name was eventually changed to Royalites after the first producing well. According to the Turner Valley Historical Society, "American drillers called it 'Little Chicago' because its first store was located on the shores of a large slough, which they dubbed 'Lake Michigan'." The story is that "there was a gas flare in every backyard and it was almost brighter at

> **DID YOU KNOW?**
> Highwood Pass is the highest paved highway in Canada at 2206 metres or 7239 feet.

103

OFF THE BEATEN PATH FROM LONGVIEW

Hogg Park – Located on the Highwood River on land donated by Janet and Archie Hogg. The park hosts an abundance of bird and wildlife species. Drive east of Longview on the Coal Trail for 11.5 KM to 64 Street. Turn right (south) for six KM to the park.

Highwood Junction and Kananaskis Country – Head west of Longview on Secondary Hwy. 541 for 43 KM to the Highwood Junction. The road winds through spectacular ranching country (see sidebar page 109 on historic ranches along this route) into the foothills, with several good spots for picnicking and camping. There is a gas station and store with washrooms at the Junction. From here you can return to Hwy. 22 or take Hwy. 40 for 105 KM over the Highwood Pass to connect with Hwy. 1 and then east again to Hwy. 22. This is a back way to access several partners on or close to Hwy. 40 (see Chapter 6). It is also one of the most scenic drives in the entire country, with excellent hiking, picnicking, and camping spots along the way. The southern portion of Hwy. 40, from the Junction to Kananaskis Lakes Trail, is closed each year from December 1 to June 15 for the annual elk migration in the area.

FLORES HAD A MIND OF HER OWN

Her real name was Grace Bensell and she grew up in a privileged home, the daughter of a prominent American judge. When her father let her take riding and roping lessons at a local sta-

Flores La Due performing fancy rope trick at Calgary Stampede in 1912 on Prince.
GLENBOW ARCHIVES NA-628-4

ble, he had no idea she would decide to become a Wild West show performer. Needless to say, Grace's career aspirations weren't popular with her family, so Grace left home in the middle of the night and joined a travelling circus, taking the stage name of Flores La Due. While touring the southern states with Colonel Cumming's Vaudeville Show, she met and married a handsome cowboy named Guy Weadick. Weadick would eventually go on to become a well-known promoter who is credited with creating the Calgary Stampede. Although La Due's story is often over-

shadowed by her famous husband's, she is remembered as one of the finest rodeo performers in North America. The inscription on her riding saddle sums it up: "Flores La Due World Champion Lady Fancy Roper, Calgary 1912-1919, Winnipeg 1913, New York 1915, Retired Undefeated." The saddle is a treasured possession of local rancher Lenore McLean, who inherited it from Mrs. Weadick on her death in 1951.

night than during the day. The vibration from the flares was so great that businessmen had to put a string across merchandise shelves to keep their contents from spilling onto the floor." At its height, "Little Chicago" had a population of 1,700, but as drilling completed it dried up to nothing. Longview continued to exist even

Eliminator — a bucking bull that is hard to ride

after the closure of the plant in 1964. Today it is a popular destination for travellers along the Cowboy Trail who stop for a meal at one of its many restaurants or to stock up on its famous Longview Beef Jerky.

The Cowboy Trail is actually the main street of Longview, where you will find a number of partners.

Blue Sky Motel

Ron and Leslie Skitch
Hwy. 22, P.O. Box 66, Longview, AB, T0L 1H0
T: 403-558-3655
ACCEPTS D, V, MC, TC
Open all year

Located right on Hwy. 22, the motel is at the gateway to Kananaskis Country and is a popular stop for hikers, hunters, and snowmobilers heading into the wilderness areas just west of town. Over the years, Longview has been a prime location for a number of well-known movie and TV productions, including *Superman*, *Unforgiven*, *Open Range*, and *Little House on the Prairie*. Blue Sky has hosted its share of movie crews and celebrities, but has kept its secrets well.

WHAT THEY OFFER: "A good sleep and a clean room." The motel has ten units, each featuring a new queen-size bed, fridge, microwave, DVD player, and cable TV.

Twin Cities Hotel was built by three National Hockey League players in 1938.
L. ANDREWS

Twin Cities Hotel and Café

Rob and Suzi Kissick

Hwy. 22, P.O. Box 306, Longview, AB, T0L 1H0

T: Hotel: 403-558-3787; Café: 403-558-3786

ACCEPTS D, V, MC

Saloon open Friday and Saturday 11:00 AM to 1:00 AM; Monday to Thursday 11:00 AM to midnight; Sunday noon to 8:00 PM. **Café open** Monday to Thursday 11:00 AM to 8:00 PM; Friday to Sunday 11:00 AM to 9:00 PM. **Hotel open** all year.

The hotel is a popular watering hole for local cowboys stopping for a cool one and a game of pool. It was built in 1938 by three National Hockey League players, "Red" Dutton, Cecil (Tiny) Thompson, and his brother Paul. They called it the Twin Cities Hotel because of the close proximity of "Little New York" and "Little Chicago" to the north. The two communities had sprung up practically overnight after oil discoveries in the area in the 1930s.

Calgary Herald reporter Ken Hull, in an article on the hotel, quoted Stan Gallup (an early Little New York storekeeper): "You'd walk into the hotel lobby and all of a sudden a body would come flying through the beer parlour doors. Those boys were plenty tough. Nobody tangled with a driller, except, of course, another driller." The saloon isn't quite as wild these days, but you can still get in on some foot-stompin' entertainment every Friday and Saturday in the summer, when live bands get the place hoppin'. You might even get lucky and catch well-

APPALOOSA — "THE SPOTTED HORSE"

The Appaloosa is the only true-blooded stock horse in North America, refined and bred by North American Indians. It is believed they were brought to Mexico by the Spanish. The breed eventually spread to the Northwest, where they were acquired by the Nez Perce Indians in the 1700s. They bred these hardy ponies in the area along the Palouse River in what is now Oregon and Washington. Early settlers called them "a Palouse horse," a name eventually shortened to Appaloosa.

The Nez Perce used selective breeding to develop their horses into intelligent animals known for their speed, stamina, and distinctive coat patterns. When the tribe was forced onto a reservation in the late 1870s, their horses were rounded up, sold to the government, or simply destroyed. Tragically, the breed was almost wiped out. Through the efforts of cowboys in Canada and the US, breeding programs were established to revive the Appaloosa to its former stature.

Speckel Boy won a string of awards over his lifetime.
DONNA WYATT

The Appaloosa Horse Club of Canada was formed in 1954, as a result of the efforts of James Wyatt, a rancher north of Longview, and Dr. Grant MacEwan, a well-known historian. Both Wyatt and his horse Speckel Boy are in the Appaloosa Hall of Fame (located in Claresholm). Speckel Boy won a string of awards over his lifetime, including World Champion Appaloosa Performance Horse at the US Nationals. He was never beaten in an open reining class after he turned four.

known cowboy singer Ian Tyson, who lives just east of town, on one of his rare impromptu appearances.

WHAT THEY OFFER: Clean, comfortable rooms at reasonable rates by the day or by the week; two rooms with private bathrooms, otherwise on a shared basis; ATM and laundromat; café has a good selection of appetizers, soups, salads, wraps, burgers, hot sandwiches, and pizza.

Memories Inn Restaurant

Kathy Saminelis and John Vlismas

Hwy. 22, P.O. Box 447, Longview, AB, T0L 1H0

T: 403-558-3665

ACCEPTS V, MC

Open Monday to Saturday 11:00 AM to 10:00 PM; Sunday Noon to 9:00 PM

Greek spoken

When Bernard (Rudy) Vallee – yes, his uncle was the well-known singer – opened his restaurant in the former Longview Trading Post on July 4, 1990, he had no idea that one year later the cast and crew of the Oscar-winning film *Unforgiven* would literally walk in the door, catapulting the little restaurant to instant fame, or that it would eventually become a Longview legend with an international reputation.

Memories Inn Restaurant is a Longview legend.
L. ANDREWS

The movie was filmed west of the Bar U Ranch, just down the road. John Scott, a local wrangler and stuntman with a worldwide reputation for his work on such movies as *Little Big Man*, *Buffalo Bill and the Indians*, *Legends of the Fall*, and *Lord of the Rings*, brought Clint Eastwood and his crew into the restaurant, and the rest, as they say, is history. The place quickly became an Alberta landmark, known as much for its impressive guest list as its good food and friendly service.

BREAD PUDDING AND WHISKEY SAUCE FROM MEMORIES INN

Combine 6–8 cups (1,500 –2,000 ml) of stale French bread crumbs, 4 cups (1,000 ml) milk, 2 cups (500 ml) sugar, 8 Tbsp (120 ml) melted butter, 3 eggs, 2 Tbsp (30 ml) vanilla, 1 cup (250 ml) raisins, 1 cup (250 ml) shredded coconut, 1 cup (250 ml) chopped pecans, 1 tsp (5 ml) cinnamon, and 1 tsp (5 ml) nutmeg. The mixture should be very moist but not soupy. Pour into a buttered 9 x 12 or larger baking dish. Place into a non-preheated oven and bake at 350F (175C) for about 1 hour and 15 minutes until the top is golden brown. Serve warm with whiskey sauce. For the sauce, cream ½ cup (125 ml) butter and 1½ cup (375 ml) powdered sugar over medium heat until all butter is absorbed. Remove from heat and blend in 2 egg yolks. Pour in ½ cup (125 ml) whiskey or rum gradually (to your own taste), stirring constantly. Sauce will thicken as it cools. Serve warm over bread pudding.

Over the years, Rudy amassed an eclectic collection of cowboy and movie memorabilia, and now every available piece of wall space seems full. Everything has a story to tell, from the rack of hats belonging to such cowboys as Ian Tyson, who lives just down the road, to the china plates signed by Gene Hackman and Jon Voight. The padded red metal chair that Eastwood sat in when he stopped to eat during the filming of *Unforgiven* is even hanging from the ceiling, and the outhouse from the set, a gift from Clint, sits out back. Rudy sold the restaurant to Kathy and her brother John in 2002, once he was sure he had found someone who would deliver what he had delivered for 12 years – good food and good friendship.

WHAT THEY OFFER: Their famous prime rib and beef rib buffet every Friday and Saturday night; also a good selection of seafood, chicken, pasta, and house specialties reflecting the Greek heritage of the new owners.

HISTORIC RANCHES STILL EXIST

Just west of Longview on Secondary Hwy. 541, three historic ranches continue to operate. You can see the gates to these properties as you drive down the road, but they are privately owned, so there is no public access. Started by O.H. Smith and Lafayette French in 1883, the OH Ranch is considered one of the first ranches in southern Alberta. Smith and French sold the ranch to Walter and Fred Ings, two brothers from Prince Edward Island who had made some money on mining properties in Spain. They renamed the ranch Rio Alto, Spanish for "High River." The ranch has had a number of owners, including Pat Burns and Bert Sheppard, who worked for George Lane at the Bar U.

Down the road, the Buffalo Head Ranch – named for its buffalo head horse brand – was founded in 1903 by George Pocaterra, a young Italian who stepped off the train in Winnipeg with $3.75 in his pocket. Pocaterra was adopted by the local Stoney Indians. His friendship started one day when he suddenly saw five Indians standing behind him, every man armed with a rifle. He later recalled, "I managed not to be startled; one living in those early conditions was usually set and ready to meet sudden crises. I smiled . . . and said, 'Have a smoke with me.' All five suddenly broke into a smile, and one of them said to the others [in Stoney], "This white man is not afraid of anything." He became a blood brother and friend of Spotted Wolf for over 50 years, travelling the wild country of the Rockies and learning the ancient trails. In the 1930s he sold out to English author R.M. Patterson, who established one of the first dude ranches in Canada, which he ran along with the main ranching operations.

Further west, the Stampede Ranch was once the home of famous Calgary Stampede rodeo promoter Guy Weadick and his wife Florence (see sidebar page 104). They turned it into a guest ranch, welcoming visitors from all over the world. The ranch became the setting for several Hollywood westerns, including the first feature film to be shot in Alberta in 1925. With a little searching you might still be able to find two of the movies filmed here – *Northwest Stampede* and *Chip of the Flying U*.

Heidi's Food Saloon

Heidi Herrmann

Hwy. 22, P.O. Box 261, Longview, AB, T0L 1H0

T: 403-558-2008

E: warrior3@telusplanet.net

ACCEPTS V, MC, AMEX, TC

Open 6:00 AM to 3:00 PM seven days a week

German spoken

Don't be surprised if you see some real cowboys at the next table. The place is a popular stop for the boys from the nearby OH Ranch.

WHAT THEY OFFER: All-day breakfast specials, including traditional bacon and eggs, omelettes, and pancakes. Heidi's reputation has spread as far as Utah. She recently had visitors from the state who made a special point of stopping after friends told them to make sure not to miss it. Lunch specials include homemade soup (often sold out before lunch is over, so don't come late) and a good selection of salads, sandwiches, and burgers. The western art is from a German friend who was so impressed with the "real west" he found here, he was inspired to create the paintings that now hang on the walls.

Black Cat: The Swiss Restaurant

Hans and Yolanda Hiltbrand

Hwy. 22, P.O. Box 314, Longview, AB, T0L 1H0

T: 403-558-0000

E: blackcatswiss@telus.net

ACCEPTS D, V, MC

Open daily except Wednesday for lunch and dinner

German spoken

Hans and Yolanda Hiltbrand moved to Longview from Switzerland in 1999. Their restaurant is located in a unique log building where "Freddy," a huge buffalo head mounted on the wall overlooking the dining room, keeps an eye on the comings and goings of the guests. Along with Freddy, the Hiltbrands' personal collection of downhill skis, snowshoes, sleds, and skates, which they brought from their home in Switzerland, are displayed on the walls of the restaurant.

WHAT THEY OFFER: European specialties such as pork schnitzel Viennese, veal bratwurst rosti, and traditional Cervelat salad with real Swiss cheese and sausage; a good selection of steaks, burgers, and sandwiches for the less adventurous. Regulars come for the home-made soups that are made from scratch each day – according to Yolanda, "we don't have a tin opener." And the Swiss-style cream pies are always in demand. Cowboys can order a Cowboy Omelette, and the Cowboy Trail Coffee is a treat at the end of a hard day in the saddle. The cow-boy version has whiskey; cow-girls have their choice of Kahlua or Galliano and whipped cream.

The Hiltbrands' collection of skis and snowshoes from Switzerland.
BLACK CAT RESTAURANT

Other Grub Stops in Longview

Four Winds, Highway 22, 403-558-3776; Ian Tyson's Navajo Mug, Highway 22, 403-558-2272; Longview Steakhouse, Highway 22, 403-558-2000.

Other Points of Interest in Longview

Tourist Information Centre
Highway 22 at the north end of town
T: 403-558-2046
Open daily July and August, 10:00 AM to 6:00 PM; weekends only from long weekend in May to end of June and September to Canadian Thanksgiving in October, 10:00 AM to 6:00 PM. Public washrooms are also available year-round at the Tails and Trails Campground behind the Information Centre.

As you drive north on Hwy. 22 from Longview, the rolling hills flanking the road are dotted with cattle and horses sharing their space with well sites and pumpjacks, suck-ing the precious oil from the ground. Beneath the surface is the southern edge of the large oil and gas field that put Turner Valley on the map in 1914. At 538 Avenue, watch for the monument on the left (west) side of the road, marking the site of the former town of Royalties or "Little Chicago" (see page 103). Further north, just before you reach Black Diamond, you will pass the access road to another Cowboy Trail partner.

Welcome Acres Bed and Breakfast

Shirley Mundell

Box 7, Site 2, R.R. #1, Okotoks, AB, T1S 1A1

T: 403-933-7529

E: welcome_acres@yahoo.com

ACCEPTS TC

Open all year

As soon as you drive into Welcome Acres, you will know there is an animal lover on the premises. Shirley and her husband run a cow/calf and grain operation, but Shirley also raises and supplies animals for kids' petting zoos. The farm is a popular spot for school groups, with a large collection of donkeys, llamas, goats, pigs, lambs, chickens, and peacocks, sure to delight visitors of all ages. Part of the original house was used as a hospital during the oil boom days, and the barn was once a hardware store.

Butler Cabin at Welcome Acres — just like Grandma used to have.
SHIRLEY MUNDELL

WHAT THEY OFFER: There are three guest bedrooms with shared bathrooms; private sitting room with TV/VCR; playground, trampoline, fire pit, and horseshoes; full hot breakfast with evening snacks. As well, the restored Butler Cabin, moved from Black Diamond, is a log cabin "just like Grandma used to have," with a comfy pine log bed, woodstove, coal oil lamps, and its own private outhouse.

GETTING THERE: From Hwy. 22, drive west on 466 Avenue for 0.8 KM. The farm is on the right (north) side of the road.

Black Diamond
www.town.blackdiamond.ab.ca

T: 403-933-4348

Sarcee name (for Black Diamond and Turner Valley) — *klas-hlath-tidi*, meaning "white mud," for the white clay deposits in the area.

The name Black Diamond refers to the abundant black coal found in the area.

Ranching activity began in the 1880s, but it wasn't until Addison McPherson opened the Black Diamond coal mine in 1899 that miners began moving in. The ridge where the mine was situated is visible on your right as you drive west out of town. By 1907 Herb Arnold, the first postmaster, had opened his store near the present site of the Black Diamond Hotel. The mine closed in 1925, but the discovery of oil and gas in nearby Turner Valley fuelled a construction boom as the population surged to over 1,000. It is said that the gas flares from the oilfields were so bright, they were able to build houses 24 hours a day. After a devastating fire in 1949, many buildings from towns like Little New York and Little Chicago were moved in. Through the Alberta Main Street Program, the town has preserved the architecture of the "Boomtown Era," where false wooden storefronts were the preferred style. Several prime examples, like the MtView Theatre and the Black Store, can still be seen. It's a great place to stop for a meal and a stroll down main street, where you can enjoy the unusual pocket gardens tucked between the historic buildings or view some of the oldest and rarest examples of commercial signs in town. They were discovered under layers of siding during restorations in 2004 on the building that now houses Cataract Creek Clothing. The town offers an eclectic mix of craft and antique shops, including two Cowboy Trail partners.

SO WHAT'S A "SLICK FORK" ANYWAYS?

Like most things western, there is a peculiar lingo that has developed to describe the parts of a saddle. The saddletree (made of wood and covered with rawhide) is the foundation on which the saddle is built. The fork is the piece attached to the front of the saddle. The horn is attached to the upper centre of the fork and usually made of steel. In the early days, the fork was often actually made from the fork of a tree, the horn and fork being cut from one piece of wood. The fork has seen several evolutions, from the slick "A" fork, to the 24-inch "freak," or wide-swell, fork. Swells extend outside the attachment point of the fork to the tree. Bronc riders found they could get a better grip with a wider swell. The result was the "freak," so-called because of its exaggerated size. Ropers generally prefer a slick or narrow fork since the rope can catch under a wide swell and slow down the speed of their dismount in professional competitions.

The cantle is the upright part at the back of the saddle that keeps the rider from falling off the back end of his mount. When the Spaniards brought horses to the New World in the 1500s, their saddles had high protective forks and cantles designed to keep an armoured warrior securely in his seat. Over the years, the height of the cantle was gradually reduced until, in the late 1800s, high-back cantles gained favour with cowboys who spent long hours in the saddle, trailing cattle herds from Texas to Montana and into Alberta. They've become more popular in recent years for modern cowboys who appreciate the support of a higher cantle on long rides out on the range.

Black Diamond Bakery and Coffee Shop

George Nielsen

119 Centre Avenue, P.O. Box 487, Black Diamond, AB, T0L 0H0

T: 403-933-4503

E: nielsen_geo@hotmail.com

ACCEPTS D, V, MC, AMEX

Open Monday to Saturday 7:00 AM to 6:00 PM

Black Diamond Bakery and Coffee Shop
L. ANDREWS

WHAT THEY OFFER: Housed in an old schoolhouse moved in from Longview, the bakery is a popular spot for the locals, which is usually a good sign. Rancher's breakfast has four pancakes, three bacon or sausages, two eggs, hashbrowns, and toast; smaller versions include Straw Boss and Little Lady; daily homemade soups and chili; Friday is perogie day, with specials on Saturdays. People come all the way from Calgary for the special Danish rye bread, but there are plenty of others, including Trail of the Cowboy sourdough. The cinnamon buns are rumoured to be "to die for," and the eccles cakes (rounds of rich puff pastry with currants, sugar, and cinnamon) are a perennial favourite

Marv's Classic Soda Shop and Diner   www.marvsclassics.ca

Marvin Garriott

121 Centre Avenue, P.O. Box 1059, Black Diamond, AB, T0L 0H0

T: 403-933-7001

E: marvsoda@telus.net

ACCEPTS D, V, MC

Open June to early September, Tuesday to Saturday 10:00 AM to 9:00 PM; Sunday and Monday 11:00 AM to 5:30 PM; winter hours Tuesday to Saturday 10:00 AM to 5:30 PM; Sunday and Monday 11:00 AM to 5:30 PM.

Elvis has definitely not left the building! Don't be surprised if you see Marv in his Elvis costume, crooning your favourite oldies from "The King" or any number of '50s tunes. Located in the restored MtView Theatre (moved in from the town of

Royalties), the shop boasts Canada's only working soda fountain and one of the few remaining Nickelodeon player pianos in the country. Western Wheel's 2005 Readers' Choice Awards voted Marv's #1 for ice cream in the foothills and #2 for desserts.

WHAT THEY OFFER: This is boomer heaven, with a large selection of vintage antiques, collectibles, and books, including '50s dinette sets, custom-made diner booths, poodle skirts, saddle shoes, and cat's-eye glasses; old-fashioned candy store features over 150 products like Beemans and Black Jack gum, Smith Brothers cough drops, stick candy, and licorice from around the world. Marv is famous for his old-fashioned malts made from scratch and his Chicago-style hot dogs prepared exclusively for the diner with Alberta beef, but with a full menu of burgers, salads, and sandwiches, there is no shortage of options. Choose from the James Dean Burger or maybe the Bopper Whopper, wash it down with a Black Cow Soda or an All Shook Up Shake, then top it off with a traditional banana split or a Cowboy Trail Saskatoon Sundae.

Stastia Carry in Sparks Circus 1923.
GLENBOW ARCHIVE PA-3457-41

Other Grub Stops in Black Diamond

Black Diamond Hotel Café, 105 Centre Street, 403-933-5078; Blakeman's Store and Deli, 206 Government Road, 403-933-4724; Diamond Valley Restaurant, 202 Centre Avenue, 403-933-3122; Foothills Pizza and Pasta, 117 Centre Avenue, 403-933-4848; Subway, 201 Government Road, 403-933-3333; The Stop Coffee House, 123 Government Road, 403-933-3002; Yum Yum, 102 Centre Avenue, 403-933-3283.

OFF THE BEATEN PATH FROM BLACK DIAMOND

River Ford at Three Point Creek and Christ Church – The ford is one of the last maintained river fords in the province. To reach it, drive west out of Black Diamond on Hwy. 22 towards Turner Valley. After the bridge, turn right (north) on 160 Street to the ford. Just north of the ford, at the junction of Secondary Hwy. 549, is the Christ Anglican Church. Built with vertical unpeeled logs in 1896, the church is still in active use. Be sure to stop and have a look at the stained-glass window and the beautiful grounds that are maintained by the Millarville Horticultural Club. You can retrace your route back to Hwy. 22 and proceed to Turner Valley, or continue west on Secondary Hwy. 549 to hook up with Hwy. 22 north of

Okotoks Big Rock is one of the largest glacier erratics in North America.
L. ANDREWS

Millarville. (If you don't want to chance the ford, you can still see the church by following Hwy. 22 through Turner Valley, past Millarville, and then taking Secondary Hwy. 549 east.)

Okotoks Big Rock – At 16,500 tons, the Okotoks "Big Rock" is one of the largest glacial erratics (boulders dumped off by a passing glacier) found in North America, and has been designated a Provincial Historic Site. At the four-way stop in Black Diamond, take Hwy. 7 east for 11 KM. The rock is on the left (north) side of the road. There is good parking and washrooms on-site.

Christ Anglican Church, built in 1896, is still active.
L. ANDREWS

River Ford at Three Point Creek is one of the last maintianed river fords in the province.
L. ANDREWS

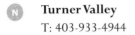

Turner Valley
T: 403-933-4944

www.turnervalley.ca

Three Turner cousins, Robert, John, and James, ran stock in the valley that became known as Turner's Valley. But it was the "Dingman No. 1" strike in 1914 that put Turner Valley on the map, creating a boomtown practically overnight. The story is that the well had been promoted by William Herron, an Okotoks rancher who managed to convince some wealthy businessmen to invest in his company by cooking eggs and bacon over a fire he lit from gas seepages in the area. The boom was cut short by World War I, but in 1924 the Royalite Company struck a major oil and gas reservoir. The well burst into flames and specialists from Oklahoma were finally called in to put the blaze out with dynamite. The waste natural gas was flared off in a coulee that came to be called Hell's Half Acre. At night, the flames could be seen all the way to Calgary. The second Turner Valley boom was on! The last boom began in 1936, when oil was discovered south of town at the site of Royalties ("Little Chicago").

> ### DID YOU KNOW?
> A doodlebugger is an amateur geologist.
>
> ### DID YOU KNOW?
> Because of the way Turner Valley was drilled – wells were crowded together and natural gas, regarded at the time as a worthless by-product, was flared, depleting the gas pressure in the reservoir – it is estimated that over 80 per cent of the oil still remains but is unrecoverable with present-day technology.
>
> ### DID YOU KNOW?
> At one time, Turner Valley was the largest producing gas field in the British Empire.

Turner Valley is still a bustling community with a growing number of resident artisans, and is well-known as a musical mecca, hosting regular concerts at the Flare and Derrick Centre. It is also a jumping-off point for access to Kananaskis Country to the west. The historic Turner Valley gas plant, located in the centre of town, is no longer operational, but guided tours are available.

Turner Valley Gas Plant National and Provincial Historic Site

www.cd.gov.ab.ca

425 Sunset Blvd., P.O. Box 593, Turner Valley, AB, T0L 2A0
T: 403-933-7487
E: tvgphs@hotmail.com
Open daily May 15 to Labour Day weekend 10:00 AM to 6:00 PM
ADMISSION BY DONATION

When Okotoks rancher William S. Heron and his company Calgary Petroleum Products, struck sweet wet gas on May 14, 1914, they put Turner Valley on the world map. The well was Dingman No. 1 (named after the chief driller, A.W. Dingman). Newspapers predicted the oil field would be "second to none in North America." A boom ensued that saw the formation of over 500 oil companies within a few days of the strike. The boom was short-lived, with the outbreak of World War I in August of the same year. When Royalite No. 4 struck sour gas in 1924, it dramatically changed the nature of the gas plant, with the installation of new separators and new scrubbers to remove the hydrogen sulfide from the gas. The discovery of oil in 1936 in the south end of the oilfield, north of Longview, triggered a drilling boom that was fuelled by the start of World War II in 1939. At its peak, in 1942, the oilfield produced in excess of 10 million barrels of oil to assist the war effort.

Between 1914 and 1947, the Turner Valley field accounted for 97 per cent of Alberta's oil and gas production. The gas plant at Turner Valley is the earliest and only surviving example of its kind in Canada and was the first high-pressure absorption gas extraction plant in Canada. The plant continued in operation until 1985. It was designated a Provincial Historic Resource in 1989 and a National Historic Site in 1995.

Access to the site is restricted and visitors must be accompanied by an interpreter. Tours start from the trailer located on the site. (Large groups should book ahead.) The Turner Valley Oilfield Society has developed a good display of information about the area and the plant that is worth a look before you start your tour. Don't miss the short video called *Roughnecks, Wildcats, and Doodlebugs*. It provides an excellent orientation to the history and some great stories about the locals, like the Matlock brothers, who ate glass and picked up chairs with their teeth. The tour gives a good overview of how the gas plant actually worked, as well as insights into the people and the communities that were shaped by the oil and gas industry in the area. You may want to pick up a copy of the excellent "Turner Valley District Driving Tour" booklet, which is for sale at the gas plant. Even if you don't drive the whole tour, it provides a wealth of information about the area from Longview to Millarville.

Chuckwagon Café and Grill

Terry Myhre

105 Sunset Blvd., P.O. Box 442, Turner Valley, AB, T0L 2A0

T: 403-933-0003

ACCEPTS CASH ONLY

Open Monday to Friday 7:30 AM to 2:30 PM; Saturday and Sunday 7:30 AM to 3:30 PM

The little red barn at the four-way stop in Turner Valley is popular with the local cowboys, who come for the all-day breakfast. But you don't have to be a real cowboy to enjoy the country music playing in the background or the wonderful collection of local western art, antique saddles, and fishing rods that fill every nook and cranny in the place. Local restaurant reviewer John Gilchrist liked the food enough to include a listing in his *Cheap Eats Calgary* book, and in 2005 the café won the Western Wheel's Readers' Choice awards for best burger, best Sunday brunch, and best place for lunch.

Chuckwagon Café and Grill is a popular stop with the local cowboys.
L. ANDREWS

WHAT THEY OFFER: An all-day breakfast, including omelettes, pancakes, steak and eggs, and the Ranchman's special; the smoked salmon eggs benedict and breakfast burrito are popular with weekend visitors; homemade burgers include beef, elk, and buffalo; pies are homemade, with banana cream a perennial favourite. You'll even find a grown-up grilled cheese, and the basil on the club sandwich just makes it better

OFF THE BEATEN PATH FROM TURNER VALLEY

Bighorn Sheep Sanctuary and Kananaskis Country – if you head west on Secondary Hwy. 546 at the four-way stop, it is a short 15 kilometre drive into K-Country, where a wide variety of hiking, picnicking, and camping options await. There is an information centre on the right (north) side of the road as you enter the area. Locals recommend a stop at the Bighorn Sheep Sanctuary, which is home to a large herd of bighorn sheep, or maybe a picnic at Sheep River Falls. There is something here for everyone, from short interpretive strolls, to equestrian trails, to overnight backcountry treks, even an outside skating rink that is maintained during the winter. It is also one of the best areas in the province for observing migrating birds of prey, which follow the foothill ridges.

Other Grub Stops in Turner Valley

Coyote Moon Cantina and Espresso Bar, 202 Main Street, 403-933-3363; Eloise's Fresh Fruit Pies & Baking, 140 Main Street, 403-933-4492; Granny's Pizza, 110 Main Street; 403-933-4000; Ralph's Place, 101 Sunset Blvd., 403-933-7901; Route 40 Soup Co., 146 Main Street, 403-933-7676; Turner Inn Family Restaurant, 101 Sunset Blvd., 403-933-5061; Turner Valley Golf and Country Club, 700 Imperial Dr., 403-933-4721; Turner Valley Lodge Spit Fire Grill, 112 Kennedy Dr., 403-933-7878

Fenders — a leather shield attached to the stirrup leather on a saddle to protect the rider's legs

Just outside the entrance to K-Country is another Cowboy Trail partner.

Anchor D Guiding and Outfitting
www.anchord.com

Dewey and Jan Matthews

P.O. Box 656, Black Diamond, AB, T0L 0H0

T: 403-933-2867

E: anchord@anchord.com

ACCEPTS V, MC, TC

Accommodations open all year; riding trips from June 1 to mid-September.

Dewey couldn't believe his luck when he was able to buy the property once home-steaded by well-known one-legged cowboy Bob Carry (see sidebar page 123). The ranch sits in the shadow of Carry Ridge, a ten-minute drive from the Sandy McNabb recreation area and the gateway to some of the most incredible mountain wilderness in the Rockies. Dewey, who has been outfitting in the area for 20 years, admits he probably has more horses than he needs — the current count is 110 — but he has no complaints about his commute to work. "Just saddle up a good horse and head out."

WHAT THEY OFFER: Two-hour, half-day, or full-day trail rides at the ranch or in the mountains (including lunch), steak dinners with advance notice. Flexible ranch vacations with accommodations in Grandpa's Cabin, a cozy, fully self-contained two-bedroom log cabin, plus riding, hiking, cross-country skiing, or relaxing.

The Weekender, four-day Adventurer, and seven-day Explorer, feature daily rides from one high mountain base camp with wall tents, cots, cooking/dining tent, and bathroom tent; Women's Western Wilderness Weekend promises "no men, no

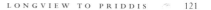

Dewey enjoys the view.
ANCHOR D GUIDING AND OUTFITTING

macho, and all the fun you can stand." The Five-day "Meanwhile . . . Back at the Ranch" trip lets you stay in luxury at the ranch, with day riding in the mountains.

Six- or seven-day moving trips use draft horses and covered wagons to transport food and camp supplies; choose from Great Divide Ride, Lost Trail Trip, Rocky Mountain High, and North Rim to Ranch Ride, with pre-and post-accommodation and transportation. Custom pack and hunting trips, including spring black bear hunt and elk, moose, and deer hunts in the fall.

GETTING THERE: from the four-way stop at Turner Valley (where Hwy. 22 turns north), take Secondary Hwy. 546 west for 13 KM. The ranch is on the right (north) side of the road.

CHRISTINE'S BUFFALO CHUCKWAGON CHILI
FROM THE HEAD COOK AT ANCHOR D

Christine uses this popular recipe when she's cooking on the trail. Brown ten lbs (4,540 g) ground buffalo meat and two chopped onions. Then add one large can brown beans, one large can kidney beans (drained), two cans mushrooms (drained), one or two 28-oz cans tomato sauce, two tsp (10 ml) chili powder, salt and pepper to taste, and three Tbsp (45 ml) brown sugar, and simmer. Serves 30 with baked potatoes, coleslaw, and buns.

ONE-LEGGED COWBOY WAS THE "SQUAREST SHOOTER THAT EVER LIVED"

In 1912 Bob Carry homesteaded west of Turner Valley at the foot of what would eventually be called Carry Ridge, near the current entrance to Kananaskis Country. Author and cowboy Bert Sheppard described Carry as "a 'Cowboy' in the true sense of the word – a working cowboy, who throughout his life exemplified 'mind over matter' to the very highest degree." He lost his leg in World War I at the Battle of the Somme, where he was forced to make a tourniquet with his bayonet and cut off the shattered limb with his knife. For the rest of his life, his particular brand of determination to "do or die" meant that having one leg never stopped him from riding broncs, branding by himself, and fighting his way home through deep snow when set afoot. Sheppard recalls, "He was buried at Christ Church, Millarville, where a host of his friends congregated to pay their respects to one who served his country well, and a man they all believed to be 'The Squarest Shooter That Ever Lived'."

Millarville

As you drive north on Hwy. 22 from Turner Valley, the road winds through a valley dotted with hay fields, aspen groves, and acreages full of horses. The long arm of development is reaching out from Calgary, as more people opt for the beauty of the countryside just a short drive from the edge of the city. The tiny hamlet of Millarville is just west of Hwy. 22 on Secondary Hwy. 549. It was named after Malcolm Miller, who operated a trading post and post office from his ranch house northeast of the present townsite. Millarville was also affected by the oil boom – Home Millarville No. 2 was the first well in Canada to produce one million barrels of oil. The hamlet still has a general store and post office, and a growing collection of huge estate homes built by Calgary commuters. You will also find another Cowboy Trail partner in this area.

The Barn on Whiskey Hill Bed and Breakfast   www.thebarnonwhiskeyhill.com
The Dolans

P.O. Box 17, Site 6, R.R. 1, Millarville, AB, T0L 1K0
T: 403-931-3657
E: hrdolan@yahoo.co.uk
ACCEPTS TC, MO, CC
Open all year

The Dolans still lived in England when they bought this 20-acre parcel of land in 1972. When visiting, they saw the stunning view over the valley from the top of the hill, and they knew they had found a special place. Each summer the family came out to picnic and dream about what their house would eventually look like.

BLACK COWBOY RESPECTED BY ALL WHO KNEW HIM

John Ware was a former South Carolina slave who managed to work his way north on cattle drives from Texas. In 1882 he signed on with Tom Lynch to help trail 3,000 head of cattle from Idaho to the Bar U ranch in southern Alberta. Ware was a big man with enormous strength. His ability with horses was the stuff of legend. When he signed on with Lynch, he was given a docile old nag and a beat-up saddle and told to ride the night herd. When he asked for a better saddle and a worse horse, the cowboys tested him with the worst outlaw in the bunch. Grant MacEwan, in his book *John Ware's Cow Country*, describes the ride. "The wicked horse was released. [It] kicked, pitched, sunfished and did unnamed contortions in the air." Gradually the horse gave up its fight. "Cowboys, forgetting their plot to create some fun at Ware's expense, knew they were seeing an exhibition of rough-riding such as to fill every one of them with admiration and, indeed, envy." Over the years, John's exceptional ability with horses, his hard work, and his honesty earned the respect of all who knew him. He homesteaded

John Ware and family c. 1896
GLENBOW ARCHIVES NA-263-1

*John Ware cairn marks the site of
the original Ware homestead*
L. ANDREWS

southwest of Millarville near what became known as Ware Creek at the foot of Ware Ridge. Ironically, he was killed in 1905 when his horse stumbled in a hole and fell on him. His funeral was the largest held in Calgary up to that time.

In 1993 the dream became a reality. The family wrote down 25 things that had to be in the house and faxed the list to an architect. Five years earlier, the architect had sat on the hill and listened to Helen describe her vision and philosophy of "the simplicity of our forebears" that she wanted the house to reflect. The architect sent back a design, which didn't change through-

Helen's dream house.
THE BARN ON WHISKEY HILL BED AND BREAKFAST

out the entire building process. During a quick one-week trip to Canada, Helen chose the builder and all the fixtures, then arrived back at Easter to see the final product. She added one window but changed nothing else.

WHAT THEY OFFER: Three rooms, with private bath and separate entrance, plus a choice of continental or full Western breakfast; enjoy the spectacular view of the valley from kitchen and open sitting room with baby grand piano and antique organ once owned by Senator Pat Burns; indoor slide (on the original list of 25 "must haves") allows kids of all ages to bypass the stairs down to the private sitting area and TV room; outdoor hot tub, fire pit, horse swing, and walking trails.

GETTING THERE: From Hwy. 22, go west on Plummers Road for 3 KM. At the T-intersection, turn left (south) and drive 5.6 KM to 280 Street. Turn right (north) and watch for the sign on the left (west) side of the road.

Priddis

As you head north past the turnoff for Millarville, you will pass the High Country Café on the left (west) side of the road, a popular stop for breakfast and lunch. The Trail continues north, then jogs west towards the village of Bragg Creek. As you head west you will see the sign for the hamlet of Priddis, just a short drive south of the highway. It is worth stopping to see the St. James Anglican Church, which was 100 years old in 2004. It was built on land donated by Charles Priddis, who homesteaded near here. There are picnic tables by the hall, as well as a coffee and gift shop, restaurant, and gas station.

From Priddis, head back to Hwy. 22. There is a Cowboy Trail partner located just off the highway as you drive west towards Bragg Creek.

John Ware Cairn – Drive west from Hwy. 22 on Secondary Hwy. 549 for 11 KM to the turnoff for Secondary Hwy. 762. Turn left (south) and go to the T-intersection. Turn right (west) and follow the crest of the hill. The cairn is on your left side (on private property), just before the log house on the right. You can retrace your route to Hwy. 22 or take Secondary Hwy. 762 north to Bragg Creek, a delightful drive through forests and rolling hills.

Millarville Race Track and Farmer's Market – From Hwy. 22, drive east on Secondary Hwy. 549 for 3 KM, then turn right (south) and follow the road to the entrance. The farmer's market is one of the largest in Alberta and runs every Saturday morning from mid-June to early October, rain or shine. The Millarville Races are a July 1 tradition that started in

Starting Line at the Millarville Races – 1920
MILLARVILLE HISTORICAL SOCIETY

1905 and continue to be one of the most important social events of the season. If you didn't venture across the Three Point Creek ford north of Black Diamond to see the Christ Church (see sidebar page 116), you can continue east on Secondary Hwy. 549 another 5 KM. The church, built in 1896, is still in active use.

Brown Lowery Provincial Park – This is one of the best-kept secrets in Alberta. From Hwy. 22, turn left (west) at Plummer's Road for 11.4 KM. The park entrance is on the left (south) side of the road, but is very easy to miss. There is a small parking area with toilets.

St. James Anglican Church in Priddis is over 100 years old.
L. ANDREWS

Hilltop Ranch Bed and Breakfast   www.hilltopranch.net

Gary and Barbara Zorn

P.O. Box 54, Priddis, AB, T0L 1W0

T: 1-800-801-0451

E: gary@hilltopranch.net

ACCEPTS V, MC

Open all year

Barbara and Gary Zorn had always wanted to open a B&B, so when they moved from Yellowknife and purchased their 57-acre hobby farm near Priddis, they decided to give it a try. The large ranch-style bungalow sits on a hilltop with a spectacular view of the Rocky Mountains to the west. The house is surrounded by colourful gardens filled with birdhouses and flowers.

WHAT THEY OFFER: Three guest bedrooms (named after their sons, Murray, Mike, and Marvin), with large windows and ensuite bathrooms; guest lounge has fireplace, TV/VCR; and deck; full hot breakfast served; "horse motel" with eight new box stalls and good quality hay and water; horse-drawn carriage and sleigh rides if Gary happens to hitch up the team.

GETTING THERE: The ranch is 3 KM west of the Priddis turnoff, just past 240 Street. You will see a red barn with "Hilltop" on it. Turn right (north) down the driveway to the ranch.

Cowboy Trail partners for this area added just prior to press time

Leighton Art Centre Museum and Gallery   www.leightoncentre.org
Calgary, Alberta
T: 403-931-3633
E: info@leightoncentre.org

Millarville Racing and Agricultural Society   www.millarville.ab.ca
Millarville, Alberta
T: 403-931-3411
E: mras@millarville.ab.ca

Tumbleweed Mercantile and Design   www.tumbleweedmercantile.com
Black Diamond, Alberta
T: 403-933-2288
E: tumbleweed@platinum.ca

Wonders Coffee House and Gift Shop
Black Diamond, Alberta
T: 403-933-2347

THE ETIQUETTE OF THE RANGE

According to local history book *Leaves From the Medicine Tree*, "When a stranger rode into a cowcamp, he was invited to 'pull his saddle off and come an' eat,' but he was never asked his name, or where he came from. Range etiquette did not allow it. He was taken at face value and later judged by his actions. If a hand found it necessary to make a fast getaway on a ranch horse, he was honour bound to return that horse. Loyalty to the brand for which he worked was one of the outstanding characteristics of the old time cowboys. Men were known to starve, freeze, fight and die for the outfit that employed them."

CRITTER WATCH: BIGHORN SHEEP

The Bighorn Sheep is Alberta's provincial mammal. They are sometimes confused with mountain goats, but once you've seen a ram with its magnificent curling brown horns, you won't forget it. The horns aren't used for defence, but for "love." During the mating season in October and November, the rams literally go head-to-head, crashing and smashing horns with their rivals to establish a breeding hierarchy. Other than this once-a-year ritual, the massive horns are mainly ornamental. Ewes tend to have shorter curved horns. Bighorns have a tan coat with a white rump patch and a beardless chin, while mountain goats are white with bearded chins and short, black, dagger-like horns. Bighorns are well known for their agility on steep slopes and rocky ledges, but they are also commonly seen along roadsides in the parks. The townsite at Waterton Lakes National Park or the Bighorn Sheep Sanctuary west of Turner Valley are good viewing spots.

The Bighorn Sheep is Alberta's provincial manmal.
JANET NASH

Recommended Reading

Cowgirls: 100 Years of Writing the Range edited by Thelma Poirier
John Ware's Cow Country by Grant MacEwan
Just About Nothing by Bert Sheppard
Kananaskis Country Trail Guide: Volume 2 by Gillean Daffern
Letters From a Lady Rancher by Monica Hopkins
R.M. Patterson: A Life of Great Adventure by David Finch
Spitzee Days by Bert Sheppard
The Buffalo Head by R.M. Patterson

Gee — a verbal command to turn a horse to the right; (the opposite of "haw" or left)

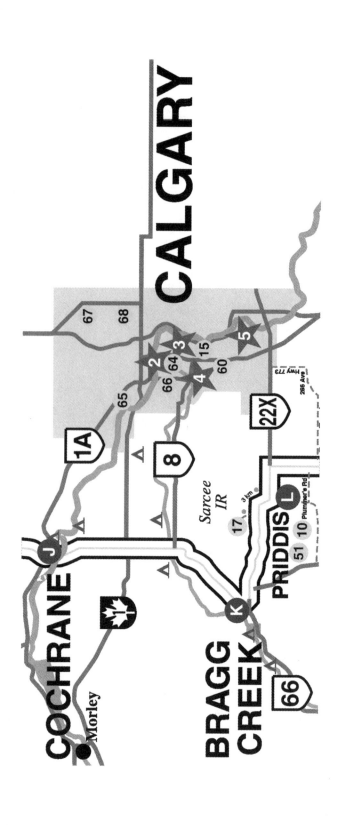

5 : BRAGG CREEK AND AREA

"A man should count himself lucky if he can look back on his life and say that he had at least one great horse, one exceptional dog, and one true friend." —Ted Stone, *Cowboy Logic*

Communities

- Ⓚ Bragg Creek

Accommodations

- ⑮ The Glenmore Inn and Convention Centre

Attractions & Events

- ⑥⓪ Ranchman's Dance Hall and Emporium

Outfitters

- Ⓚ Inside Out Experience
- ⑤① Moose Mountain Adventures

Rafting & Water Adventures

- Ⓚ Inside Out Experience

Restaurants

- Ⓚ Bragg Creek Shopping Centre
- Ⓚ Madrina's Ristorante
- Ⓚ The Bavarian Inn Restaurant
- ⑮ The Glenmore Inn and Convention Centre
- ★3 Calgary Exhibition and Stampede
- ⑥⓪ Ranchman's Dance Hall and Emporium
- ★4 Heritage Park Historical Village
- ★5 The Ranche Restaurant; Annie's Bakery and Café

Shopping, Antiques & Artisans

- Ⓚ Archer's Antiques and Pine Classics
- Ⓚ Bragg Creek Shopping Centre
- Ⓚ Bragg Creek Trading Post
- ⑮ The Glenmore Inn and Convention Centre
- ⑥④ Smithbilt Hats
- ★3 Calgary Exhibition and Stampede
- ★2 Glenbow Museum
- ★4 Heritage Park Historical Village

Icon Attractions

- ★3 Calgary Exhibition and Stampede
- ★2 Glenbow Museum
- ★4 Heritage Park Historical Village
- ★5 The Ranche Restaurant; Annie's Bakery and Café

MAJOR EVENTS ALONG THE TRAIL

(check www.thecowboytrail.com for a complete listing)

March
Rodeo Royal, Calgary Stampede

May
Festival of Quilts, Heritage Park

June
Frontier Pastimes, Heritage Park
Railway Days, Heritage Park

July
Bragg Creek Days, Bragg Creek
Calgary Exhibition and Stampede, Calgary Stampede
Tsuu T'ina Classic Pow Wow and Rodeo, Bragg Creek

August
Heritage Day, Heritage Park
Rural Roots, Heritage Park

September
Canadian Country Music Week, Calgary Stampede
Fall Fair, Heritage Park

October
Octoberwest, Heritage Park

Hang up — when a bareback or bull rider is unable to get his
hand out of the rigging or bull rope

5 :   B R A G G   C R E E K   A N D   A R E A

Bragg Creek and Area   www.braggcreekchamber.com; www.braggcreek.ca
T: 403-949-0004

The official story is that the creek and the hamlet were named after Warren Bragg, who came west from Truro, Nova Scotia, and settled here briefly in 1894. But Marilyn Bragg Symons has a more personal version: "Bragg Creek was named for my great uncle Albert Warren Bragg *and* my grandfather, John Thomas Bragg. What has never been told was that Uncle Warren was about 17 at the time and Grandpa John was 12 in 1894. I think that makes the story much more interesting. A kind of Canadian Tom and Huck adventure. The boys had run away from their home in Oxford Junction, Nova Scotia, over a disagreement with their new (and very young) stepmother. The boys had made application to prove a homestead – they were not squatters. They left because they got homesick, not because of the bad weather." Both boys eventually returned to Alberta to ranch, Warren at Rosebud and John at Rockyford.

The hamlet sits at the gateway to Kananaskis Country, which is located just west of town on Hwy. 66. With pristine wilderness literally on the doorstep and the city of Calgary just a short 30-minute drive to the east, it was probably inevitable that it would become a popular spot for commuters who choose to live here and make the daily trek into work. Despite the influx of new residents, Bragg Creek has somehow managed to maintain a rural flavour, attracting a variety of artists and craftspeople who have chosen to call it home. It makes for an interesting collection of art and craft shops, antique specialty stores, and a destination spot for fine dining.

Bragg Creek may be drawing a new kind of urban "settler," but from the beginning the area attracted many visitors. The historic Stoney Indian Trail runs through the heart of the community. The Stoney tribe used the trail as they travelled the Eastern slopes of the Rockies, hunting and trading. In fact, it was probably the presence of the trail that brought the first homesteaders to the area. They quickly learned that the higher altitude brought early frosts and a shorter growing season that discouraged

> **DID YOU KNOW?**
> The first church in southern Alberta, the "Our Lady of Peace Mission," was built about 1872. It was north and west of the present site of Bragg Creek, which did not have a church of its own during the early settlement. A cairn commemorates the site of the church. As you drive north on Hwy. 22 from Bragg Creek, watch for the sign pointing left (west). You can follow the road to the cairn.

133

cropping. So they turned to ranching, taking advantage of the good grass. Some families, like the Fullertons and the Robinsons, have been ranching here for over 100 years and are now into their third and fourth generation on the land.

OFF THE BEATEN PATH FROM BRAGG CREEK

Bragg Creek Provincial Park – Follow White Avenue west out of town to the park. It is available for day use and is a great spot for picnics.

Kananaskis Country – Bragg Creek is located on the doorstep of K-Country. As you head west on Hwy. 66, you will pass an information centre on the right (north) side of the road, where you can find detailed maps and information about everything the area has to offer. On the drive west, you will climb the so-called "Stairway to Heaven" through grasslands, aspen parklands, and subalpine forest to views of the high alpine. The area boasts something for everyone, from paved bike and interpretive trails, to mountain biking and hiking trails that offer challenging overnight backcountry treks. The McLean Creek Off-Highway Vehicle Zone has trails and camping facilities designated for those looking to explore the area on trail motorbikes and four-wheel drive vehicles.

Locals Recommend: You don't have to be an avid hiker or biker to enjoy yourself here. There are a number of beautiful picnic and fishing spots and easy interpretive walks within a short distance of Bragg Creek. Here are a few recommendations from the locals:

Elbow Falls: Good picnic spots; a paved walking trail offers spectacular views of the falls and the river

Allen Bill Pond: A great spot to do some fishing or just relax and eat your picnic by the pond

Fullerton Loop Trail: An easy 5 KM trail (mountain bikers prohibited).

Despite its small size, there are several Cowboy Trail partners located in town.

Inside Out Experience www.insideoutexperience.com

Andrew Pratt

P.O. Box 987, Bragg Creek, AB, T0L 0K0

T: 1-877-999-7238

E: info@insideoutexperience.com

ACCEPTS D, V, MC

Open all year

Andrew is a transplanted Aussie who first travelled to Calgary to take the Outdoor Pursuits program at the University of Calgary. He used that training to establish an outdoor recreation program at a private school in Australia, but eventually returned to Canada to go into business for himself. Now he is doing what he loves best – bringing people from inside the city to the outdoors to experience true learning adventures, hence the name Inside Out Experience.

WHAT THEY OFFER: Half-day and full-day adventures in rafting, hiking, mountain biking, and horseback riding in the summer, and snowshoeing and cross-country skiing in the winter; full-day trips, and several of the half-day options,

Rafting the rapids in Kananaskis Country.
INSIDE OUT EXPERIENCE

include lunch; half-day rafting trip has choice of a gourmet lunch or dinner; full-day combos include lunch and choice of hike and raft, mountain bike and raft, or saddle 'n paddle. As well, there are family rafting trips good for kids aged five and up, and youth rafting for ages 12 to 16 every Friday from July 1 to August 31.

"Cattle, rattle, paddle, and saddle" features two days at the Calgary Stampede, riding, rafting, and a barbecue steak lunch. Inside Out Experience teams up with several hotels, B&Bs, and resorts in the Kananaskis Valley and Banff, as well as the Red Deer River Ranch (see page 193) near Sundre, to offer accommodations and a variety of hiking, rafting, biking, and skiing options.

 Archer's Antiques and Pine Classics

Steve Archer

 24 White Avenue, P.O. Box 602, Bragg Creek, AB, T0L 0K0

T: 1-877-949-3655

ACCEPTS V

Open Thursday to Sunday, Noon to 5:00 PM, or by appointment or chance,

Between Steve and his grandfather, they have been in the business of restoring early Canadian furniture for 45 years. Their showroom is located in a renovated 1912 arts and craft home and offers quality restored antiques from across Canada.

Archer's Antiques offers quality restored antiques from across Canada.
STEVE ARCHER

According to Steve, he has more pre-Confederation furniture than anyone else in Canada. Because of the shortage of good quality pieces, Steve has decided to reproduce the "pine classics," using original craftsmanship and museum-quality finishes to bring his customers the history and heritage of Canada's past. He also carries a selection of finely crafted Hutterite, Mennonite, and Doukhobor pieces that are unique to the prairies.

Bragg Creek Shopping Centre
22 Balsam Avenue, Bragg Creek, AB, T0L 0K0

Located on Balsam Avenue, this is the main shopping centre for the hamlet. The covered wooden boardwalk lends a distinctly western flair to the variety of shops and restaurants located here. Shops include:

Aztec Interiors/Durango Trail Furniture, 403-949-3266
Boardwalk Coffee and Wine Bar, 403-949-2842
Bragg Creek Bottle Depot, 403-949-2260
Bragg Creek Food Town, 403-949-3747
Bragg Creek Health Foods, 403-949-3581
Bragg Creek Husky, 403-949-3525
Bragg Creek Leather Shop, 403-949-2468
Bragg Creek Video and Gifts, 403-949-3881
Canada Post Postal Outlet, 403-949-2339
Curves for Women, 403-949-8267
Daisy Door, Flowers and More, 403-949-4212
Frontier Candy and Ice Cream, 403-949-3575
Moose Mountain Diner, 403-949-2606

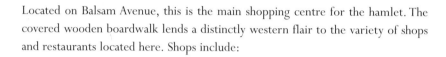

Jingle — to round up a herd of cattle or horses

Mountain Bistro and Pizzeria, 403-949-3800
One of a Kind Art and Gift Gallery, 403-949-2592
Powderhorn Saloon, 403-949-3946
Rock 'n Berry's Bar 'n Grille/Joey's Only Seafood, 403-949-3336
Spirits West Liquor and Wine Merchants, 403-949-2497
Sutton Group CanWest Realty, 403-949-4100
The Beehive, Handmade Soaps, 403-949-5660
The Kiln Gallery, 403-949-3938
Wicker Tea and Spice, 403-949-4262

The Bragg Creek Trading Post is a local landmark.
L. ANDREWS

Bragg Creek Trading Post

Barbara Teghtmeyer

117 White Avenue, P.O. Box 415, Bragg Creek, AB, T0L 0K0

T: 403-949-3737

ACCEPTS D, V, MC, AMEX

Open daily 10:00 AM to 6:00 PM

Walk in the door of this wonderful old building and you will be surrounded by the rich, earthy smell of tanned leather hides and the warmth of a wood-burning heater. The store was originally called the Upper Elbow General Store. It was built by Guy Coates in 1925 and operated by his wife Tina until 1940, when it was sold to Jack Eldson. Jack renamed it the Trading Post, and it has since become a local landmark. The Trading Post is now owned and operated by Jack's daughter Barbara, who has maintained the original log building and still uses the original scales, glass showcases, and gas pump.

WHAT THEY OFFER: Besides gas, Barbara sells finely crafted moccasins, mukluks, and other leather goods made by Natives from the local Stoney tribe as well as the Sarcee, Cree, and Ojibway who regularly stop to do business. But that's not all. You're as likely to find a T-bone steak as a Cowichan sweater, a pair of gumboots, or a fishing license.

Madrina's Ristorante

www.madrinasristorante.com

Louise-Marie Eagar

20 Balsam Avenue, P.O. Box 1094, Bragg Creek, AB, T0L 0K0

T: 403-949-2750

E: madrinas@telusplanet.net

ACCEPTS D, V, MC

Open for lunch Tuesday to Saturday 11:30 AM to 3:00 PM and Sunday 1:30 PM to 3:00 PM; for Sunday brunch 11:00 AM to 1:30 PM; for dinner Tuesday to Thursday 5:00 PM to 9:00 PM, Friday and Saturday 5:00 PM to 10:00 PM, Sunday 4:30 PM to 8:00 PM.

Madrina's Ristorante focuses on authentic Italian dishes.
L. ANDREWS

WHAT THEY OFFER: Casual and formal dining with a focus on authentic Italian dishes, including antipasti, traditional Italian thin-crust pizza, panini, and pasta. According to Louise-Marie, the Roseline Al Forno (smoked ham and mozzarella rolled in pasta and baked in a rosé sauce) is a perennial favourite, as are the Caesar salad (prepared at your table) and the beef tenderloin. The broad menu includes a good selection of salads, soup, beef, chicken, veal, lamb, and vegetarian choices, while desserts feature homemade sorbets and gelatos.

The Bavarian Inn Restaurant

www.thebavarianinn.com

Charlie Holschuh and Pamela Shewchuk

75 White Avenue, P.O. Box 808, Bragg Creek, AB, T0L 0K0

T: 403-949-3611

E: info@TheBavarianInn.com

ACCEPTS D, V, MC

Open for dinner Tuesday to Sunday 5:00 PM to close; for lunch Sunday 11:30 AM to 2:30 PM

German spoken

Like many Germans, Charlie got hooked on the western way of life he found during a vacation spent visiting friends. He was 35 at the time and felt he was still young enough to make one more big change in his life. So he made the move, and purchased the Bavarian Inn a year later, in 1989. From its beginning, almost 30 years ago, the restaurant has had a reputation for excellence, consistency, and the

Bavarian hospitality that Charlie and his wife, Pamela, have continued to maintain. Charlie trained as a chef in the Rhine Valley and Bavaria, working in several European countries before he moved to Canada.

WHAT THEY OFFER: German and alpine specialties such as Bratwurst with sauerkraut and Bavarian potato cakes or wiener schnitzel; Alberta Grade AAA steak and tenderloin dishes, as well as a selection of veal, fish, vegetarian fare, wild game, and seafood dishes; the weekly Chef's Selection menu offers seasonal specialties. Reservations are recommended.

Other Grub Stops in Bragg Creek

Bragg Creek Steak Pit, 50 White Avenue, 403-949-3633; Cinnamon Spoon, 1 White Avenue, 403-949-4110; Creek Bakery, BC Village Centre, 403-949-2818; Dave's Pizza and Family Restaurant, BC Village Centre, 403-949-2002; El Gringo's Restaurant and Lounge, 127 Balsam Avenue, 403-949-8226; Infusion, 23 Balsam Avenue, 403-949-3898; Subway, 21 White Avenue, 403-949-5654.

CRITTER WATCH: COUGAR (MOUNTAIN LION)

Cougars, mountain lions, or catamounts (short for "cat of the mountains") have been called the most efficient predator in the world. They are capable of bringing down an elk or a bull moose, but generally feed on mule or white-tailed deer, bighorn sheep, and smaller animals such as beaver and mountain goats. They depend on the element of surprise, leaping onto the animal's shoulders and biting deeply into the back of the neck, suffocating them by wrapping their claws around the windpipe. Cougars will feed on a large deer for a week or more, burying the carcass between feedings. It is actually possible for these big cats to starve during very cold winters if the carcasses of their prey freeze solid before they have the chance to get

more than one meal, because their jaws are designed for slicing and they have difficulty chewing frozen meat. Cougars were once common throughout the province, but there are now believed to be less than 700 breeding adults in all of Alberta. Cougar sightings are extremely rare. Some of the likeliest spots are in the Sheep River area on the eastern edge of Kananaskis country, west of Bragg Creek and Turner Valley, as well as the area from Sundre to Nordegg.

Cougars are one of the most efficient predators in the world.
JANET NASH

Other Points of Interest in Bragg Creek

Public washrooms located by the Husky service station on Balsam Avenue.

Located just south of Bragg Creek, Moose Mountain Adventures starts many of its horseback riding trips from Kananaskis Country.

Moose Mountain Adventures   www.packtrips.ca

Neil MacLaine

P.O. Box 285, Bragg Creek, AB, T0L 0K0

T: 1-866-513-RIDE (7433)

E: info@packtrips.ca

ACCEPTS V, MC

Open all year

Since 1991, Neil has been guiding horse enthusiasts and adventurers looking to experience the Rockies with a well-trained, responsive horse. Neil's philosophy is to encourage respect for your horse and the wilderness.

WHAT THEY OFFER: Hourly, half-day, and full-day rides, and off-season riding on the ranch property or in Kananaskis Country just west of the ranch from mid-May to mid-October; Moose Mountain Ranch Club offers experienced riders with no

Riders enjoy the beauty of Kananaskis Country.
MOOSE MOUNTAIN ADVENTURES

horse, a winter season's pass for unlimited, unguided horseback riding in the off-season.

The packages include three-day pack trips, five-day expeditions, or the eight-day Longrider; Saddle and Paddle combines riding and canoeing; the Mountains and High Plains Combo includes mountain pack trip and competitive trail ride in the Milk River country south of Lethbridge; the six-day High Plains Drifter travels from the Sweetgrass Hills on the Montana border to the Cypress Hills in Saskatchewan, including historic Fort Walsh; pre- and post-trip bed and breakfast accommodation at local establishments can be arranged for any of the trips.

GETTING THERE: From Hwy. 22, drive south on Secondary Hwy. 762 for 10 KM. Watch for the log entrance gate on the left (east) side of the road. You can also access the ranch from Secondary Hwy. 549 heading west past Millarville. At the junction with Secondary Hwy. 762, turn right (north) and go for 12 KM. The entrance is on the right (east) side of the road.

Several Cowboy Trail Icon Attractions and partners are located within the city of Calgary. They are easily accessible from Hwy. 22 north of Bragg Creek via Hwy. 8 or Hwy. 1, or via Hwy. 1A from Cochrane. For excellent information on Calgary, check out www.tourismcalgary.com or call toll-free 1-800-661-1678.

The Glenmore Inn and Convention Centre   www.glenmoreinn.com
2720 Glenmore Trail SE, Calgary, AB, T2C 2E6

T: 1-800-661-3163

ACCEPTS ALL MAJOR CREDIT CARDS

Open all year

This is a full-service hotel and convention centre located in the southeast sector of Calgary, a short drive from the Calgary International Airport and four of the Cowboy Trail Icon attractions – the Calgary Exhibition and Stampede, Heritage Park, the Glenbow Museum, and The Ranche Restaurant.

WHAT THEY OFFER: 169 rooms offer a variety of choices from standard doubles to studios, Jacuzzi rooms, and business and executive suites; the Carving Board Café serves breakfast, lunch, and dinner from 6:00 AM; the Garden Court is well known for its buffets and Sunday brunches presented in a lush, tropical garden setting; on-site liquor store and gift shop; guests have access to fitness room, sauna, and hot tub; new indoor pool and waterslide added in 2005.

GETTING THERE: From Macleod Trail, take Glenmore Trail east until you reach the Inn.

54 Smithbilt Hats Ltd.   www.smithbilthats.com
Wade Schultz
1235 – 10th Avenue SW, Calgary, AB, T3C 0J3 (factory – no sales outlet)
T: 403-244-9131
E: info@smithbilthats.com

Smithbilt hats are sold at over 300 stores across Canada. Morris Shumiatcher came to western Canada from Russia in 1909. When the family arrived in Calgary, they decided to shorten their name to Smith, and Morris started looking for a business to own. In 1919 he bought the Calgary Hat Works after his brother Harry agreed to co-sign on a loan for $300. Morris soon earned a reputation as a fine hat maker, and in 1926, when several of his clients asked him to make a top-of-the-line western hat, Morris took up the challenge. His designs were so popular, he could barely keep up with the demand.

CALGARY'S WHITE HAT AND THE "WHITE HATTER" CEREMONY

In 1947 oilman William S. Heron and his family took the "best dressed" prize at the Calgary Stampede Parade. They wore matching white hats made by Morris Shumiatcher of Smithbilt Hats Ltd. as part of their prize-winning outfit. According to Herron, the only place where they could find stock that was truly white was from a supplier in (then) USSR. The hats were a hit and were worn the next year by fans who attended the Grey Cup game in Toronto as part of a promotion spearheaded by radio announcer Don Mackay. White hats were everywhere as the Calgarians treated the Eastern dudes to Cowboy breakfasts and rode their horses into the bars for a drink. When Mackay became mayor in 1950, he began the tradition of presenting the white hat as a symbol of civic welcome to visiting dignitaries. Since then thousands of guests have been "white hatted" and have taken the

The famous white Smithbilt Cowboy Hat.
CALGARY CONVENTION AND VISITORS BUREAU

"oath of allegiance" (see page 148) during their visit to the city. Almost every prime minister and president of the last 50 years has been white hatted, as well as a long list of celebrities, including Kevin Costner, Wayne Gretzky, Oprah Winfrey, and Vladimir Putin.

In 1946 the Calgary Stampede approached Morris to help them develop a plan to get Calgarians to wear and promote cowboy hats during the Stampede. Morris decided to tap into the rage for light colours that had been created by a shortage of materials during the war. The result was the legendary champagne white Smithbilt cowboy hat that is used by the City of Calgary in its famous white hat ceremony to welcome visiting celebrities and dignitaries. The symbol of the white hat has since become synonymous with the Calgary Stampede and western hospitality (see sidebar page 143).

WHAT THEY OFFER: Men's and ladies' western hats in beaver, beaver blends, fur and wool felt, and straw. Styles include a buckaroo, a wrangler, a Billy the Kid, and an outlaw; sold at over 300 stores across Canada.

Calgary Exhibition and Stampede

www.calgarystampede.com

Stampede Park, 1410 Olympic Way SE, P.O. Box 1060, Stn M, Calgary, AB, T2P 2K8

T: 1-800-661-1767 (for tickets)

1-800-661-1260 (main reception) – toll-free anywhere in North America

ACCEPTS ALL MAJOR CREDIT CARDS FOR TICKETS ADMISSION CHARGED

ADMISSION; CASH AVAILABLE THROUGH ON-SITE ATMS

Show runs for ten days each year from the first Friday in July

From its modest beginnings in 1912, the Calgary Stampede has evolved into "The Greatest Outdoor Show on Earth," attracting over one million visitors each year. For ten days each July, the show transforms this otherwise conservative city into the stage for the wildest western show in the world. It may seem a bit audacious for Calgarians to tout their show as the Greatest on Earth, but here are a few reasons why they do.

You can see the world's rodeo elite compete for $1,000,000 – the richest

The Young Canadians entertain at the evening grandstand show.
CALGARY EXHIBITION AND STAMPEDE

regular season professional rodeo purse in the world. The final day of competition includes a sudden-death ride-off, with $75,000 up for grabs in each of the six main events – steer wrestling, tie-down roping, saddle bronc riding, bareback bronc riding, bull riding, and barrel racing. You can see the world-famous Rangeland Derby – where the top 36 chuckwagons in the world compete each evening in a nail-biting display of spectacular driving ability.

You can see an agricultural exhibition that has maintained its reputation for excellence for over 115 years, one of the oldest exhibitions of its kind in North America. You can watch some of the finest cutting horses, working cow horses, stock dogs, and beef cattle on the continent compete for top prizes. You can travel

WHAT'S IN A NAME?

The word rodeo comes from the Spanish *rodear*, meaning "to go around." As far back as the 1500s, Mexican vaqueros or cowboys learned to work cattle from the backs of horses introduced by the Spaniards. They created the tradition of riding and roping that evolved into the practice of rodeo as a way to show off their skills. The first rodeo is said to have happened in the streets of Sante Fe, New Mexico, in 1847. In Canada the cowboys weren't much different, gathering on a day off to bust a few broncs and rope a few cattle for a friendly wager. This was serious bronc busting – there was no time limit. It lasted until the cowboy rode the horse to a standstill or was bucked off.

THE BIG FOUR

In the summer of 1912 Guy Weadick (see page 109) met with four big area ranch-ers at Calgary's exclusive Ranchmen's Club to make a pitch for $100,000. Weadick want-ed to stage a Wild West show that he claimed would "make Buffalo Bill's Wild West Extravaganza look like a sideshow." Calgary had been holding agricultural exhibitions since 1886. It wasn't until Weadick, an American cowboy and business promoter, con-vinced the "Big Four" – George Lane, Archie McLean, Pat Burns, and A.E. Cross – to back his idea for a Wild West cowboy show, that the Calgary Stampede was born. The first Stampede, held in September 1912, wasn't a resounding success – poor weather and organizational problems meant the "Big Four" lost money on the venture. But they saw the potential for success and agreed to try again.

The "Big Four" were honoured in 1959 when the Big Four building was erected on the Stampede grounds in Calgary, and in 1963 when their portraits were hung in the Canadian Agricultural Hall of Fame in Toronto, but they each left their own imprint on the history of southern Alberta.

Pat Burns started out as a farm boy from Ontario who came west when he was 22 to homestead. He settled in Winnipeg, where he worked on the construction of the Canadian Pacific Railway, following the railway west to Calgary around 1890. Burns fig-

The Big Four – left to right, Pat Burns, George Lane,
Prince of Wales, A.J. McLean, A.E. Cross –
at EP Ranch, October 1924.
GLENBOW ARCHIVES NA-2043-1

ured he could make more money supplying beef to the Indian reserves, construction gangs, and mining and lumbering camps than he ever could farming, so he turned his attention to building up his beef contracts. He started out with a small slaughterhouse, where he also slept. By the time he was done, Burns owned one of the largest meat-packing and food provision-ing businesses in the world. But he didn't stop at meat-packing. He

slowly expanded into ranching. At one time, his landholdings totalled about 182,000 hectares (450,000 acres). It was said he could ride from the international boundary to Calgary without ever leaving his land.

George Lane was born on a farm near Des Moines, Iowa, moving west to work on a ranch in Montana when he was 16. In 1884 he was hired by the North West Cattle Company to become the foreman of the Bar U Ranch. He eventually left the Bar U to pursue his own ranching interests, acquiring the Flying E on Willow Creek and the YT on the Little Bow River. Under his careful management, the YT grew to include 16,000 hectares (40,000 acres) of deeded and leased land.

When the Bar U came up for sale in 1902, Lane brought in the meat-packing firm of Gordon, Ironsides and Fares to help finance the deal. Valued at $250,000, it was the largest ranch transaction in the North West to that date. The Calgary Herald noted, "There is a touch of romance in the deal, inasmuch as Mr. Lane originally came to Alberta to work for this very outfit. He struck the country with exactly $100 and started to work for the Bar U outfit for $100 a month . . . he has by his own unaided efforts become one of the most wealthy and substantial men in Alberta. From a plain cowboy he has risen to be one of the largest, if not the largest, cattle ranch owner in Western Canada." Lane would go on to develop the largest and most respected herd of purebred Percheron horses in the world.

Alfred Ernest (A.E.) Cross trained as a veterinary surgeon and came west in 1884 to work on the Cochrane Ranch, located near the present-day town of Cochrane. He soon left the Cochrane to establish his own ranch in the Porcupine Hills west of Nanton. His original brand application was for "a1," to indicate that stock with this brand were top quality. But brand officials felt the brand would be too easy for rustlers to alter, so it was changed to a7 – there were seven brothers in the Cross family. The a7 brand still remains in the Cross family. The story is told that when Cross asked Lane if some of the Bar U cowboys could help separate a herd that the two outfits had run together, Lane said he would have to wait because his boys were too busy. Cross went to the cowboys and offered them five dollars a month more in wages, whereupon they all quit and went to work at the a7. Lane admired Cross's gumption and the two men remained good friends. Cross helped in the formation of the Western Stock Growers Association and was a founding member of the exclusive Ranchmen's Club. For all his many accomplishments, Cross is probably best known as the man who started the Calgary Brewing and Malt Company, the first brewery in what was then the Northwest Territories.

Archie McLean was born in Ontario in 1860. He settled near Virden, Manitoba, in his early twenties, where he built up a good trade in horses. In 1886 he headed west to southern Alberta to become manager and a partner in the Cypress Cattle Company (CY) northwest of Taber. He also established a cattle exporting firm under the name Bater and McLean. By the early 1900s the CY succumbed to the pressure of settlers coming into the district and McLean sold the operation. He moved into politics in 1909 and was public works minister by 1919, when the Big Four met once again to back Weadick's First World War Victory Stampede. It was his service in public works that earned him recognition as architect of Alberta's provincial highway system. When he died in 1933 at the age of 73, the Macleod Gazette claimed his memorial service was "probably the largest funeral ever held in southern Alberta."

back in time to an authentic Indian Village where members of Plains Indian tribes allow visitors the privilege of entering their tipis and experiencing first-hand their culture and traditional way of life. The Stampede Pow Wow features the best native dancers on the continent competing for cash prizes.

Of course the Stampede offers its visitors a whole host of other attractions over the ten days of the Exhibition. There is everything from the opening-day parade that regularly attracts well over 250,000 spectators, to the World Blacksmith Competition, the midway, the corn dogs, the evening grandstand show and spectacular fireworks display, the Stampede Casino, the western art showcase, to the non-stop music and entertainment at Nashville North – to name a few.

The Stampede doesn't stop at the gates. Head in any direction from the park and you'll see an entire city gone western, from the traditional white hat to the well-worn cowboy boots. Businesses all over the city compete for "best western" prizes, so it's worth a stroll around to have a look at the amazing transformation of a city as hay bales, corrals, and saddles suddenly appear in the most unlikely places. Stephen Avenue, in the centre of the city, is the site of everything from hat-stomping contests to (staged) gunfights. Each morning, free flapjacks and bacon are served hot

High-tail – to take off in a hurry

off the griddle from the back of authentic Rangeland Derby chuckwagons. Rope Square presents marching bands, dancers, fiddlers, and the Great Western Flapjack Flip. And if you can't make it downtown, roving caravans offer free pancakes and western entertainment each morning at shopping malls around the city.

If you aren't lucky enough to be in Calgary during the Stampede, don't despair. Be sure to check out the current show list at the park. They host a variety of western events throughout the year – everything from bull riding shows to rodeos to horse competitions.

GETTING THERE: Stampede Park is located on the east side of Macleod Trail between the Elbow River and 14th Avenue SE, just south of downtown. Since parking is always at a premium, consider using the city's excellent bus or light rail transit system.

CALGARY STAMPEDE'S HALF MILE OF HELL!

Calgary's famous Rangeland Derby was the brainchild of Stampede promoter Guy Weadick. No one knows for sure where he got the idea, but one of the best stories is told by Dick Cosgrave (who won the championship ten times), in Art Belanger's book on the "chucks." Cosgrave related, "It was Pat Burns's birthday during the 1919 Stampede and they were throwin' a buffalo steak dinner, served chuckwagon style, in front of the Grandstand. The wagons were all grouped together with the horses tied up at the side. After the meal, the drivers hitched up the horses, loaded in their gear and raced once around the track. Weadick was there and decided it was just what the Stampede needed."

The first chuckwagon races were held at the 1923 Calgary Stampede. Each wagon had a driver and four mounted men called outriders. Contestants were required to dismantle an eight-foot tent fly, load branding irons and a stove, cut a figure eight around two barrels in front of the grandstand, and cut across the infield. They entered the racetrack at the centre of the backstretch and ran the last quarter mile. When they reached the infield "campground," they stopped beside their barrel, unhitched the team, set up the tent fly, unloaded the stove, and started a fire. The first outfit to produce smoke was the winner.

The races proved so popular, they have been a tradition ever since. The essentials of the race remain the same. At the sound of the Klaxon, the

Chuckwagons round the turn in the famous Rangeland Derby.
CALGARY STAMPEDE

outriders throw tent poles and a stove (now made out of rubber for safety reasons) into the wagon. The outfits perform a figure eight around the barrels and then run like hell for the finish line. The first across isn't necessarily the winner – time penalties can be assessed for a number of infractions, including knocking over a barrel or a late outrider. Fires were eventually dispensed with for a much more exciting four-wagon dash over the finish line.

THE RULES OF THE RODEO

Ever wonder why a cowboy was disqualified in an event or got a low score, when his ride looked good to you? In each of the saddle bronc, bareback, and bull riding events, the first basic rule is that the cowboy must manage to stay on for eight seconds, but there is much more to it than that. The rider's ability is only half of the story. The rodeo judges award points based on the rider and the bucking action of the horse or the bull. The animal is assigned through a draw system, so the cowboy quite literally depends on the "luck of the draw" to pull an animal that will help him earn a high score. In theory, there are 100 points available, where 70 is considered average, 80 is very good, and 90 or higher is exceptional.

Here's a quick roundup of the rules behind the events you are likely to see at one of the many rodeos held throughout the summer in towns and villages all along the Cowboy Trail.

Saddle Bronc Riding – The rider is required to have his spurs over the break of the shoulders until the horse completes his first jump out of the chute. He must maintain a good rhythm in time with the bucking action of the horse, spurring from the animal's neck in a full swing toward the back of the saddle with this toes pointed outwards. Spurs must have dull rowels so the horse is not injured by the spurring action. Touching the animal or the equipment or losing a stirrup means automatic disqualification.

Bareback Riding – A double-thick leather pad called a rigging is cinched to the horse. The cowboy hangs on to the leather handhold of the rigging and must ride using only one hand, with no stirrups or reins. The rider cannot touch the animal or the equipment with his free hand. He must keep his spurs over the break of the horse's shoulders until the first jump out of the chute is completed, and must spur the horse on each jump by reaching as far forward as he can and bringing his ankles up to the rigging.

Bull Riding – This is probably the most dangerous event. The cowboy uses a braided manilla rope, wrapped loosely around the bull, with a weighted cowbell hanging underneath. Once the ride is over, the cowbell is designed to pull the rope free so no one has to tackle the bull to get the rigging off. The rope is the cowboy's only anchor to the bull, and he is disqualified if he touches the animal or bucks off before the end of eight seconds. Since it is a feat just to stay on one of these ornery critters for the full time, riders don't have to spur.

Tie-down Roping – This is a timed event where horse and rider must work as a team to score well. The cowboy and his horse start backed into a chute with a rope barrier. The calf must cross the scoreline before the rider breaks the barrier or he will be hit with a ten-second penalty. The rider ropes the calf, runs down the rope, and throws the standing animal by hand. He then ties any three legs of the calf with a piggin' string. The tie must hold for six seconds. A good roping horse has to be able to judge the speed of the calf, stop on cue, and then hold the rope taut while the roper runs to the calf.

Ride 'em cowboy!
CALGARY EXHIBITION AND STAMPEDE

Steer Wrestling – Sometimes called bull doggin', this is a timed event requiring strength and coordination. The steer must cross the scoreline before the rider breaks the barrier or a ten-second penalty will be added to the time. The horse runs beside the steer and continues to run by as the steer wrestler grabs the right horn and hits the ground with his legs extended forward. He throws the steer to the ground, where it must be flat on its side before an official time is recorded. An extra horse called a hazer helps keep the steer running as straight as possible.

Ladies' Barrel Racing – This is the only event in which cowgirls compete in a professional rodeo. The rider must cross the scoreline, run a cloverleaf pattern around three barrels, and then head back across the scoreline. Knocking down a barrel will result in a five-second penalty, but riders are allowed to hold a barrel from falling. Run times are calibrated to the hundredths of a second.

Team Roping – Two cowboys, a "header" and a "heeler," work against the clock to rope a steer. The header must give the steer a head start, or the team will be assessed a ten-second penalty. The header ropes the steer with one of three allowed head catches, then turns left. The heeler ropes both hind legs (five seconds are added if he only gets one leg). The time flag drops when the slack is out of both ropes and the riders face each other.

Head south of the Stampede grounds on Macleod Trail and you'll find Canada's self-proclaimed #1 country and western dance hall. As the official hospitality location of the Canadian Professional Rodeo Association, the Ranchman's is a popular cowboy gathering place, not just at Stampede time, but at any time of the year.

Ranchman's Dance Hall and Emporium   www.ranchmans.com

9615 Macleod Trail South, Calgary, AB, T2J 0P6

T: 403-253-1100

E: ranchmans@ranchmans.com

ACCEPTS D, V, MC, AMEX, DC

Open Monday to Saturday 10:30 AM to close; last call at 2:00 AM; available for private functions with groups over 100 on Sunday.

For over 30 years the Ranchman's has been synonymous with cowboys and Alberta's rodeo heritage. Photographs and rodeo memorabilia are proudly displayed throughout the restaurant and dance hall, including over 90 championship saddles and bronzes of Canadian and World Champion cowboys such as Jim Gladstone and Winston Bruce. And with one of the biggest dance floors in the city, it's a great place to dance to some real country music. A long list of country music legends have performed on the Ranchman's stage, including Kenny Rogers, Loretta Lynn, and Ian Tyson, while country stars like Neal McCoy, Paul Brandt, Lisa Brokop, Sons of the Desert, and Farmer's Daughter "cut their teeth" here. In fact, the Ranchman's has been voted the Canadian Country Music Association's Country Club of the Year three times.

WHAT THEY OFFER: Grade AAA beef is definitely the specialty, with plenty of steaks and BBQ rib dishes to choose from, but there are lots of options including a large selection of appetizers (the Virgins on Horseback are actually scallops wrapped in bacon), chicken, wraps, burgers, sandwiches, and all-day breakfast. You can even find comfort food (turkey dinner, meat loaf, and pot roast) just like Mom used to make. Live country music entertainment is featured Thursday to Saturday evenings. World-champion dance instructors offer the latest in country dancing every Monday to Friday.

GETTING THERE: look for the big sign on the west side of Macleod Trail

MAN OF VISION

In the 1940s, lawyer, rancher, and oilman Eric Harvie had purchased mineral rights to 197,000 hectares (486,000 acres) in the Leduc area. When the Leduc discovery well blew in, his earnings became the basis of a fortune estimated at $100 million. But unlike most people who amass huge wealth, Harvie was a philanthropist. According to a *Time* magazine article, he "gave everything back, and then some," eventually donating millions to the province of Alberta in support of art, history, and scientific research. He was keenly aware of the need to preserve the heritage of the West, and though he was often asked, "What do you want with those old things?" he thankfully ignored the question and kept on buying. His collections were the basis for what has become Western Canada's largest museum, the Glenbow, which he named after his "beloved" ranch of the same name. Well-known author Peter Newman described Harvie as, "the only rich Canadian who leaves behind a popular legacy. His magpie instinct for collecting anything and everything he happened to see has endowed his foundations with the finest collection of western artifacts and general trivia anywhere." Newman recalls one bit of advice that he was able to extract from Harvie during one of his rare interviews. "Never throw away old socks, old underwear, or old cars."

Glenbow Museum www.glenbow.org
130 – 9th Avenue SE, Calgary, AB, T2G 0P3
T: 403-268-4100
E: glenbow@glenbow.org
ACCEPTS D, V, MC, AMEX, TC ADMISSION CHARGED
Museum open Monday to Sunday 9:00 AM to 5:00 PM, Thursday 9:00 AM to 9:00 PM;
Museum shop open Monday to Sunday 10:00 AM to 5:30 PM, Thursday 10:00 AM to 9:00 PM.

When Eric Harvie instructed members of his staff to "go out there and collect like drunken sailors," he meant what he said. He was following his own advice. Harvie was a Calgary lawyer, rancher, oilman, and world traveller, whose penchant for collecting eventually resulted in the Glenbow, western Canada's largest museum.

The Otter flag tipi of the Siksika Nation.
GLENBOW MUSEUM

It was the 1950s when Harvie began his shopping spree. Soon, boxes and crates filled with treasures from every corner of the world began arriving in Calgary. The collection was eclectic to say the least – everything from Queen Victoria's royal bloomers, to 3,000 volumes on the horse, to the drum played at Sitting Bull's command before the Battle of the Little Bighorn. He eventually focused his priorities on the objects and history of western Canada, especially the pioneers and aboriginal peoples before 1911.

Horse-skinner – a horse driver who uses his whip severely

In 1966 Harvie donated his entire collection of paintings and artifacts, together with $5 million, to the people of Alberta to commemorate the 1967 Centennial of Canada. A partial list of the collection at the time of the gift included 14,000 works of art, 10,000 pioneer objects, 4,000 military items, 20,000 books and pamphlets, 70,000 negatives, and 24,000 natural history specimens. Since then, this extraordinary gift has grown to include more than two million objects and has made the Glenbow one of Canada's top cultural institutions.

Glenbow Museum normally features six permanent galleries, but 2006 will be a year of transition as one of the main galleries is closed to make way for a new permanent exhibition called *Mavericks: An Incorrigible History of Alberta*. Inspired by the book by noted Alberta author Aritha van Herk, the 30,000-square-foot gallery is slated for opening in February 2007. It will trace the history of southern Alberta through the legendary and colourful personalities who shaped and defined Alberta's history and who embody Alberta's well-known "maverick" nature. The new gallery will build on the existing *Nitsitapiisinni: Our Way of Life*, which will remain open during renovations. If you have any interest at all in the culture and heritage of the west, this exhibition is a must-see. It depicts the story of the three main tribes of the Blackfoot People – the Kainai (or Blood), the Pikani (or Peigan), and the Siksika (or Blackfoot). The entrance to the gallery is dominated by the authentic Otter flag tipi of the Siksika Nation. The tipi reflects the unique collaboration that went into the creation of the exhibition. Senior Blackfoot leaders and teachers from the Blackfoot Confederacy decided how to tell their story, and museum staff created the space to deliver their message. The result is an outstanding display that tells of the Blackfoot world, their stories and their way of life, both before the coming of the white man and after the end of the buffalo days. Four additional permanent galleries reflect the unusual breadth and scope of the collection, largely because of Harvie's inability to say no to anything that looked interesting. The exhibitions include: *Warriors: A Global Journey Through Five Centuries*, *Where Symbols Meet: A Celebration of West African Achievement*; *Treasures of the Mineral World*; and *Many Faces, Many Paths*, an exhibition of the sacred objects from the Buddhist and Hindu cultures of Asia. Special presentations throughout the year welcome the best of international travelling exhibitions, as well as drawing from the museum's extensive collection. When you are finished your explorations, don't miss the museum shop. It has an outstanding selection of books and hand-crafted gifts and souvenirs.

BLACKFOOT TIPI DESIGNS

Niitoy-yiss is Blackfoot for "tipi." The designs on Blackfoot tipis are not just decorations, but are often given by Spirit Beings to people in their dreams "so that prosperity, harmony, and long lives would come to those inside the tipi." A formal public ritual is used to transfer the right from one individual to another to paint a tipi design.

DID YOU KNOW?

The Glenbow has the largest non-government archives in Canada. More than two million images capture the life and times of Alberta. The library houses over 100,000 books, periodicals and newspapers, including rare books on horses from the 15th century.

GETTING THERE: The museum entrance is located downtown across the street from the Calgary Tower, where there is ample parking.

Heritage Park Historical Village   www.heritagepark.ca

1900 Heritage Drive SW, Calgary, AB, T2V 2X3

T: 403-268-8500

E: reception@heritagepark.ab.ca

ACCEPTS V, MC, AMEX, TC   ADMISSION CHARGED

Open Mid-May through September long weekend, 9:00 AM to 5:00 PM daily, then weekends only to Canadian Thanksgiving in October.

It is hard to say what old Sam Livingston would think of the 66-acre historical village that sits next to the spot where his original farm was flooded by the Glenmore Reservoir. But by all accounts his ghost (see sidebar page 157) is a friendly one, and Sam would probably be pleased to see that his house and barn have been restored and now sit in one of North America's largest and most successful living history facilities.

The village occupies a peninsula of prime parkland, surrounded on three sides by the reservoir and a stunning view of the Rocky Mountains to the west. Heritage Park tells the story of the settlement of Western Canada from the fur trade to World War I through the three communities contained within its boundaries: a

Riding the rails.
HERITAGE PARK HISTORICAL VILLAGE

Heritage Park claims to have several resident ghosts, but one of the more famous is a mischievous spirit who has become known as Sam – named after Sam Livingston. According to the official ghost story book published by the park, "All kinds of people say they have seen him. Psychics have come into the building [the Canmore Opera House] and sensed there is something there, and perhaps more than one spirit. Certainly the one that is most visible to everybody is an elderly gentleman. He never says anything – he just walks about. When he is asked to leave, he just gets up and leaves." Maybe it's Sam trying to find his way home. Part of his farm was flooded for the 1929 construction of the Glenmore Dam and Reservoir next to Heritage Park, and his house, which now sits in the park, was originally located just south of the Canmore Opera House.

Sam had a long line of firsts attached to his name. He was the first dairy farmer in Calgary, had the first cattle herd, and was the first to peddle milk in the streets of the settlement. He is also credited with being the first to use mechanized farming equipment for threshing and mowing and to plant fruit trees that actually survived. He cut a colourful figure with his long shoulder-length hair, buckskins, and wide-brimmed hat, and was well-known for his hospitality. He was remembered as the "warm-hearted pioneer, whose latch-string always hangs out for the virtuous wayfarer."

circa 1860 Hudson's Bay Company trading fort, a circa 1880 pre-Railway Settlement, and a circa 1910 Railway Prairie Town. The ranching era is depicted in its own setting complete with the 1904 Burnside ranch house, 1907 Copithorne barn (with resident farm animals), rodeo arena, and sheds. The park also features a number of special festivals and celebrations throughout the season, including a Festival of Quilts in May, Railway Days in June, Fall Fair in September, and Octoberwest in October.

The park opened its doors to the public on July 1, 1964, with 27 exhibits and some assorted rail stock. When it celebrated its fortieth anniversary in 2004, the park boasted 150 exhibits and service structures (50 per cent of which are relocated and restored originals), 45,000 artifacts, livestock, an antique midway, an original steam engine, the SS Moyie sternwheeler, and a fleet of fully restored and operational antique vehicles.

There is too much to enjoy here in only one day, so allow yourself plenty of time to take in as much as you can. Depending on where you park, you can hop on the electric streetcar that will take you directly to the front entrance to begin your adventure. If you plan your arrival before 10:00 AM, you can get in on the free western breakfast, but be sure to leave room for a few treats along the way. Don't miss out on a cone at the Vulcan Ice Cream Parlour or the fresh-baked gingerbread cookies and other goodies at the Alberta Bakery. You'll have to pace yourself –

there are plenty of spots for a snack, and the Wainwright Hotel in the centre of town offers excellent meals at a reasonable price. You can also bring your own lunch and enjoy the beautifully maintained gardens and picnic spots along the way.

As you wander through the village, it's not hard to imagine that you have been transported back in time to another era. Costumed interpreters and antique vehicles scooting around the park on errands bring the entire place to life. Each piece in the 11,000-item replica costume collection has been researched to accurately portray the historical eras depicted at the park. You can opt to walk, or if your feet need a rest, you can hop on the train at one of the restored train stations and take a ride to the next stop. Tired feet are always a good excuse to take a wagon ride, cruise the reservoir on the antique sternwheeler SS Moyie (she is environmentally friendly – the hydraulic propulsion system was converted to use canola oil), or sit and watch the kids enjoy the beautifully restored Bowness carousel and the fully operational antique midway rides. There are so many exceptional exhibits here that there is really no way to recommend one over the others. The vintage train collection in the railway roundhouse is a must for train buffs, and the outstanding assortment of restored gasoline pumps that line Gasoline Alley probably represents one of the best collections of its kind anywhere. The Queen Anne–style Prince House, with its splendid gardens and gazebo, is always a popular stop, probably as much for the ghost stories that draw the curious as the wonderful collection of artifacts housed inside. The park has something for everyone to enjoy.

> **DID YOU KNOW?**
> Heritage Park has 4,300 feet of railway track. Making 32 circuits per day over an operating season of about 126 days, the train travels about 5,300 kilometres each year.

GETTING THERE: Heritage Park is located at the end of Heritage Drive on the west side of 14th Street SW. There is ample on-site parking.

> **COWBOY TRAIL CONNECTIONS**
> There are several buildings in Heritage Park that came from locations on the Cowboy Trail. St. Martin's Church came from the Livingstone district near Pincher Creek. The original building cost $110 and although the church had a belfry there was never a bell in it – probably because it cost too much. The Windsor Hotel in Lundbreck became famous for its two-storey outhouse that now sits next to the Wainwright Hotel. The bottom level was for the bar patrons and the top for the hotel guests so they could nip out to the privy without going downstairs and through the bar.

Latigo — descriptive of a variety of leather straps attached to a saddle

The elegant Queen Anne–style house at the former Bow Valley Ranch has been restored.
THE RANCHE RESTAURANT

The Ranche Restaurant; Annie's Bakery and Café   www.theranche.com

Fish Creek Provincial Park, 15979 Bow Bottom Trail SE, Calgary, AB,

T: 403-225-3939

E: info@theranche.com

ACCEPTS D, V, MC, AMEX, DC

Open Monday to Thursday 11:30 AM to 9:00 PM; Friday 11:30 AM to 10:00 PM; Saturday 5:00 PM to 10:00 PM; Sunday Brunch 10:30 AM to 2:30 PM; Sunday dinner 5:00 PM to 9:00 PM; Annie's is open daily in the summer 10:00 AM to 6:00 PM; weekends 10:00 AM to 4:00 PM in the winter.

When it was built in 1896 by rancher and businessman William Roper Hull, the elegant house at the Bow Valley Ranch "represented the height of country luxury and grace." The house is no longer in the country, but thanks to the dedicated efforts of the The Ranche at Fish Creek Restoration Society, it still reflects its original turn-of-the-century grandeur. Located in the spectacular setting of Fish Creek Provincial Park at the southern edge of the city, the house continues to welcome visitors from every corner of the world, just like it did when Hull built it to entertain the social elite of a booming settlement called Calgary.

Hull was a prominent entrepreneur in the meat-packing business who bought the 4,000-acre ranch from the lieutenant-governor of Quebec, Theodore Robitaille, to use as a place to finish cattle for slaughter. Robitaille had purchased

CHARLIE WAS A BOW VALLEY RANCH FIXTURE FOR MORE THAN 50 YEARS

According to a Calgary Herald article dated September 21, 1997, "Yuen Chow, or Charlie Yuen, [was] the Chinese cook, gardener and caretaker who kept the house and fed the ranch hands there for more than 50 years ... He kept the house a showpiece for visitors and was always in the kitchen, as comfortable cooking for dignitaries as he was for the ranch hands." Annie and Billy Bannister lived in the foreman's house, which is now the site of Annie's Bakery & Café. After the Bannisters moved to Inglewood where Billy was head of the Burns stockyards, "Annie often brought her children out to visit their friend, the Chinese cook." Annie's daughter Maude recalls, "She used to bring us all out for a piece of his pie – we always looked forward to Charlie's pie." Maude credits Charlie with the design of the ranch table with the rotating middle that is still in use at the restaurant. "My Dad built this [table] but he must have got the idea from Charlie. [The design was, and still is, common in Chinese restaurants]. Maude remembers, "When we came out to visit Charlie, we always sat around this table."

the property (known as Indian Supply Farm #24) in 1883 from the Dominion Government for three dollars per acre. The government had established the farm to train Native Indians on farming techniques, but when the operation proved less than successful, Robitaille snapped it up for speculative purposes. His plans were stymied by a general depression, but he eventually managed to sell it to Hull in 1892 for a rumoured price of $30,000.

CONK COVER?

Whether you call it a conk cover, a lid, or a hair case, a cowboy's hat is one of the most distinctive and useful parts of his outfit. Its brim protects from the sun and the rain, and the high crown helps keep heads cool in hot summer weather. It can substitute as a bellows to get a fire going, and a good whack on the rump with it can give an incentive to a slow horse or an ornery steer to get moving. In a pinch, it makes a good water trough or even a pillow to catch a few winks of sleep out on the trail.

Probably more than any other piece of a cowboy's gear, the hat has become a symbol of the western way of life. It is often said that the particular way in which an individual chooses to crease it, bend it, and decorate it lets everyone know what kind of person is underneath it. Contrary to popular opinion, a real cowboy doesn't pay a high price for his hat out of vanity, but because he knows he will need a good one to withstand a lot of rough use over a long period of time. As one western writer notes, "He may throw it on the floor and hang his spurs on a nail, for he knows a good hat can be tromped on without hurting it, while tromping on a spur does neither the tromper nor the spur any good."

BRAISED BISON SHORT RIBS WITH GLAZED
ONIONS AND ROOT VEGETABLES

For the Ribs: Preheat oven to 280F (140C). Brown 910 g bison short ribs on all sides; season with salt and pepper and set aside. In the same pan, without cleaning off the bits of rib meat, cook two medium carrots, two celery stalks, one small onion, one bay leaf, two sprigs rosemary, and four sprigs thyme over medium heat for 15 minutes, until soft. Deglaze the pan with 200 ml red wine, add all ingredients with 1 L game stock reduction and 300 ml chicken stock, cover and cook in oven for six to eight hours until meat falls off the bone. Do the ribs a day or so in advance, leaving the ribs in the braising liquid to cool, for maximum flavour and moisture retention. Remove them, strain the liquid, and reduce until it coats the back of a spoon. When ready to serve, add the ribs to the liquid and gently heat the ribs in the sauce.

For the Vegetables: Preheat the oven to 375F (190C). Blanch one diced celery root, one diced parsnip, 85 ml pearl onions, and four peeled baby carrots. Add 100 ml chicken stock, 50 ml honey, 50 ml wine or cider vinegar, and salt and pepper, and bring to a simmer. Place the entire pan in the oven and cook for 10 minutes, basting with the liquid every two minutes. Add 30 ml unsalted butter, cut into pieces, and swirl in to melt. Reduce sauce on stovetop until liquid is syrupy and viscous.

To Serve: Place the braised ribs over the vegetables, then spoon the reduced braising liquid over all. Serve with simple mashed or roasted potatoes and sprinkle with a good quality finishing salt just prior to serving.

Hull developed the ranch into a showplace that attracted influential visitors from around the world. He wanted a home that would properly reflect his social stature, so he hired James Llewellyn Wilson, a distinguished Calgary architect, to design the house. Originally built for $4,000 in the Queen Ann style, it is recognized as the "finest country home in the Territories during that era and a unique piece of architecture." In 1902 Hull sold the entire property to Patrick Burns (see sidebar page 146), who renamed it Bow Valley Farm. It became the headquarters for Burns' vast ranching empire. During the Burns tenure, the house saw extensive renovations, but was not the social centre it had been during the Hull years. In 1973 the property was acquired by the Government of Alberta as part of Fish Creek Provincial Park, and by 1978, the house was boarded up and vacant. From the initial vision provided by Calgarians Larry and Mitzie Wasyliw in 1995, The Ranche at Fish Creek Restoration Society took on the daunting task of restoring the dilapidated house to its former glory. In 1999 the dream became a reality when the historic building once again opened its doors as The Ranche Restaurant. In 2001 the Ranche House and adjacent land was designated as a Provincial Historic Resource.

Now you can enjoy fine dining in the Grand Salon or the more intimate

Formal Room with its bay window and wood-burning fireplace. Charlie's Room (see sidebar page 160) is now a lounge, but it was originally where the ranch hands ate their meals at the special dining table constructed by Billy Bannister, the ranch's foreman. The table had a spinning centre piece that allowed cowhands to pick off what they needed as the food rotated past them. The table is one of the few original pieces of furniture left in the house and is still used by diners. The restaurant specializes in wild game such as elk, bison, and caribou, raised on a local game ranch just south of the city. Menus are changed seasonally, but there is a large selection to choose from, including Alberta beef, braised rabbit, lamb, chicken, pork, and bison. A popular brunch offering is the seared buffalo skillet, featuring buffalo tenderloin tips. The Rocky Mountain charcuterie board, which includes a selection of smoked/cured game and fish, and the roasted scallops with fresh horseradish, are perennial favourites. In 2005 well-known restaurant critic John Gilchrist rated the restaurant at a nine out of ten for dinner.

If you are looking for a lighter meal, follow the tree-lined Ranche Promenade, (with its 15 cast iron gas lamps), to Annie's Bakery & Café, the restored home of Annie and Billy Bannister, the ranch foreman. Here you'll find a selection of cookies, muffins, and scones baked fresh daily at The Ranche, as well as sandwiches, homemade soups and stew, and mini fruit pies. It's a popular stop for bikers and hikers enjoying the park.

Don't miss the Native Gardens, located along the laneway between the two restaurants. It contains native plants and grasses from the late 1800s, including trembling aspens, Saskatoon bushes, native roses, and hundreds of wildflowers. A bronze statue entitled "Egg Money" honours the spirit of the Pioneer Women, the unrecognized heroes in the opening of the West.

GETTING THERE: The restaurant is located on the west side of Bow Bottom Trail in Fish Creek Provincial Park.

Recommended Reading

A Brand of its Own: The 100-Year History of the Calgary Exhibition and Stampede by James
    H. Gray

Calgary Stampede and the Canadian West by Patrick Tivy

Chuckwagon Racing: Calgary Stampede's Half Mile of Hell by Art Belanger

Come 'n Get it: Cowboys and Chuckwagons by B.M. Barss

The Cowboy Spirit: Guy Weadick and the Calgary Stampede by Donna Livingstone

Nitsitapiisinni: The Story of the Blackfoot People by the Blackfoot Gallery Committee of
    the Glenbow Museum

Wild Ride: Three Journeys Down the Rodeo Road by David Poulsen

The Bucking Chute

Noel Burles

Saddles and rosin.
And flat braided ropes.
Each man arrives
Full of high hopes.
Bright colored shirts
Spurs and high boots.
The cowboys all gather
Behind the Buck Chutes.

The gates are all oiled
And the crew set to go.
And the man in the booth
Says, "Let's Rodeo"
And all work together
With cheers and some hoots
And the rough stock comes in
To those old Buckin' Chutes.

Now it comes down
To an eight second ride.
Be it bareback or saddle
Or some bull's loose hide.
Most are young men
But they're all tough old coots,
As the gate swings wide open
From those old Buckin' Chutes.

The Rodeo's over
Come the close of the day.
And all those involved
Have gone their own way.
Some pockets are empty
And some full of loot
And silence prevails
On those Old Buckin' Chutes.

REPRINTED WITH THE PERMISSION OF NOEL BURLES

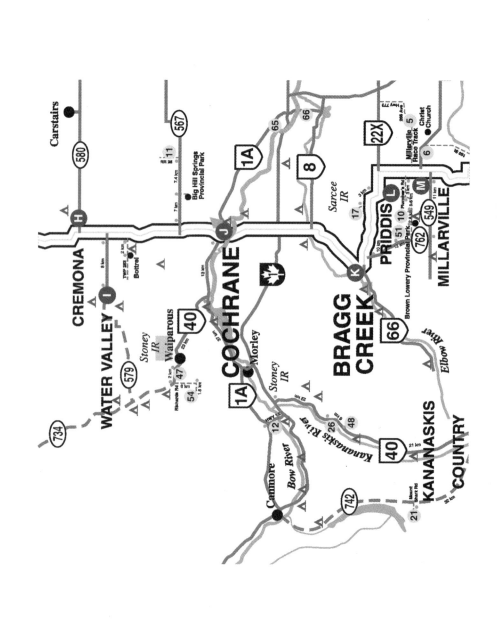

6 : COCHRANE TO CREMONA

"Have trust in your fellow man, but be sure to brand your calves."

—Ted Stone, *Cowboy Logic*

Communities

- (J) Cochrane
- (I) Water Valley
- (H) Cremona

Accommodations

- (J) Rockyview Hotel and Canyon Rose Steakhouse
- (26) Sundance Lodges
- (21) Mount Engadine Lodge
- (12) Brewster's Kananaskis Guest Ranch
- (47) Bar C Ranch Resort
- (11) Big Springs Estate Bed and Breakfast Inn

Outfitters

- (48) Boundary Ranch / Guinn Outfitting
- (12) Brewster's Kananaskis Guest Ranch
- (47) Bar C Ranch Resort
- (54) Saddle Peak Trail Rides

Camping

- (26) Sundance Lodges
- (J) Bow Rivers Edge Campground

Restaurants

- (J) Rockyview Hotel and Canyon Rose Steakhouse
- (48) Boundary Ranch
- (12) Brewster's Kananaskis Guest Ranch
- (47) Bar C Ranch Resort

Shopping, Antiques & Artisans

- (26) Sundance Lodges
- (48) Boundary Ranch
- (12) Brewster's Kananaskis Guest Ranch
- (47) Bar C Ranch Resort

MAJOR EVENTS ALONG THE TRAIL

(check www.thecowboytrail.com for a complete listing)

May
Water Valley Rodeo, Water Valley

September
Cochrane Fast Draw Championships and Rodeo, Cochrane

War bag — a small canvas bag used by a
rider to carry personal items

6 : COCHRANE TO CREMONA

Cochrane www.cochrane.ca

T: 403-932-1193

Sarcee name – *nitah-sitah-tay* meaning "sitting bobcat," for the big hill that dominates the area.

Cochrane sits at the base of the Big Hill in the valley of the Bow River, with sweeping views of the mountains to the west. The Canadian Pacific Railway named its station located there after the huge Cochrane Ranch (see sidebar page 171), which had been started by Senator Matthew Cochrane in 1881. It was actually the presence of the ranch, which held vast leaseholdings in the area, combined with the establishment of the town of Mitford a few miles west, that impeded Cochrane's development for several years. When Tom Cochrane (a distant relative of the senator) and his wife, Adela, started a sawmill operation in the area, a village complete with post office, saloon, and store soon sprang up. The tiny settlement was named Mitford, but the site turned out to be too far from good timber stands, and the grade was too steep for the railway to haul the logs out. When Tom and Adela tried their hands at coal mining and brick manufacturing ventures, they failed too. Eventually the citizens of Mitford moved to the present site of Cochrane. The new hamlet provided services to the growing urban and rural community, and

100 YEARS AND STILL COUNTING

The historic Rockyview Hotel in the centre of Cochrane celebrated its 100th birthday in 2004. It started out as a two-storey wooden box with a sloped roof, but later improvements added a brick veneer and a western-style verandah. When the hotel first opened its doors to the public, the *Cochrane Advocate* noted, "The bar-room has been lavishly furnished but beauty does not appeal to a thirsty man; he seeks something of a more succulent nature, a glass of foaming ale or a touch of Scotch." During prohibition years from 1916 to 1923, the ground floor was converted to a bakery, confectionery, and tea room, but it soon reverted to dispensing liquor when the dry years finally ended. The current owners have renovated it to evoke a turn-of-the-century theme, with cedar walls, hardwood floors, and a 40-foot carved oak Brunswick bar in the Stageline Saloon.

became home to a stone quarry, a sawmill, and four brick plants. The shortage of workers during World War I forced an end to many local industries, and until the early 1970s the town remained essentially a service centre for the local ranchers, with a population of less than 1,000.

Cochrane's proximity to Calgary has seen it grow at an astonishing rate over the past decade – at one point, it was the fastest growing town in Canada – but the main street has still managed to maintain a distinctly western flavour and is a haven for a number of artisans, antique stores, and galleries. It's an ideal place to poke around the shops, then treat yourself to an ice cream at the famous McKay's Ice Cream Store, a Cochrane institution established by Jimmy McKay in 1948 and still operated by his daughters.

Rockyview Hotel and Canyon Rose Steakhouse   www.rockyviewhotel.com
304 – 1st Street West, P.O. Box 237, Cochrane, AB, T4C 1A5
T: 403-932-2442
E: aha@Albertahotels.ab.ca
ACCEPTS D, V, MC
Open all year, Restaurant 10:00 AM to 10:00 PM Monday to Friday, 9:00 AM to 10:00 PM Saturday and Sunday; Saloon 10:00 AM to 3:00 AM daily.

What They Offer: Clean, comfortable rooms at a reasonable rate, with or without private bathroom; Stageline Saloon has a large dance floor with live country bands Thursday to Saturday; Canyon Rose Steakhouse specializes in fine Alberta beef and buffalo, but offers a wide variety of other choices. Marline's fresh homemade pies are reported to be "to die for."

Points of Interest in Cochrane

Visitor Information Centre and Cochrane Ranch Historic Site: Both are located in the same building on the left (north) side of Hwy. 1A just east of Hwy. 22. (Telephone: 403-932-1193.) A trail with interpretive signs winds around the site, which is located at the original headquarters of the famous Cochrane Ranch. Displays about the ranch's history can also be viewed in the information centre. You can wander the trails on your own, or take one of the tours led by staff members from the centre. The building is open daily 9:00 AM to 5:00 PM from the May long weekend to the September long weekend. Paths are open all year but are not maintained in the winter. The Cochrane Historical and Archival Preservation Society (CHAPS) has developed a walking or driving tour that includes a number of the historic buildings in Cochrane.

Guide booklets can be purchased at the Information Centre.

Men of Vision Statue – This overlooks the Cochrane Ranch site and a stunning view of the Bow River and the Rocky Mountains. The statue is accessed by a trail located at the site.

Studio West Bronze Foundry and Art Gallery: 205 – 2nd Avenue SE. This is a working bronze foundry owned by well-known sculptors Don and Shirley Begg. Visitors are

Men of Vision statute, located at the Cochrane Ranch site, is a tribute to the early pioneers.
L. ANDREWS

welcome to tour the facilities and watch the work in progress. The foundry and gallery are open Monday to Friday 8:00 AM to 5:00 PM; Saturdays from 9:00 AM to 4:00 PM; Sundays by appointment. Shirley has a pioneer women exhibit above the gallery, which she is happy to share with visitors. Telephone 403-932-2611.

Westlands Bookstore: Located at 118 –2nd Avenue West, it has one of the best selections of books on ranching and western heritage you are likely to find anywhere.

Grub Stop

AC's 2 for 1 Pizza and Pasta, #8, 205 3rd Avenue W, 403-932-5333; Blue Dog Café, Live Blues, 110 3rd Avenue W, 403-932-4282; Cochrane Café, 318 Main Street, 403-932-2521; Cochrane Coffee Traders, 114 2nd Avenue, 403-932-1695; COTO Japanese Restaurant, #13, 205 1st Street E, 403-932-2926; Cumbrian Arms Neighbourhood Pub, 57 West Aarsby Road, 403-932-4523; DJ's Prime Rib & Steak House, 521 1st Street W, 403-932-4030; Ducks on the Roof, 205 3rd Avenue W, 403-932-5959; Friends Coffee Shoppe, 118 1st Avenue W, 403-932-1915; Great Wall Fortune Chinese Restaurant, #1, 214 Grand Blvd., 403-932-0012; Guy's Café and Bakery, #6, 201 Grand Blvd., 403-851-9955, HQ Cookhouse and Pie Emporium, 216 1st Street W, 403-932-2111, KK's Kitchen Chinese, 22 Westside Drive, 403-932-3292; Lord Fin Fish & Chips, 416 1st Street W, 403-851-0393; McKay's Ice Cream, 220 1st Street W, 403-932-2455; Omega Family Restaurant, 205 1st Street W, 403-851-8112; Panini's Italian Eatery, #1, 204 5th Avenue W. 403-932-6339; Peking House Chinese Restaurant, #8, 122 4th Avenue W, 403-932-2868; Poco Loco Pizza, 521 1st Street W, 403-932-2020; Porterhouse Pub, #9, 205 1st Street E, 403-851-1023; Portofino Italian

> **DID YOU KNOW?**
> At one time, Cochrane had the only grass racetrack west of Winnipeg. On race days, the Canadian Pacific Railway ran special trains between Cochrane and Calgary to accommodate the horse racing fans.

THE COWBOY'S SIGN LANGUAGE

Branding was not a North American invention. It was introduced by the Spaniards, who brought the custom, along with the first horses and cattle, from Europe to Mexico in the early 1500s. Cortez, the Spanish conqueror of the New World, is often credited with having the first official brand in North America. It was called the three Christian crosses, symbolizing the Holy Trinity. The Spanish brands were very intricate and complicated. They could not be "read" and were often not named. Cowboys referred to them as a "skillet of snakes" because of their detailed designs. They were totally impractical on the huge unfenced grasslands of North America and were replaced by a system that was simple, direct, and easy to understand.

The North West Mounted Police began recording brands at Fort Macleod in 1876, but they had no legal status until 1878, when the Territorial Government made brand registration the law in the West. In 1880 an official Brand Recorder was appointed, and on January 18 of that year, the first recorded brand in Western Canada, the "71," was registered by Percy Neal and Samuel Steele of Fort Macleod. On May 16, 1882, the "70" on the left rib was registered to Charles Kettles. He had retired from the NWMP to ranch near Pincher Creek. The "70" remains the oldest brand currently registered to a family member with the same surname. Allan Kettles, Charles's great-grandson, purchased the brand to ensure that it remains in the family.

WHAT'S A WHANGDOODLE ANYWAYS?

The ability to read a brand quickly separates the real cowboy from the greenhorn. There are definite rules for reading brands. They are read from left to right, from top to bottom, and from the outside to the inside. Cattle brands are registered in six positions, on the left or right shoulder, rib and hip, and must be in capital letters so they are easy to read.

Over the years, a very distinct and colourful jargon has evolved to describe the symbols used in a brand. A symbol can be "forked" with a V-shaped prong attached to a letter or figure. Or it can be a "whangdoodle," a group of interlocking wings with no central flying figure. A letter can be "lazy" by lying down, "crazy" by standing on its head, or "reverse" by facing in the wrong direction. It can "rock" when the bottom touches the inside of a curve, "fly" with wings attached, "walk" by putting feet on it, "swing" by joining a quarter circle to the top of it, "tumble" as though it were falling over, or "hang" from another letter. Here's some examples of how these letters can look when they are part of a brand:

Lazy B   ◻

Crazy A   ∀

Reverse R   Я

Rocking F   𝖥

Walking R   ℞

Tumbling T   ⅄

HARD LUCK STORY

Perhaps he should have listened to the advice of someone who knew what he was talking about, but Senator Matthew Cochrane had his own ideas about ranching in the Canadian West. Cochrane had met Kootenai Brown (see sidebar page 27) on a land scouting trip in the area south of Waterton Lakes. Brown had settled near the lakes in the late 1870s and knew the country well, later becoming the first Superintendent of Waterton Lakes National Park. Cochrane believed that land that had once supported vast buffalo herds should be able to support cattle, and that they should not require additional feed because the warm chinook winds kept the plains free of snow during the winter. Brown didn't agree. He knew the ferocity of the winters and that chinooks didn't always arrive when you needed them.

But Cochrane had to learn the hard way. A well-known cattle breeder from the east, he established the Cochrane Ranch, the first of the big corporate ranches, in 1881 at Big Hill (eventually the site of the town of Cochrane). Over the next two years, he brought in almost 12,000 head of cattle from Montana, but bad management and two hard winters in a row, with few chinooks, left the ranch with only 4,000 animals. In fact, after the winter of 1882–83, it is said that some of the long ravines were so filled with carcasses that a man could go from top to bottom and throughout the entire length without ever stepping off a dead cow. In 1883 the cattle were moved to leases held on land south of Waterton Lakes. Although the early years were tough, this operation eventually developed into a well-run venture. The Big Hill leases were sold to the British American Ranch Company in 1884, with Cochrane as one of its shareholders. The ranch ran sheep but lost many to prairie fires and one particularly severe blizzard. When the lands of the Big Hill lease reverted to the Crown, they were settled by homesteaders and smaller ranchers. In the south, much of the land was purchased by Mormons who had come from Utah.

"TOP GUNS"

Cochrane is home to two of the fastest shooters in the world. Richard Benedictson has competed in fast-draw championships for over 35 years, winning a string of championships – including second "Top Gun" in the World in his division in 1998 and 2002 at the World Fast Draw Championship, second in the Canadian Championship in 2002 and 2003 and first in 2004. His wife, Linda, has only been shooting since 1998, but was 2002 Women's World Champion and 2003 and 2004 Women's Canadian Champion in her division. Every year since 1999, they have hosted the Canadian Fast Draw Championships in Cochrane on the Labour Day weekend in September. The competition is one of only three sanctioned championships in the world and attracts participants from across North America. Since 1999, 35 world records have been set at the Cochrane contest.

Ristorante, #18, 205 1st Street E, 403-932-1777; Prairie Smoke, 19 Westside Drive, 403-932-9001; Salt and Pepper Mexican Restaurantes, 114 3rd Avenue W, 403-932-7772; Texas Gate, 113 Railway Street W, 403-932-6666; Tom's Hideout Lounge, #3, 204 5th Avenue W, 403-932-4441; Walla Walla Pizza Inc., 521 1st Street W, 403-932-2020

FOUNDER OF ALBERTA'S CATTLE INDUSTRY

John McDougall was a Methodist missionary who is probably most remembered for his work amongst the Stoney Indians. In 1873 he established a mission and settlement at Morley, 27 kilometres west of Cochrane. In 1874, he travelled south to Montana and brought back some Texas steers, in an attempt to make the mission self-sufficient. Although McDougall didn't plan a commercial venture, the mission became the site of the first cattle-raising attempt in western Canada, and McDougall is credited as one of the founders of the cattle industry in southern Alberta. Today, you can visit the old church at the mission site.

From Cochrane you can continue your drive north on Hwy. 22, but there are also several Cowboy Trail partners located to the west of town.

26 **Sundance Lodges** www.sundancelodges.com

Sheryl and Brian Green
P.O. Box 190, Kanaskis Village, AB, T0L 2H0
T: 403-591-7122

E: info@sundancelodges.com
ACCEPTS D, V, MC, AMEX, TC
Open May long weekend to end of September

It all started back in 1983, when Brian Green read an article on tipis in an outdoor magazine. It piqued his interest to the point where he finally bought one in 1988 for the family to use. He and his wife, Sheryl, painted it and put it up in the Porcupine Hills west of Claresholm. Once it was up, people started asking if they could stay in it. One day, Brian suddenly imagined a campground filled with tipis, and the idea was born. Kananaskis Country seemed like the ideal place to do it.

WHAT THEY OFFER: Ten large (sleep four) and three small (sleep two) Sioux-design tipis with authentic hand-painted canvases; private sites include picnic table and fire pit; tipis have wooden floor, wood-frame beds with foam mattresses sealed in plastic, a small kerosene heater and lantern; 17 trapper's tents (sleep four) have similar furnishings plus deck and awning; basic camping gear (sheets, pillows, duvet, towels, camp stove, cots, and cooking/utensil kit) available for rent — ideal option for oversees visitors; also 30 unserviced RV and tent sites with chemical toilets and access to showers/toilets.

Trading Post offers basic groceries, coin laundry, Internet access, hot showers, sports equipment rental, and gift shop; on-site volleyball, soccer, football, badminton, and horseshoes; nearby hiking, biking, rafting, and horseback riding

GETTING THERE: From Hwy. 22 south of Cochrane, head west on Hwy. 1 to the junction with Hwy. 40. Go 22 KM south on Hwy. 40 to Sundance Road (watch for the sign). Turn right (west) to the lodges. Or from Hwy. 22 at Longview, head west on Secondary Hwy. 541 for 43 KM to the junction with Hwy. 40. Drive north 78 KM to the Kananaskis Village. Go 2.5 KM past the Village to Sundance Road, turn left (west) and follow the road in.

An authentic Sioux-design tipi.
SUNDANCE LODGES

THE SUN DANCE

In midsummer the Blackfoot bands came together for the Sun Dance. It was considered the major tribal ceremony and was the only time of the year when all the people of the tribe assembled in one place. As explained by Mike Mountain Horse in *My People the Bloods*, "The Sun Dance originated among my people long before the advent of the white race. It is an annual tribal ceremony held in the summertime to propitiate the Sun and other lesser spirits." The form of the Sun Dance differed from tribe to tribe, but involved several days of preliminary rituals followed by the erection of the ceremonial lodge and the selection of the centre pole. Among the Blackfoot, the festival was organized by a virtuous woman who oversaw the erection of the Sun Dance lodge and the gathering of buffalo tongues, which were used as sacred food at the ceremony. Fasting, prayers, and songs of thanksgiving were accompanied by dancing. Many of the men and women's societies performed the dances, and none of the dancers would break the fast until the entire ceremony was completed. The Blackfoot often performed rituals of self-torture, sometimes called "the making of a brave," in which the dancer was pierced in the breast and fastened to the centre pole with leather thongs until he freed himself. Young men seeking admission into the warrior societies would often participate in this part of the dance. The scars were regarded as marks of honour.

The Kiska Lodge is a great spot for group events.
BOUNDARY RANCH/GUINN OUTFITTING

Boundary Ranch/Guinn Outfitting Ltd.   www.boundaryranch.com

Denise and Rick Guinn

P.O. Box 44, Kananaskis Village, AB, T0L 2H0

T: 1-877-591-7177

E: info@boundaryranch.com

ACCEPTS D, V, MC, AMEX, TC

Open early May–early October (year-round for group events)

Rick grew up on the back of a horse, helping his family operate a guest ranch in the area, roaming the mountains, and learning everything he could about horses and outfitting. (Guinn's Pass is named after his father, Alvin.) Rick and Denise set up Boundary Ranch in 1987, at one point living in tents while Rick started cutting trails and building fences, corrals, and a ranch house. From its humble start, the ranch has grown into a facility that hosts thousands of visitors each year.

WHAT THEY OFFER: Hourly, half-day, and full-day rides with lunch; two-hour ridge ride and steak lunch; full-day surf and saddle combines riding and whitewater

---

DID YOU KNOW?

A Stoney tipi was usually smaller and lower than that of the Blackfoot. The woman of the household owned it, and it was her job to put it up and take it down. It consisted of ten to sixteen poles, and was assembled by binding three poles in a tripod and then leaning the other poles against it. Two more poles slipped into tiny pockets sewn into the ear flaps, which were shifted to control the draft and the smoke.

---

rafting, with barbecue lunch. Two- and three-day pack trips use Happy Valley base camp; five- or six-day trips use different camps, and include all meals and accommodation in wall tents with foam mattresses. Pre-and post-trip accommodations available at nearby hotels and campgrounds as well as Cochrane and Canmore. And group events include Wild West rodeo, barbecues, country hoedown, even gunfights.

GETTING THERE: From Hwy. 22 south of Cochrane, head west on Hwy. 1 to the junction with Hwy. 40. Go 28 KM south on Hwy. 40 (3 KM from the Village). The ranch is on the left side of the road. Or from Hwy. 22 at Longview, head west on Secondary Hwy. 541 for 43 KM to the junction with Hwy. 40. Drive north 75 KM to the ranch entrance on the right side of the road.

Mount Engadine Lodge

www.mountengadine.com

Andrew and Sharisse Kyle
P.O. Box 40025, Canmore, AB, T1W 3H9
T: 403-678-4080
E: lodge@mountengadine.com
ACCEPTS V, MC, TC. PC
Open all year

The lodge overlooks the Smuts Creek Valley, and is a prime location for spotting moose attracted by the natural salt lick in the meadows bordering the creek. Nearby Mount Engadine lends its name to the lodge.

WHAT THEY OFFER: Single or double rooms in the lodge for up to 12 people, with shared bathroom and showers; three cabins with private washrooms and decks with a magnificent view of the valley; two cabins accommodate two people, one has two bedrooms for a family of four or two couples; two suites overlook the meadows and feature queen-size beds, private bathrooms, gas fireplace, and sitting area; lodge has two stone fireplaces, large comfortable sitting areas, a piano, and deck with hot tub.

The meals are a culinary extravaganza. Rates include a two-course buffet breakfast, build-it-yourself lunch with fresh-baked bread, meats, cheeses, fruits, and homemade treats to enjoy on the trail or at the lodge, afternoon tea, and a gourmet dinner.

Mount Engadine Lodge overlooks Smuts Creek Valley.
L. ANDREWS

The guided hiking program is offered Monday, Wednesday, and Friday in July and August; a weekly dinner combined with interpretive program on Karelian "Bear" dogs in the summer can be booked in advance by the general public; the lodge is close to some of the finest hiking, birding, fishing, biking, and skiing venues in the country.

GETTING THERE: From Hwy. 22 south of Cochrane, head west on Hwy. 1 to the junction with Hwy. 40. Go left (south) for 50 KM to the Kananaskis Lakes Trail. Turn right (west) and go two KM to the Smith Dorrien Road (Secondary Hwy. 742). Turn right (north) and follow the gravel road for 30 KM north to the Mt. Shark Road. Turn left and follow the signs to the lodge. Or from Hwy. 22 at Longview, head west on Secondary Hwy. 541 for 43 KM to the junction with Hwy. 40. Drive 54 KM north on Hwy. 40 to the turnoff for the Kananaskis Lakes Trail. Turn left (west) and follow the directions as noted above. (Hwy. 40 is closed each year from December 1 to June 15 from the junction with Secondary Hwy. 541 to the Kananaskis Lakes Trail.)

OFF THE BEATEN PATH FROM HIGHWAY 40

For the length of Hwy. 40 from the junction with Secondary Hwy. 541 to Hwy. 1 (a distance of 105 KM), you will pass many scenic pull-outs, picnic and hiking spots. This is one of the most spectacular drives in the Rocky Mountains. For a good overview of the area and the many things to do and see, be sure to stop at the Peter Lougheed Visitor Centre, located about 3.5 KM off Hwy. 40 on the Kananaskis Lakes Trail. It is open Monday to Friday 9:00 AM to 5:00 PM and weekends from 9:00 AM to 6:00 PM in the summer, with reduced hours in the winter (telephone 403-591-6322). The centre features informative displays on chinooks and avalanches, as well as local wildlife including grizzlies, cougars, and wolves. (A portion of the road from Secondary Hwy. 541 to the Kananaskis Lakes Trail is closed from December 1 to June 15 each year.)

Brewster's Kananaskis Guest Ranch

Janet Brewster-Stanton

P.O. Box 340, Exshaw, AB, T0L 2C0

T: 1-800-691-5085

E: horses@kananaskisguestranch.com

ACCEPTS V, MC, AMEX, TC

Open mid-May to early October

www.kananaskisguestranch.com

The Brewster family has been in the outfitting business in the area for over 100 years. The guest ranch is actually located on the site of John Brewster's original homestead, where he kept a dairy herd to service the growing community of Banff. Janet is part of the fifth generation of the family that continues to be involved in a number of local businesses.

Hitting the trail in Kananaskis Country.
BREWSTER'S KANANASKIS GUEST RANCH

WHAT THEY OFFER: Private cabins and chalets with full baths and antique furnishings, including breakfast and dinner; access to licensed dining room, lounge, pool table, gift shop, and whirlpool, as well as a nine-hole golf course and nearby rafting, hiking, canoeing, and fishing.

Options include hourly and full-day trail riding, ride and raft combinations with lunch, and half-day guided fishing trips; two- and four-day pack trips include wilderness cabin accommodations and all meals; all-inclusive adventure

---

STILL IN THE FAMILY

Bill and Jim Brewster began their outfitting business almost by chance. When the manager of the Banff Springs Hotel was unable to find a guide for a couple of English anglers, John Brewster suggested his two sons. It was the beginning of a family business that continues to this day, spanning five generations and including practically every aspect of transport and tourist service in Banff for over 100 years. In fact, one of the businesses – Brewster Transport, which was owned and operated by a family member for 73 years – is believed to have been the largest privately owned sightseeing company in the world.

package (minimum 15 people) offers two nights of accommodation, most meals, and your choice of three from a long list of activities – horseback riding, rafting, golf, hiking, fly fishing, or canoe float; one-night Spikes and Spurs offers breakfast, dinner, golf, and riding; one-night Giddy Up Girlfriends (minimum 10 people) features breakfast, dinner, and choice of two activities. There are rodeos and barbecues for groups.

GETTING THERE: From Cochrane, drive west on Hwy. 1A for 50 KM to Hwy. 1X. Turn left (south) and continue 2 KM to the ranch entrance on the right (west) side.

47 Bar C Ranch Resort   www.bar-c.com

Lawrence Cowan
P.O. Box 1720, Cochrane, AB, T4C 1B6
T: 1-877-932-BarC (2272)
E: info@bar-c.com
ACCEPTS D, V, MC, TC, US CASH
Open May to September

This is a working cattle ranch that has been in operation since 1904. The Bar C runs about 300 head of Herefords and Red Angus.

WHAT THEY OFFER: 34 log cabins with bathroom, fireplace, and all linens; authentic Sioux tipis (sleeping bags, foam pads, and pillows can be rented), with a modern bathhouse complete with laundry facilities close by; Bar C Saloon is open daily for meals; Ghost River Trading Post offers postal services, tourist information, and a gift store.

There are trail rides to suit your preference; once a week "cattle checks" provide a full day checking cattle, plus lunch on the trail; sundowner barbecue rides feature barbecue steak supper and a wagon ride to the site; entertainment nights can include country music, line-dancing lessons, native dancing, or storytelling around the campfire; two-night, three-day pack trips use tent accommodations (custom trips can be arranged for groups of six or more); all-inclusive packages include accommodations, all meals, trail riding, and ranch activities.

GETTING THERE: From Cochrane, drive 13 KM west on Hwy. 1A to the Forestry Trunk Road (Hwy. 40). Turn right (north) and go for 23 KM to the ranch on the left side of the road.

Owl hoot — a trail used by bandits to rob unsuspecting travellers

Saddle Peak Trail Rides

Dave and Jacquie Richards

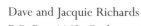

P.O. Box 1463, Cochrane, AB, T4C 1B4

T: 403-932-3299

E: okcorral@telusplanet.net

ACCEPTS D, V, MC, TC

Open late April to mid-October

www.saddle-peak.com

It's not too surprising that Dave ended up as a guide and outfitter. After all, his father, Audley, was an old-time horseman, guider, and packer who ran as many as 400 head of horses with his brothers, Jim, Edgar, and Bill. During the 1940s, Audley packed and guided for Ruth and Claude Brewster out of Banff. It was here that he met his future wife, Esther. She was a trail cook for 28 years, cooking for up to 100 guests with a wood stove! She even cooked for the movie crew of *River of No Return*, starring Marilyn Monroe and Robert Mitchum, which was shot on location in the area. In 1934 Audley homesteaded a small foothills ranch close to the Ghost River and east of Devil's Gap. Today it is the headquarters for the Saddle Peak operation.

Trailing into the backcountry.
SADDLE PEAK TRAIL RIDES

WHAT THEY OFFER: Hourly riding; guided day rides include a steak dinner afternoon or evening ride, a brunch ride, a half-day Pringle Mountain Ridge ride (you can add in a steak dinner), or a full-day Ghost River ride with lunch.

The three-day Devil's Head pack trip includes two nights at the base tent camp and expedition-style canvas wall tents with foam sleeping pads (you bring a ground cloth and sleeping bag); combine three-day pack trip with a one-day ranch stay in one of two rustic cabins (equipped with wood stove and electricity, but no running water) and dinner in the main ranch house. A two-day Ghost River option includes cabin accommodation, a day ride to Ghost River (with picnic lunch on the trail and barbecue steak dinner), and a half-day ride to Pringle Mountain the next day (with lunch at the ranch); two-day getaways combine cabin accommodations, an evening ride and supper, and a half-day Pringle Mountain ride the next day; five-day Explorer features three-day pack trip with two days of whitewater rafting on the Red Deer River, or try the two-day option with riding and rafting; three-day fall colour ride provides great photo opportunities with all-day rides and cabin accommodations. The Sundance Hall can cater for up to 150 guests for family reunions or groups.

GETTING THERE: From Cochrane, drive west on Hwy. 1A for 13 KM to the Forestry Trunk Road (Hwy. 40). Turn right (north) and go 25 KM to Richards Road. At the sign, turn left (south), go 8 KM, then turn right (west) at the sign and go 1.6 KM to the ranch.

Outrider — one of four mounted riders that follows the chuckwagon in a race

OFF THE BEATEN PATH FROM COCHRANE

As you head north on Hwy. 22 from Cochrane, the country opens up to some stunning vistas of the Rockies to the west. Along the road, there are some interesting spots that are just a little off the beaten path from the highway, but well worth a look.

Big Hill Springs Provincial Park: From Hwy. 22 head east on Secondary Hwy. 567 for seven KM. Turn right (south) at the sign and follow the road into the park. This is a day-use area only, with good picnic spots and an interpretive trail. The centre of the park is a steep-walled valley where Bighill Creek trickles through and over tufa ledges to form a number of small waterfalls. Tufa is a spongy limestone. It often hosts multi-hued algae that can make the waterfalls look quite colourful.

Bottrel General Store: Located 2 kilometres west of Hwy. 22 on TWP 283, the store was established in 1901 and continues to be a popular stop for the locals. Apparently, the name came from a misspelled version of Edward Botterell, an early settler. The family campground beside the store straddles Dog Pound Creek, and is a good spot for birders or fishing enthusiasts.

As you continue driving on Hwy. 22 north of Cochrane, you will find another Cowboy Trail partner.

Big Springs Estate Bed and Breakfast Inn   www.bigsprings-bb.com
Earle and Carol Whittaker
R.R. 1, Airdrie, AB, T4B 2A3
T: 1-888-948-5851
E: bigsprings@bigsprings-bb.com
ACCEPTS V, MC, AMEX
Open all year

Cowboys never had it so good! Earle and Carol's promise is "elegance in the Wild West for discriminating guests who seek and appreciate excellence." So if you are looking to be pampered, this is the spot.

WHAT THEY OFFER: Private gated property; two suites — one with king-size canopy bed, gas fireplace, minibar, two bathrooms, and private sunroom; the other features a free-standing claw-foot tub and wood-burning fireplace; both overlook extensive gardens and provide the ultimate in comfort and luxury. (The ultra-masseur tubs have 40 air jets and heated headrest.) Two additional rooms offer private bath and distinctive furnishings. Guests have access to a private English Garden Lounge, separate TV room, and private nature trail. Breakfast is a five-course culinary event — Carol is a certified journeyman cook who loves to experiment.

Elegance in the Wild West.
BIG SPRINGS ESTATE

The packages include a two-night romantic getaway; a two-night Rocky Mountain Adventure with choice of two half-day hiking, biking, horseback riding, or whitewater rafting adventures; or choose from one of seven self-guided day trips designed for guests staying a minimum of two nights.

GETTING THERE: From Hwy. 22, drive east on Secondary Hwy. 567 for 14.4 KM. Turn left (north) at RR25 and follow the sign in.

HOME SWEET HOME

The sod house was warm in the winter, cool in the summer, and easy to build. Strips of sod about four inches thick were cut with a plough, and the grass was left on to hold it together. The slabs were laid to form a wall about three feet thick. The roof was built out of wood if possible, or sod was laid across the rafters. The interior walls were whitewashed to help keep the bugs out until it rained, and the mud dispensed with any pretence of white walls.

Sod house with pile of buffalo skulls in front, 1910.
GLENBOW ARCHIVES NA-520-67

Water Valley

Water Valley and Skunk Hollow – the tiny little hamlet of Water Valley is a short eight kilmetre drive west of Hwy. 22 on Secondary Hwy. 579. The general store serves ice cream and coffee, and the Long Winter Country Crafts and Collectibles features a delightful selection of crafts and gifts. Continue west for another five kilometres across the bridge, make a sharp right on RR5.4, and then a left on a road signed William J. Bagnall Wilderness Park. The area was once the site of a thriving mining community called Skunk Hollow, with a post office, general store, and dance hall. No one is sure where the unusual name came from, but you might want to keep your eyes open for signs of the black and white "stink kitty."

Cremona

As you head north on Hwy. 22 towards Sundre, you will pass the village of Cremona. Lillian and Smith Jackson opened the post office there in 1906 and suggested the name, after the Italian city famous for it violins.

Cowboy Trail partner for this area added just prior to press time:

Bow Rivers Edge Campground   www.bowriversedge.com
Cochrane, Alberta
T: 403-932-4675
E: info@bowriversedge.com

CRITTER WATCH: MULE DEER

Muleys are common across the province and are easy to spot in open areas. Mule deer have large mule-sized ears with a distinct black trim. Their ears are adapted to living

Mule deer or "muleys" exhibit a bouncing gait called "stotting" or "pronking."
JANET NASH

in open areas where sound tends to travel farther. They are sometimes confused with the white-tailed deer, which are redder in colour with a brown rump and a fringed white tail that shows all white only when it is raised. Mule deer have a large whitish rump patch that is divided by a short, black-tipped tail. Muleys have a distinctive bouncing gait called "stotting" or "pronking." When a mule deer stots, it bounds and lands on all four legs simultaneously, an adaptation that helps it navigate the obstructions it commonly encounters in its habitat. They can seem quite tame and gentle, but if threatened, they can lash out viciously with sharp hooves. Snorting and feet stomping are a good sign that you are too close.

Recommended Reading

Banff, The Rockies and the West: Tales of the Early Days by F.O. "Pat" Brewster
Brewster Story: From Pack Train to Tour Bus by E.J. Hart
Canmore and Kananaskis History Explorer by Ernie Lakusta
Horses and Other Loves: The Life of Ivor Clarke by Brenda Giesbrecht
Kananaskis Country Trail Guide Volume 1 by Gillean Daffern
My Valley, The Kananaskis by Ruth Oltman
The Indian Tipi – Its History, Construction and Use by Reginald and Gladys Laubin

Pickup man – a mounted cowboy who helps a rider off a bucking horse

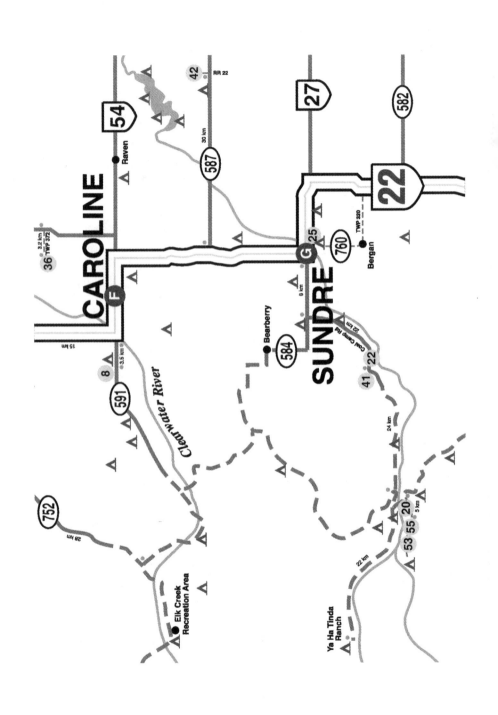

7 : SUNDRE TO CAROLINE AND AREA

"Never take a bull by the horns. Take him by the tail. That way you can let go."

—Ted Stone, *Cowboy Logic*

Communities

- Ⓖ Sundre
- Ⓕ Caroline

Accommodations

- 25 Rustlers Guest Lodge
- Ⓖ Sundre Hotel
- 22 Myown River Ranch
- 20 Mountain-Aire Lodge Motel and Campground
- 55 Sunset Horseback Holidays
- 53 Panther River Adventures
- 8 Art on the Range Gallery Studio Bed & Breakfast & Bale

Attractions & Events

- Ⓖ Sundre Pioneer Village Museum
- Ⓕ Caroline Wheels of Time Museum

Farm & Ranch Vacations

- 22 Myown River Ranch
- 41 Red Deer River Ranches
- 42 Red Lodge Outfitters and Guest Ranch
- 36 Lazy M Ranch

Outfitters

- 55 Sunset Horseback Holidays
- 53 Panther River Adventures
- 42 Red Lodge Outfitters and Guest Ranch
- 36 Lazy M Ranch

Bring Your Own Horse

- 20 Mountain-Aire Lodge Motel and Campground
- 55 Sunset Horseback Holidays
- 53 Panther River Adventures
- 8 Art on the Range Gallery Studio Bed & Breakfast & Bale

Camping

- 20 Mountain-Aire Lodge Motel and Campground
- 55 Sunset Horseback Holidays
- 53 Panther River Adventures
- 42 Red Lodge Outfitters and Guest Ranch

Rafting & Water Adventures

- Ⓖ Otter Rafting Adventures Inc.

Restaurants

- 20 Mountain-Aire Lodge Motel and Campground
- 42 Red Lodge Outfitters and Guest Ranch

Shopping, Antiques & Artisans

- Ⓖ Otter Rafting Adventures Inc.
- 20 Mountain-Aire Lodge Motel and Campground
- 8 Art on the Range Gallery Studio Bed & Breakfast & Bale

MAJOR EVENTS ALONG THE TRAIL

(check www.thecowboytrail.com for a complete listing)

May
Big Horn Rodeo, Caroline

June
Sundre Pro Rodeo, Sundre

July
A Taste of the West – Cowboy Music and Poets, Sundre Pioneer Village Museum
Go Wild, Go West, Sundre
Red Deer River Festival, Sundre

August
Chuckwagon Endurance Race, Sundre
Super Six Team Roping, Sundre

September
Bearberry Horseback Poker Rally and Steak Fry, Bearberry
Sundre Agricultural Society Fair, Sundre

Palaver – profuse or idle talk

As you drive north from Cochrane and Cremona towards Sundre, you are entering a region of the province called the aspen parkland, an area of intermingled prairie and groves of aspen, white spruce, and paper birch. It is a transitional zone between prairie to the south and boreal forest to the north. It tended to attract settlers later than the prairie region, because the land required more clearing to make it viable. The area supports mixed farming, and there aren't as many of the vast spreads that you find in the south. But don't be fooled. There are still plenty of cattle, horses, and cowboys here, as any jaunt off the main highway will confirm.

Sundre
www.sundre.com
T: 403-638-3551

The town was named after the Norwegian birthplace of Nels Hagen, who opened a combined post office, store, dance hall, and rooming house in 1906. But long before this, explorer David Thompson had christened the spot "The Plain of the Grand View" during a trip in October 1800. His route on this journey often intersected the current course of Hwy. 22. At the future townsite of Sundre, Thompson's journal notes, "Here we had a grand view of the Rocky Mountains. All its snowy cliffs to the Southward were bright with the Beams of the Sun, while the most northern were darkened by Tempest . . ." As you head west along a short jog of Hwy. 27 into town, the view of the Rockies truly is quite "grand."

Just west of town, in an area that came to be called McDougall Flats, David McDougall was the first white man to live and ranch in the area. He was the

David Thompson called the future site of Sundre "The Plain of the Grand View" during a trip to the area in 1800.
SUNDRE PIONEER VILLAGE MUSEUM

COWBOY BANDANAS: USES AND ABUSES

A bandana, or a "101," is said to have 101 uses. Lee Thomson, in his hilarious saga *Bandanas Uses and Abuses*, does a mighty fine job of telling us what they all are. Consider this partial list of practical uses for the humble kerchief no self-respecting cowboy would be without. Bandanas can wipe off dust when you're trailing the herd, flick off horseflies and mosquitoes, and strain the surprises out of the water. They are good neck warmers when it's cold and a wet bandana can keep you cool in the heat. First-aid bandanas can make a sling, a tourniquet, or an eye patch. They can cover a dirty neck, a hickey, or an unsightly bullet hole in your jacket. They can save you from the sun when you've lost your Smithbilt or cover up a bad hair day. Bandits love to hide behind them, and they come in handy to mask certain, shall we say, unpleasant odours in the barn and the bunkhouse. And that's only 15! Irene Lyle, a long-time resident of Sundre, probably saved her own life with some quick thinking and her polka-dot bandana. When she was out hunting, she injured herself with an accidental gunshot wound that cut a main artery in her hand. By using her teeth and her good hand, she tightened the bandana around her wrist and rode the five kilometres home at a brisk lope. She lived to tell the tale in her book *Gram's 'ventures: Irene Lyle*.

brother of well-known missionary John McDougall (see sidebar page 172), who had established a mission for the Stoneys at Morley. David suffered substantial cattle losses during the disastrous winter of 1906–7 and decided to sell out to Nels Hagen, who came from North Dakota. When Mrs. Hagen saw the state of the old log cabin that was to be their home — cattle had been wandering in and out of it — she told the drayman not to bother unloading the furniture. Her husband convinced her to give it a try. They settled here for many years, and are often called the founders of Sundre.

As you drive west into Sundre on Hwy. 27, you will pass a Cowboy Trail partner located just across from the golf course.

Rustlers Guest Lodge   www.rustlers-lodge.com

Stephen and Paula Dodwell

P.O. Box 2032, Sundre, AB, T0M 1X0

T: 403-638-4389

E: rustlers@telusplanet.net

ACCEPTS D, V, MC, AMEX, PC

Open all year

WHAT THEY OFFER: Six spacious rooms located off a private guest sitting room that features TV/VCR and small kitchenette with fridge and complimentary beverages. As well, a full hot breakfast served in the 1,700 square-foot cedar-lined pool house with full-size swimming pool and hot tub; direct access to patio with barbecue and tables and chairs. There are four acres of secluded forest adjacent to Sundre Golf Course. Catering for private functions such as weddings and reunions.

GETTING THERE: From Hwy. 22, turn left (west) on Hwy. 27 towards Sundre. The lodge is on the left (south) side of the highway, across from the Sundre Golf Course. Watch for the log gateway and sign.

When you are in town, don't miss the Sundre Museum. It offers an outstanding introduction to the area's history and is a great place to start your visit.

Sundre Pioneer Village Museum   www.geocities.com/sundre_museum
Sundre and District Historical Society
211 – 1st Avenue SW, P.O. Box 314, Sundre, AB, T0M 1X0
T: 403-638-3233
E: sundremuseum@telus.net
Summer hours: 10:00 AM to 5:00 PM daily from May long weekend to September long weekend; Winter hours: 10:00 AM to 4:00 PM Thursday to Saturday or by appointment.
ADMISSION CHARGED

WHAT THEY OFFER: Located on four acres of land in the centre of town. A new 7,300 square-foot Reception Centre features semi-permanent and "floating exhibits" depicting many aspects of local pioneer life. The Pioneer Village includes the old Bergen school, a 1913 log cabin and a 1930s ranger station from west of Sundre, an old blacksmith's shop, and the Garrington ferry man's house. The barn houses arti-facts and exhibits of general historical significance. The Youth Museum (built by the youth of Sundre for the town's youth) has a functional "Fountain of Youth" and displays dedicated to anything of interest to young people.

A new 5,000 square-foot Wildlife Exhibit, slated for opening in 2006, will house an extensive wildlife collection donated by a local Sundre

Pioneer Village.
SUNDRE PIONEER VILLAGE MUSEUM

hunter. This world-class exhibit will feature over 200 animals collected from countries around the world, such as Africa, Russia, New Zealand, Australia, the Arctic, and, of course, Canada. All of the animals will be housed in replicas of their own natural habitat.

PUNCH AND JUDY WERE BUFFALO?

Russ Greenwood with his team of trained buffalo, Punch and Judy.
SUNDRE MUSEUM

Greenwood Campground in Sundre is named after Russ Greenwood, a well-known Sundre pioneer. According to Reuben Olson, an old-time rancher from the area, "Russ could train anything." Greenwood had a horse that would walk on its hind feet, a coyote that would ride his Jersey steer, and a team of buffalo named Punch and Judy that he had trained to pull a cart – they were a popular entry in the Sundre and Calgary Stampede parades for many years. Olson recalls talking to Greenwood one day when he had brought the buffalo downtown with the cart. "They took off and Russ had to run after them to get them stopped." The buffalo cart is on display at the Sundre Museum.

Other Points of Interest in Sundre

Visitor Information Centre

604 Main Avenue East

T: 403-638-3245

Open Sunday to Wednesday 10:00 AM to 6:00 PM; Thursday to Saturday 10:00 AM to 8:00 PM, from the May long weekend to the September long weekend. Be sure to stop and pick up a free copy of the excellent "West Country Driving Tour" booklet for a great introduction to some short driving trips in the area.

TALL TALES

Dave McDougall was well-known as a storyteller – some people called his tales whoppers. Many of his stories are remembered in a book called *Folklore of Canada* by Edith Fowkes. Here's one of them: "[Dave] told me when he came to this country, the prairie was filled with buffalo. You could get out and walk for miles on the buffalo. You had to get out and pull the buffalo calves from between the spokes of the wheels to drive." Apparently, Dave told his stories so often, he actually began to believe they were true.

Grub Stop

Burger Baron, 211 Main Avenue W, 403-638-3844; Classic Lunch and Cakery, 106 Centre Street N, 403-638-2015; Cosmos, 302 Main Avenue W, 403-638-9065; Granny's Country Kitchen, #6 Prairie Creek Plaza, 403-638-2860; Harvest Moon Restaurant,

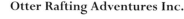 Pigging string – the rope that is used to tie a calf's legs when it has been roped

101 Main Avenue E, 403-638-3321; Koffee Binge, 102 2nd Street SW, 403-638-4009; Latte & Gifts, 105 Centre Street N, 403-638-4008; Outlaw's Bar and Grill, 250 Main Avenue E, 403-638-2882; Piros Family Restaurant, 110 Main Avenue W, 403-638-3354; Rocky Top, 407 Main Avenue, 403-638-3905; Subway, 308 Main Avenue W, 403-638-4444; Sundre Hotel Restaurant, 102 Centre Street S, 403-638-3777; Sunny Café, 103 Main Avenue E, 403-638-9105; Trendies Restaurant, 401 Main Avenue N, 403-638-2233; Wildrose Restaurant, 101 3rd Street SW, 403-638-4249.

As you head west out of Sundre, you will pass the offices of another Cowboy Trail partner.

Otter Rafting Adventures Inc.   www.otterrafting.com
David Todd
829 Main Avenue West, P.O. Box 1717, Sundre, AB, T0M 1X0
T: 1-800-661-7379
E: otter@otterrafting.com
ACCEPTS D, V, MC

Rafting open May 15 to September 15. **Pottery shop open** daily all year.

When David came west from northern Ontario, he found Alberta didn't have enough lakes, so he looked for a good river and decided to set up shop. The Red Deer River is a class-3 river, which offers plenty of fun without being terrifying. According to David, "there is a constant gradient, so there is always something happening, but it is not so wild that it wears you out."

WHAT THEY OFFER: Half- and full-day rafting and kayaking trips or scenic half-day float; full-day trips include buffet lunch. Otter supplies shuttle services and all necessary river-running equipment; wet suit rental available. The pottery shop features David's handmade decorative pottery. He uses primitive firing techniques, wood ash glazes, and salts to get dramatic and unique effects in the finished product.

OFF THE BEATEN PATH FROM SUNDRE
(ON COAL CAMP ROAD)

Ranching, logging, and petroleum remain important industries in Sundre, but it is also a world-renowned centre for activities such as horseback riding, whitewater rafting, hiking, and fishing in the wilderness areas west of town. Even if you aren't heading out to any of the Cowboy Trail partners located on the Coal Camp Road, it's worth the drive to see some of the spectacular scenery and take in a few of the stops along this historic trail.

Coal Camp Road: From the junction of Hwy. 22 and Hwy. 27, head west for eight kilometres (the road becomes Secondary Hwy. 584). Turn left at the Coal Camp Road. The road becomes gravel after about 25 kilometres. It was built to service the mining town of Coal Camp, where coal was first mined in 1898. Coal Camp also became a major logging camp from 1907–15 but still retained its name. There are several picnic and camping spots along this road, next to the Red Deer River.

Blue Hill Lookout: The lookout was built by George Pearce in the 1920s. Horses packed in every stick of timber "up hills so steep that man on foot had to have hobnail boots to stop from sliding back." This is a popular eight kilometre hike with good views. As you are driving west on Coal Camp Road, watch for the small green signs on the right (north) side of the road. The hike begins at sign number 10 just east of the Red Deer River Ranger Station and approximately 42 KM from Secondary Hwy. 584.

Ya Ha Tinda Ranch: The name comes from the Stoney for "mountain prairie" or "little prairie in the mountains," because it sits in a broad valley with the Red Deer River on the south side and wide grass-covered hills on the north. The valley is usually swept free of snow due to frequent chinooks. It is home to one of Alberta's largest elk herds during the winter and an extraordinary diversity of plant and animal life that thrive in the mild climate. Bill and Jim Brewster (see sidebar page 177) started the ranch in 1907 to winter horses used in their Banff livery operation. It was taken over by the Parks Service in 1917 and used as a breeding ranch to supply horses to the warden service. The breeding program is no longer in place, but it remains the only federally operated horse ranch in Canada. Camping is available year-round at the Big Horn Campground located close to the spectacular Big Horn Falls – you can bring your horse, too! Interpretive tours of the ranch can be booked by calling 403-668-7347. The tour features historic exhibits including the barn, the blacksmith's shop, and the bunkhouse, which are designated historic sites. To get to the ranch, follow the Coal Camp Road to Secondary Hwy. 734. Turn left and follow the road to the blue bridge. Just before the bridge, take the gravel road to the right for 22 KM to the Big Horn Campground. There is a parking lot with a large wooden interpretive sign next to the trail leading to the falls. If you are going on a tour, cross the bridge and follow the road to the ranch buildings.

HARRY DIDN'T STAY LONG

It was 1890 when Harry Graham took up squatter's rights on a piece of unspoiled wilderness on the west side of what would eventually be called Williams Creek. One of the first white men to settle in the area, Harry had no way of knowing his small beginning would eventually evolve into the Red Deer River Ranches. Harry didn't stay long. A marauding grizzly bear that played havoc with his cattle, and a sweetheart who played havoc with his heart (the story is she spurned him even after he built her a beautiful home at a spot near present-day Westward Ho), persuaded Harry to try his luck somewhere else, but the seed for the ranch had been sown. Over the years, there were many colourful owners, including Colonel Harry Snyder, who hunted big game all over the world and housed his trophies in a building on the ranch he called the "Teepee." The entire collection, which drew people from all over the world to see it, was lost in a fire in 1953. Today the ranch runs a herd of 400 mainly red Angus cross cows on a spread that includes 405 hectares (1,000 acres) of private land and over 20,200 hectares (50,000 acres) of grazing leases.

There are several Cowboy Trail partners located on Coal Camp Road, if you decide to spend more time enjoying this beautiful area.

Red Deer River Ranches   www.reddeerriverranches.com

Jason Bradley

P.O. Box 1069, Sundre, AB, T0M 1X0

T: 1-866-638-4226

E: info@reddeerriverranches.com

ACCEPTS D, V, MC, TC, PC

Open all year

WHAT THEY OFFER: Brown/Juno Creek cabins with loft, full kitchen, and bathroom for a maximum of six. And newly renovated Hunters cabin has new kitchen, toilet, queen-size bed, and bunk beds for a maximum of four. The Hauling and Williams Creek bunkhouses have wood stoves and kitchen areas, with toilet and showers close by. Access to hot tub, gas barbecues, basketball/volleyball court, badminton, and horseshoes.

There's a 1940s log barn with elevated sundeck/barbecues ideal for groups. Guided and self-guided options include half- or full-day horseback adventures with lunch, one- or two-day saddle and paddle combos, canoeing, kayaking, ATVs, fishing, hiking, biking, wild-horse viewing, and photography; can arrange shopping trips to local western shops. Custom packages, hunting trips, helicopter fly-fishing, and hiking; limited only by your imagination.

Cozy ranch cabins welcome visitors.
RED DEER RIVER RANCHES

GETTING THERE: From the junction of Hwy. 22 and Hwy. 27, head west for 8 KM (the road becomes Secondary Hwy. 584) to the Coal Camp Road. Turn left and drive southwest for 22 KM. The ranch is on the right side of the road.

WILD HORSES STILL ROAM FREE

Most people would be surprised to know it, but wild horses still roam the area west of Sundre along the Coal Camp Road and into the forest reserve. The best way to see them is on their terms on horseback, but you will occasionally be able to catch a glimpse from a truck trail in the reserve. The herds have grown from three main sources. Small, tough mine ponies hauled coal carts out of the mine at Nordegg (northwest of Sundre) and were turned out to fend for themselves when the mine closed. They have interbred with heavy horses used by the Great Western Logging Company to skid logs out of the forest west of Sundre. These giants suffered the same fate as the mine ponies when the company ceased logging operations in the 1930s. Over the years, a third bloodline has been injected into the herds from ranch quarter horses that were stolen away by the wildies. In the 1950s, the Alberta government embarked on a program to eradicate wild horses from the province, but public outcry eventually put an end to this plan. Since then, the herds have largely been left to fend for themselves.

Pull leather — to hang on to the saddle horn to keep from falling off a horse; if you ride clean, you haven't grabbed the horn

Mountain-Aire Lodge Motel and Campground

Ross Legge
P.O. Box 570, Sundre, AB, T0M 1X0
T: 1-877-637-0202
E: mountainaire@telus.net
ACCEPTS D, V, MC, AMEX
Open all year

www.mountainaire.ca

WHAT THEY OFFER: 12-unit motel, each room with gas fireplace, private bathroom, DVD or video rental, and exceptional views; access to hot tub and fitness centre. A 20-acre campground at the lodge has RV hookups, hot showers, flush toilets, laundromat, horse-shoes, horse corral, covered Quonset for groups, plus sand volleyball court, baseball, and new Pitch 'n Putt golf; also operates five Provincial Recreation Areas, including Cartier Creek and Deer Creek on the Coal Camp Road, North and South Red Deer River campgrounds on Secondary Hwy. 734, and Wild Horse campground near Ya-Ha-Tinda Ranch.

Mountain-Aire Lodge – people drive miles for the homemade burgers and fries.
L. ANDREWS

A full-service restaurant is well-known for its homecooked meals. According to Ross, people drive miles for one of their homemade hamburgers and cut fries; self-service gas station with gas, diesel, propane; grocery store and gift shop with native and western items.

GETTING THERE: From the junction of Hwy. 22 and Hwy. 27, head west for 8 KM (the road becomes Secondary Hwy. 584) to the Coal Camp Road. Turn left and drive southwest for 46 KM. Turn left at the junction with Secondary Hwy. 734. The lodge is on the right-hand side, just across the blue bridge.

Running iron – a branding iron often used to alter an existing brand (illegally)

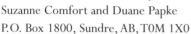

Sunset Horseback Holidays

www.sunsetholidays.net

Suzanne Comfort and Duane Papke

P.O. Box 1800, Sundre, AB, T0M 1X0

T: 1-888-637-8580

E: sunsetholidays@telus.net

ACCEPTS D, V, MC, AMEX, TC, MO

Open all year

WHAT THEY OFFER: Panther River Retreat is open year-round, with heated cabins (bring your own bedding), central shower/toilet facilities, meals taken in central cookhouse, access to hot tub; serviced RV spots.

Options include B&B, one- and two-hour rides, half-day rides with lunch, full-day rides with lunch and dinner; mountain wagon rides; Wild Rose Weekender

Riding the backcountry west of Sundre.
SUNSET HORSEBACK HOLIDAYS

offers activities such as riding, hiking, canoeing, rafting, fishing; three-day Panther trips ride in the backcountry and sleep in a bed; five-day Panther includes backcountry riding and canvas tent accommodation; wildlife/wild horse photography trips use retreat or camp as a base; five-day summer youth camp for ages 10 to 14 runs each July; winter season from December 1 to March 31 offers guided winter scenery, photography, snowmobiling, and cross-country skiing tours. Dormer Mountain Tent Camp runs June 1 to late September; options include riding, fishing, photography; five- to ten-day high-mountain pack trips take a limited number of participants.

GETTING THERE: From the junction of Hwy. 22 and Hwy. 27, head west for 8 KM (the road becomes Secondary Hwy. 584) to the Coal Camp Road. Turn left and drive southwest for 46 KM. Turn left at the junction with Secondary Hwy. 734, cross the blue bridge, then turn right (west) and drive 5 KM to the gate on the right side of the road. The route is well-signed.

Panther River Adventures

www.pantherriver.com

Terry and Laureen Safron; Alfred and Veronika Kowatsch

P.O. Box 415, Eckville, AB, T0M 0X0

T: 403-637-2920

E: panrivad@telusplanet.net

ACCEPTS D, V, MC, PC

Open all year. German spoken.

WHAT THEY OFFER: Six cozy log cabins with radiant hot-water heat and hand-crafted log furniture; immaculate shower/toilet facilities in main lodge, plus full meal service in lodge; camping spots with fire pit and table.

As well, hourly, half-day, or full-day rides with lunch; three-day trail rides that travel into the backcountry with custom-made wagon to carry supplies and tent camp for longer trips; guided hiking and full- or part-day wagon trips; custom hunting trips; quadding, snowmobiling, cross-country skiing, and horse-drawn sleigh rides offered in winter. There is a covered area with barbecue and fireplace; fishing and swimming in nearby river; natural salt lick attracts bighorn sheep.

GETTING THERE: From the junction of Hwy. 22 and Hwy. 27, head west for 8 KM (the road becomes Secondary Hwy. 584) to the Coal Camp Road. Turn left and drive southwest for 46 KM. Turn left at the junction with Secondary Hwy. 734, cross the blue

The wagon is custom-built for the rigors of the backcountry.
PANTHER RIVER ADVENTURES

bridge, then turn right (west) and drive 6 KM to the gate on the right side of the road. The route is well-signed.

DID YOU KNOW?

Hanne Christersson came with her husband from Denmark with a dream of owning land and horses. Her husband was drowned in a tragic accident in 1955, but she couldn't let her dream die. Left with two small children, she bought land near Bearberry, capturing and training wild horses, and earning a reputation for selling well-trained, gentle animals.

Bearberry Heritage and Arts Centre: From Sundre, drive west on Secondary Hwy. 584 for 25 KM to the tiny hamlet of Bearberry. Every weekend from May to September (and long-weekend Mondays), the centre showcases the talents of the area's many artisans. It is actually an old restored barn from the James River Ranger Station. The centre includes a historic display on the ground floor and a gallery in the loft, with paintings, pottery, stained glass and hand-crafted wood furniture. The Bearberry Saloon is a good spot to stop for a meal or a snack.

Bergen General Store: From Sundre, head east on Hwy. 27 out of town and turn right (south) on Secondary Hwy. 760 for 10 kilometres to this thriving rural store. They sell gas, groceries, ice cream, and gifts, but their claim to fame is their "world famous" beef jerky, which they make on the premises. You can drive east from Bergen on TWP320 to hook up again with Hwy. 22. Along the way you will cross McDougall Coulee. It is a wide open space through the trees and was part of the trail used by the Indians and early settlers in the area – a trail that old-timer Reuben Olson, who ranched near Bergen all his life, informed me was the "Real Cowboy Trail."

Rowel – a revolving disk at the end of a spur

ANNA'S STORY

In 1927 Pete and Anna Unger headed north from Oregon in a Willis overland car loaded with all their possessions. Pete had been working in Oregon, but was originally from Saskatchewan and always had a hankering to move back to Canada. When he saw an ad for a quarter section west of Bowden with a log house on it, he started a correspondence that lasted for over a year before he finally agreed to swap two lots in Oregon for the ranch, sight unseen. It became the Red Lodge Ranch, a working cattle ranch still run by Pete and Anna's grandson, Dale, and his wife, Wendy. At first, Anna wanted to go home, but it didn't take long for her to fall in love with the country and become one of its biggest supporters. In fact, she lived on the ranch until she was 92. The story is told of Anna delivering Dale's mother, Margaret, with the help of the local horse doctor, Alex McKenzie, because the midwife was away picking chokecherries. "Alex rolled up his sleeves and boiled his hands like a real doctor would do, but he became so excited when the little head appeared that he began talking to the mother and emerging child as he would to a mare and foal. 'Whoa there, steady now, easy old girl, there she comes, won't be long now.'" Even in her discomfort and pain, Anna had to smile at the urgings of this horseman doing the best he knew. Anna would remember being light-headed but enormously grateful to this man. It was typical of the hardships many women endured with precious little recognition of their contribution to the taming of the Wild West.

Once you've finished your side trips from Sundre, head north on Hwy. 22 for 15 kilometres to the junction with Secondary Hwy. 587. If you like saskatoon berries, you might want to drive east for 16 kilometres on Secondary Hwy. 587 past the James River General Store to Pearson's Berry Farm, where you can pick them yourself or indulge in a piece of homemade pie and other goodies. Located 14 kilometres east of Pearson's turnoff is another Cowboy Trail partner.

Red Lodge Outfitters and Guest Ranch   www.redlodgeoutfitters.com
Wendy and Dale Bradshaw
Box 1, Site 12, Bowden, AB, T0M 0K0
T: 403-224-3082
E: info@redlodgeoutfitters.com
ACCEPTS D, V, MC, TC, PC
Open all year

WHAT THEY OFFER: Rustic heated cabins (with space for up to 70), tent and RV sites; bedding required for cabins; shower/toilet facilities in central block; volleyball, horseshoe pits, baseball, buckin' barrel. Meals are served in licensed Round Dining Lodge; public welcome all year for the Sunday Brunch or monthly western Prime Rib supper with local country music entertainment.

There are hourly ranch rides (with or without lunch) or one-day backcountry riding in North Burnt Timber area; ranch getaways at all-inclusive daily rate; learn basic horsemanship and roping; help check and move cattle; hay and sleigh rides. The banquet hall with fireplace and kitchen is ideal for group functions.

GETTING THERE: From Hwy. 22, drive east on Secondary Hwy. 587 for 30 KM to RR22. Turn left (north) and follow the driveway to the ranch.

Caroline   www.caroline.ca
T: 403-722-3781

Further north on Hwy. 22, the sign at the entrance to the village of Caroline proudly announces you are in "Kurt Browning Country," home of the world-champion figure skater. But the town itself is actually named after Caroline Rebecca Langley, known as Reba, the only daughter of Harvey and Cynthia Langley. They opened the first post office and general store in 1908 – it was one corner of a one-room tarpaper shack that was their home. The abundance of timber in the area, and the discovery of the largest sour gas discovery in Alberta in 1986, have made logging and oil and gas important industries here, but the rolling farm and ranchland continues to support a large population of cattle and horses – and of course the occasional cowboy.

Points of Interest in Caroline

The Kurt Browning Arena on 51 Street features memorabilia from his outstanding career, in Kurt's Corner. There is a viewing room as well as a number of plaques and trophies throughout the arena honouring local cowboys.

The Caroline Wheels of Time Museum (403-722-3884, E: bbop32@yahoo.com), located one kilometre east of town next to the campground, is open daily noon to 6:00 PM from the May long weekend to the September long weekend. The tourist information centre (403-722-2210) is open daily 7:00 AM to 11:00 PM from May 15 to September 15 in the campground next to the museum; public washrooms available as well.

Locals recommend a stop at the **Long Branch Saloon** on main street for good food and a taste of some real cowboy culture. The walls are full of local rodeo and hunting trophy photos; there are even saddles hanging from the roof beams.

The Prince of Wales presenting an award to Pete Vandermeer at the EP Ranch, September 1923.
GLENBOW NB-H-16-409

BUGBEE BEAR BROKE THE RECORD

In November 1949, local rancher George Bugbee shot and killed a world-record brown grizzly bear while guiding an American hunting party. The bear had charged the group in defending a recent kill. The bear weighed 725 kilograms (1,600 pounds) and measured 2.75 metres (nine feet) from head to rump.

George Bugbee (on right) with world-record Grizzly bear.
SALLY BUGBEE

BRED TO BUCK

When a rodeo contestant climbs on to the back of a bucking bronc or bull, he's relying on more than just his ability to get a good score. The rodeo judges award 50 per cent of the points based on the bucking performance of the animal, so contractors who can supply good quality stock are in high demand. The days when contractors scoured the country for an outlaw that could score high in the arena have been replaced with sophisticated selective breeding programs that aren't that much different from those for breeding a great cutting quarter horse. In fact, there are even registries for bucking bulls. Harvey Northcott, who lives just a few miles from Caroline, has been raising quality bucking stock since 1968. Over the years, Harvey has raised more Canadian champion bucking bulls than any other contractor.

There is a Cowboy Trail partner located east of Caroline off Highway 54.

36 Lazy M Ranch   www.lazymcanada.com
Margie and Lane Moore
P.O. Box 427, Caroline, AB, T0M 0M0
T: 403-722-3053
E: info@lazymcanada.com
ACCEPTS V, MC, AMEX, PC, BANK DRAFTS
Open May to September (check website for exact dates). Off-season for group meetings and retreats.

Expect well-trained,
well-mannered mounts.
LAZY M RANCH

Visitors can expect something a little different on this working cattle ranch. With over 50 years' experience working with horses, Lane is internationally known for his non-resistant method of riding and training. The current buzzword is "horse whisperer" (see sidebar page 203). His remarkable connection with horses is obvious when he rides his horse, Stubby, in the local Caroline parade with no bridle and no saddle. Horse enthusiasts come from all over the world to take his intensive "horse sense" clinics. Visitors looking for well-trained, well-mannered horses will find them here.

WHAT THEY OFFER: Six rooms in main lodge, three double rooms with private baths, three double rooms share three bathrooms. Meals are taken in the lodge at a huge country-style table; hot tub and sunroom; verandah overlooks Stauffer Creek and magnificent view. Options include "Simply Stay" with meals and no riding; two-, three-, five- and seven-day getaways with various riding and horsemanship options. Seven- and ten-day trips travel to five-star mountain base camp or outpost camp in the Rockies. Tents have wood floors, beds, linen service; shower tent has hot water.

The Great Canadian Cowboy package offers 10, 13, or 14 nights (at two different ranches) with all accommodations, meals, lessons, ranch activities, and transfers. Spend time at Lazy M learning western horsemanship, then transfer to Willow Lane Ranch in the Porcupine Hills (see page 87) to put your expertise to work on a cattle drive.

DID YOU KNOW?
Stauffer Creek (AKA the North Raven River) is known as one of the best places in North America for brown trout fly-fishing.

GETTING THERE: From Hwy. 22, drive east on Hwy. 54 to Secondary Hwy. 761. Turn left (north) and go to the Stauffer General Store at TWP 372. Then head left (west) for 3.2 KM to the ranch. Watch for the sign.

RECIPE FOR POTATO BANNOCK
FROM MARGIE MOORE AT LAZY M

According to Margie, this hearty flatbread is good to sop up stew and chili, and great when you're on the trail. Mix 2½ cups (625 ml) flour, 2 Tbsp (30 ml) baking powder, 1 cup (250 ml) milk, ¼ cup (62 ml) sugar, 1 tsp (5 ml) baking soda, and 1 cup (250 ml) mashed potatoes. Press onto a cookie sheet and bake at 375F (190C) for about 20 minutes. Brush with melted butter to brown. On the trail, wrap it around a stick and cook over an open fire.

"HORSE WHISPERING" NOT NEW

Margie Lane of Lazy M offers her views on horse whispering. "Horse whispering is simply today's 'buzz phrase' for a non-resistant approach to training. These methods were used way back in Greek times, as well as by North American Indians and farmers who used teams for all their farm work – hence the terms 'team working,' 'pulling together,' etc. As man's relationship with horses increased for sport and pleasure rather than essential use, 'quick training' became the norm. Most of these methods are not to the benefit of the horse. Horse whispering, when done with the horse's best interest uppermost in the trainer's mind, produces well-rounded, confident, happy horses who are a pleasure to ride, drive, work with, and be around." Canadian horse whisperer Chris Irwin has become one of North America's most respected coaches in the art of non-resistance training for horses and riders, but as Margie points out, "There are many good 'horse whisperers' around and most of them are not celebrities."

CHAMPION PITCHER

Caroline native Myrna Kissick started pitching horseshoes in 1972. She has won five Canadian Championships and 15 or 16 Alberta Championships (she's not exactly sure). She ranked fifth in the world and always placed in the top ten in the world when she was still competing. She still pitches horseshoes, but now it's mostly for fun. The art of horseshoe pitching had its origins in ancient Greece, where discarded horseshoes were used as a substitute in discus throwing. It was a logical choice for a game in the early days of the West, where horseshoes were plentiful. The players, one at a time, toss the iron U-shaped "shoe" from a set point to land around or against a metal pole in the ground. The winner is the one who pitches his or her horseshoe closest to the pole the most times during play.

Raven Union Church – Head east from Caroline on Hwy. 54. Just down the road, you will see a rustic log building on the left (north) side of the road. It's worth a stop to wander through the cemetery and have a peek in the old country church that is still in use.

The Raven Union Church is still in use.
JUDY LARMOUR AND HENRY SALEY

Cowboy Trail partners for this area added just prior to press time:

F Caroline Wheels of Time Museum (featured on page 200).

8 **Art on the Range Gallery Studio Bed & Breakfast & Bale**
www.artontherange.com
Caroline, Alberta
T: 403-722-3308
E: info@artontherange.com

Myown River Ranch
www.myownriverranch.com
Sundre, Alberta
T: 403-251-6465
E: services@myownriverranch.com

Sundre Hotel
Sundre, Alberta
T: 403-638-3040
E: sunhotel@telusplanet.net

WHAT'S IN A NAME?

A Danish man met his wife in New York City and brought her back to a bush-land homestead east of Caroline. She was very homesick. The neighbours, who loved them dearly, decided to help make her feel more at home and went through the process of naming Range Road 43 "Wall Street Road." The name is recognized with a permanent green road sign on both highway 54 and 11.

Recommended Reading

Cowboy Bandanas: Uses and Abuses by Lee Thomson
Fire Lookout Hikes in the Canadian Rockies by Mike Potter
Folklore of Canada by Edith Fowke
Haze Over Blue Hill by R. Ernie Pearce
Horses Don't Lie: The Magic of Horse Whispering by Chris Irwin
On The Road With David Thompson by Joyce and Peter McCart
The Man Who Listens to Horses by Monty Roberts

Remuda — a herd of horses from which cowboys will choose those to be used for the day

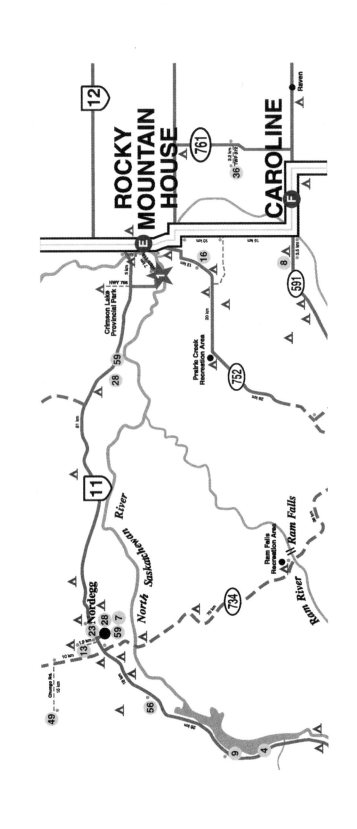

8: ROCKY MOUNTAIN HOUSE AND AREA

"The only weather prediction that'll hold true in a dry spell is that a drought always ends with a rain."   —Ted Stone, *Cowboy Logic*

Communities

(E) Rocky Mountain House

Accommodations

(E) & (59) Voyageur and Klondike
      Ventures

(E) Walking Eagle Inn and Lodge

(16) Grandview Stage Resort

(23) Nordegg Resort Lodge

(13) Cheechako Cabins

(49) Chungo Creek Outfitters

(9) Aurum Lodge and Cottages

Attractions and Events

(16) Grandview Stage Resort

(7) Nordegg Heritage Centre and
     Brazeau Collieries Industrial
     Museum

(4) Icefield Helicopter Tours

Outfitters

(E) & (59) Voyageur and Klondike
      Ventures

(49) Chungo Creek Outfitters

(56) Wild Horse Mountain Outfitters

Rafting & Water Adventures

(E) & (59) Voyageur and Klondike
      Ventures

Bring Your Own Horse

(16) Grandview Stage Resort

Camping

(16) Grandview Stage Resort

(E) & (59) Voyageur and Klondike
      Ventures

(28) Camp 'n Fun Adventures

(56) Wild Horse Mountain Outfitters

Restaurants

(16) Grandview Stage Resort

(23) Nordegg Resort Lodge

(7) Nordegg Heritage Centre and
     Brazeau Collieries Industrial
     Museum

Shopping, Antiques & Artisans

(E) Buffalo Spirit Gifts

(E) In the Beginning Antiques and
     Collectibles

★ Rocky Mountain House National
   Historic Site of Canada

(16) Grandview Stage Resort

(23) Nordegg Resort Lodge

(7) Nordegg Heritage Centre and
     Brazeau Collieries Industrial
     Museum

Icon Attraction

★ Rocky Mountain House National
   Historic Site of Canada

MAJOR EVENTS ALONG THE TRAIL
(check www.thecowboytrail.com for a complete listing)

June
Annual Bluegrass Festival, Grandview Stage Resort
Canadian Rockies Bluegrass Festival, David Thompson Resort
Rocky Mountain House Pro Rodeo, Rocky Mountain House

August
David Thompson Days Country Fair, Rocky Mountain House

September
Provincial Square and Round Dancing Championships, Rocky Mountain House

Skirt — the main part of a saddle without the seat

8 : ROCKY MOUNTAIN HOUSE AND AREA

Rocky Mountain House www.rockymtnhouse.com
Toll-free 1-800-565-3793

Blackfoot name – *apustan*, after a bridge across the Clearwater River on the trail from the fort to Blackfoot country.

Rocky Mountain House took its name from the fur-trading post that was established by the North West Company just west of the townsite in 1799. The name seems to have been a logical choice, given the incredible view of the mountains, but it wasn't without controversy. Two other proposals were put forth – "Saskatchewan City," after the North Saskatchewan River, and "Loch Ernie." The local newspaper *The Echo* had this withering comment on the second suggestion: "A person don't need to scratch their head more than once to find a better name than 'Loch Ernie.'" In the end, it seems, history and common sense won the day.

The story of Rocky Mountain House is inextricably linked to the mighty river that brought the fur traders in 1799. The Nor'Westers were rivals of the Hudson's

"LADY GUIDE OF THE HILLS"

On her tombstone in the Pine Grove Cemetery in Rocky Mountain House, the words say "Lady Guide of The Hills." Friends called her "Shorty," and for over 50 years she guided Canadian and American hunters, geologists, and travellers into the mountains west of Nordegg. By the fall of 1955, she had 15 camps, each with packer and cook, and a total of 103 head of horses. She ran a trapline, operated a sawmill – cutting and skidding the logs herself – and built her own trapper's cabin. Not only was she a seamstress who could whip up made-to-measure dresses and shirts, she also made tack for her horses, crafting the leather into bridles and halters. Over the years she won many trophies, one of the finest accomplishments being the Rocky Mountain Trophy for five years of registering the largest animals taken each season. Her name was Myrtle Sands Raivio, and she was the first woman guide and outfitter in Alberta.

Bay Company in a race to corner the lucrative fur trade with the Indian tribes of the area. The original plan was to establish trade relations with the Kootenay Indians who lived on the western side of the Rocky Mountains. But the Blackfoot tribes, who were fierce enemies of the Kootenays, thwarted these plans. The result was that the Nor'Westers used the fort as a headquarters for exploration and local trade instead. (The famous surveyor explorer, David Thompson (see sidebar page 218),

CANADIAN – "THE LITTLE IRON HORSE"

The Canadian breed is not well-known in the west, but it is actually the National Horse of Canada. The breed traces its ancestry to foundation stock brought to Acadia and New France in the 17th century and to horses introduced from the Royal Stables of French King Louis XIV in the late 1600s. They became extremely popular for their hardiness, stamina, and ability to endure the hardships of brutal winters combined with poor feed and hard work. It earned them the name of "little iron horse."

The breed became so popular that large numbers were exported into the northern United States for crossbreeding and to supply the Civil War. In Canada the numbers were reduced almost to the point of extinction. A series of breeding programs by the federal and Quebec governments helped revive the breed, and numbers have increased as breeders become aware of the traits that made them so popular in the past. Their strength and gentleness make them ideal for ranch work, packing, endurance riding, or as a family horse. Although they are more common in eastern Canada, there are some breeders along the Cowboy Trail who are hooked on their versatility, good looks, and good temperament. Willow View Canadians near Rocky Mountain House and Lazy M Ranch (see page 202) near Caroline both raise Canadians.

actually lived here for several years, using the fort as a base for his historic expeditions.) The Hudson's Bay quickly established a fort literally next door, called Acton House. When the two companies merged in 1821, Acton House was renamed Rocky Mountain House and the other site was abandoned. Over the years, three more versions of the fort would be built, until it was finally deserted in 1875.

The first homesteaders began trickling into the area as early as 1904, but it was the discovery of coal around Nordegg and the coming of the railroad in 1910 that opened the area up for settlement. As you travel north to Rocky Mountain

Sawbuck – a pack saddle using wooden crossbars from which pack boxes are hung

House on the Cowboy Trail, you will notice a change in the landscape. You have entered the boreal forest region – the largest natural region in Alberta. Because most of the annual precipitation here falls as rain, trees such as white and black spruce, balsam fir, and lodgepole pine flourish. Winters are cold and long, and muskeg is common. When settlers first arrived, they faced the back-breaking work of clearing the land. It took dogged perseverance to survive and prosper. The abundance of trees meant the land didn't lend itself to ranching in the sense that it became known further south, but eventually settlers put down deep roots and established thriving mixed farms. There is little doubt you are still in cattle country; cowboy traditions are alive and well here.

Over the years, the area's rich natural resources have sustained a diverse economy based on agriculture, trapping, logging, coal, and oil and gas. More recently, the town has recognized the value of the pristine wilderness that lies just west. Here, visitors can pursue practically any outdoor activity imaginable in one of the most spectacular settings in the province.

Check out these Cowboy Trail partners located in town.

Buffalo Spirit Gifts

www.buffalospiritgifts.com

Bev Weber

4916 – 52 Avenue, Rocky Mountain House, AB, T4T 1G7

T: 1-877-507-3144

E: blweber@telusplanet.net

ACCEPTS D, V, MC, AMEX

Open Monday, noon to 6:00 PM, Tuesday to Saturday, 11:00 to 6:00 PM, or by appointment

WHAT THEY OFFER: Native, western, and wildlife art; sterling, turquoise, and copper jewellery; apparel; excellent selection of local artwork and native handcrafts, moccasins and mukluks, beadwork, antler work, Canadian Soapstone, leather work, ceramics, and much more.

In the Beginning Antiques and Collectibles

www.inthebeginningantiques.com

Dwayne Stuart and Rene Siegrist

5027 – 45 Street, Rocky Mountain House,, AB, T4T 1B2

T: 403-845-4594

E: bev@inthebeginningantiques.com

ACCEPTS D, V, MC, AMEX

Open Monday to Saturday, 10:00 AM to 5:00 PM; Sunday, noon to 5:00 PM, in July and August

WHAT THEY OFFER: A good selection of antique furniture, lamps, jewellery, glassware, clocks, primitives, and collectibles from all over North America.

Walking Eagle Inn and Lodge

 www.walkingeagle.net

Highway 11, P.O. Box 1317, 4915 – 45 Street
Rocky Mountain House, AB, T4T 1A9
Curtis Sagmeister

T: 1-866-845-2131
E: reservations@walkingeagle.net

WHAT THEY OFFER: The lodge has 34 air-conditioned rooms with fridges and microwaves; parlour, Jacuzzi suites; executive suites with fireplaces; family suites with living room and bedroom; free continental breakfast, high-speed internet, laundromat.

Walking Eagle Inn and Lodge.
CURTIS SAGMEISTER

The inn has 78 air-conditioned rooms with fridges; parlour, Jacuzzi and executive suites; free coffee, high-speed internet, access to steam room and hot tub; also an on-site liquor store. The lodge offers a number of one- and two-night packages, including canoeing, golf, quad, and ATV adventures, whitewater rafting, horseback riding, and hiking in the summer. Dog mushing, cross country skiing, snowmobiling and Christmas concert packages in the winter; the inn offers a Romantic Getaway package.

Other Points of Interest in Rocky Mountain House

Visitor Information Centre and Rocky Mountain House Museum

5406 – 48 Street (on Hwy. 11), Rocky Mountain House, AB, T4T 1B1
T: 1-800-565-3793
Open daily, 10:00 AM to 6:00 PM on weekends; 9:00 AM to 7:00 PM Monday to Friday from beginning of May to Labour Day weekend; 9:00 AM to 5:00 PM Monday to Friday remainder of year.

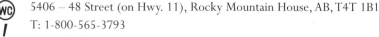

This is an award-winning information centre and it's easy to see why. Staff are extremely helpful and the selection of materials on the area is outstanding. The museum is located in the same building and is open year-round from Monday to Friday, with extended weekend hours from the May long weekend to the end of

August. There is a small admission charge, but it is worth a visit to see the excellent pioneer displays and to listen to the 1917 restored piano player – one of the staff will be happy to set up a tune for you. Gramma Gertie's Gift Gallery has a good selection of local souvenirs.

"Big Rock" is located on the town's walking trail.
PAT MCDONALD

Just north of the information centre, on the town's paved walking trail, is the "Big Rock." It is a glacial erratic deposited by a glacier many thousands of years ago. Both Alexander Henry and David Thompson mention the rock in their journals. It was a familiar marker for traders coming to the forts, which were only about two kilometres to the southwest. If you keep walking north, the town walking path system actually links up with trails that will take you all the way to Twin Lakes and Crimson Lake west of town. Pack a picnic and spend the day exploring some of the scenic spots close to town.

Grub Stop
A&W, 4504 – 47 Street, 403-845-5151; Boston Pizza, Hwy. 11 West Side, 403-846-2343; Burger Baron/Danny's 2for1 Pizza, 4840 – 45 Street, 403-845-6009; Co-op Cafeteria, Hwy. 11 East Side, 403-845-2841; Cosmopolitan Café, 4503 – 48 Avenue, 403-845-2600; Dairy Queen, 4747 – 45 Street, 403-845-2474; Grandma Bott's (seasonal), Hwy. 22 South, 403-845-6221; Grapevine Tea House, Hwy. 22 North, 403-845-5456; Kentucky Fried Chicken, 5139 – 49 Street, 403-845-3121; LaLa's Pizza, 4911 –

Snub — to tie an animal closely to a post so they can be worked on

51 Avenue, 403-845-2700; Martesa DiLume Ristorante Italiana, 4925 – 50 Street, 403-845-7197; McDonald's, 4828 – 45 Street, 403-845-2007; Merlin's Family Dining, 5203 – 50 Street, 403-845-7711; New Dragon Palace, Bighorn Plaza, 403-845-4300; Novel Ideas Coffee, 5033 – 50 Street, 403-844-2665; Panago Pizza, Hwy. 11 North, 403-310-0001; Pearl's, 5020 – 50 Street, 403-845-3120; Petro Canada (24 hrs), 4429 – 45 Street, 403-845-2002; Ritz Café, 4917 – 50 Street, 403-845-3088; Rocky Mountain Black Forest House, 4523B – 47 Avenue, 403-844-4100; Rocky Mountain Grill, Hwy. 11 East, 403-844-4430; Royal Canadian Legion, 4911 – 49 Street, 403-845-6948; Saddle Sore Saloon and Dining Lounge, 4914 – 49 Street, 403-845-5910; Smitty's Family Restaurant, 4520 – 45 Street, 403-844-4468; Subway, 5012 – 50 Street, 403-844-9442; Tamarack Motor Inn, 4904 – 45 Street, 403-845-5252; Terri's Luncheon, 5104B – 50 Avenue, 403-845-6638; The Black Stump Char Grill, Hwy. 11 Centre West, 403-844-8432; Tim Horton's (24 hrs), Hwy. 11 South, 403-845-6810.

It's a short seven-kilometre drive west of town on Hwy. 11A to the site of the old trading fort that eventually gave the town its name. (The route is well-signed.)

Rocky Mountain House National Historic Site of Canada

www.parkscanada.gc.ca/rockymountainhouse

Site 127, Comp 6, R.R. 4, Rocky Mountain House, AB, T4T 2A4
T: 403-845-2412

E: rocky.info@pc.gc.ca

ACCEPTS V, MC, AMEX   ADMISSION CHARGED

Open May long weekend to September long weekend 10:00 AM to 5:00 PM daily.

The history of Rocky Mountain House was in danger of crumbling into the dustbin of time when the local people asked the Historic Sites and Monuments Board of Canada to protect what remained of the old fort ruins. In 1980, the site became Alberta's first national historic park. There has been no attempt to reconstruct the past, only to preserve what remains as a reminder of a story that had its beginnings in 1799, when the North West Company built their fur-trading post here on the banks of the North Saskatchewan River. Over the years, there would be five fur-trade posts built at the site.

The play fort is a popular spot for the kids.
ROCKY MOUNTAIN HOUSE NATIONAL HISTORIC SITE

All that remains of the last fort, built in 1865, are remnants of two large chimneys that have been partially restored to keep them from further decay. Otherwise, the site closely resembles what it would have looked like to someone who happened to stumble upon the ruins in the early part of the 1900s. From the visitor centre, you can follow two different trails along the banks of the river. The short 0.9 kilometre walk takes you to the chimneys at the last fort site, with interpretive stops along the way at a Red River Cart, a York boat, and a fur press. A longer (3.2 kilometre) walk leads to the site of the first two competing forts built at Rocky Mountain House in 1799. Next to the original Acton House site is a display on the 1967 Centennial Voyageur Pageant and the Alberta team canoe. A portion of this trail winds along the river bank, where interpretive signs highlight local plants such as saskatoons, wolf willow, and Alberta rose bushes. Picnic tables, a walk-in tenting area, and a canoe launch are located at the end of the trail. A bison paddock is home to 15 to 30 bison. If you are lucky, you might get a good look at them from the viewing platform located close to the Acton House site.

Children will love the half-sized play fort and puppet theatre that runs weekends from mid-May to June at 2:00 PM and Wednesday to Sunday at 2:00 PM in July and August. The show commemorates the life of David Thompson, the famous cartographer and surveyor who spent time at Rocky Mountain House during his explorations of the west. The visitor centre runs films on Thompson, the voyageurs, and the famous artist Paul Kane, who visited during 1848 and painted portraits of two Assiniboine chiefs who were camped nearby. The interpretive exhibit at the centre is also well worth a visit. It offers an outstanding display of Native artifacts, as well as a replica of the trading room at the fort, complete with animal pelts and a collection of trade goods that would have been exchanged with the natives for their furs. The Trading Post store, located in the centre, carries an excellent selection of books and native crafts.

GETTING THERE: Head west from town on Hwy. 11A for 7 KM. The route is well-signed.

DID THE BEAVER REALLY OPEN THE WEST?

It has been said that the beaver "was responsible for unrolling the map of Canada." It's quite a claim. It's also quite true. The relentless quest for the lustrous pelts drew trappers and traders across an entire continent and helped give birth to a nation in the process. It was one of the main reasons the Nor' Westers and the Hudson's Bay Company established their trading posts across the west, including Rocky Mountain House. They were feeding a European fashion market that demanded high quality fur for beaver hats – it was a mania that lasted almost as long as the beaver itself. Long before it was demoted to the "tail" side of the nickel coin, the beaver pelt was quite literally a form of money. Prime beaver skins were the standard of currency, not cash. One quality skin from an adult beaver was called a "Made-beaver" and it became the standard unit of barter for over 150 years.

Another Cowboy Trail partner is located just a short drive southwest of town.

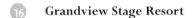

Grandview Stage Resort www.grandviewstage.com
Del and Lesley Ramage
Box 38, Site 3, R.R. 2
Rocky Mountain House, AB, T4T 2A2
T: 403-845-6404
E: gvstage@telus.net
ACCEPTS V, MC
Open all year

WHAT THEY OFFER: New 3½ Star Canada Select cabins with full bath, TV/VCR, covered porches; some with fireplace and/or kitchenette; RV sites with full hook-up. A well-stocked general store, liquor store, and gas bar; gift gallery has wide selection of arts and crafts and in-store ice cream parlour; restaurant offers home cooking at a reasonable price and is a popular spot for the locals (always a good sign); new "Hole in the Wall" addition to restaurant offers views of the mountains and deck with firepit; Country and Bluegrass Jam Night last Saturday of each month with dinner. Hike Grandview Trail to nearby Cow Lake for swimming, fishing, and annual Bluegrass Festival each June; access to nearby canoeing, fishing, hiking, biking, horseback riding, and skiing.

GETTING THERE: From Rocky Mountain House, take Secondary Hwy. 752 southwest for 12 KM. Grandview Stage is on the right side of the road just before Cow Lake.

OFF THE BEATEN TRACK FROM ROCKY MOUNTAIN HOUSE

West Country Access – Secondary Hwy. 752 provides an alternate access route to the wilderness areas west of town, including the Prairie Creek, Elk Creek, and Ram Falls Recreation Areas. The road, which becomes gravel, connects to the (gravel) Forestry Trunk Road, Secondary Hwy. 734, offering almost unlimited options in canoeing, fishing, hiking, mountain biking, quadding, and snowmobiling. Area maps are available at the Grandview Stage Resort store, and the Information Centre has excellent detailed trail summaries for hikes, bikes, quads, and horses. Locals recommend a picnic at the scenic Ram River Falls on Secondary Hwy. 734.

Ram River Falls west of Rocky Mountain House
KRIS NIELSON

From Rocky Mountain House, the David Thompson Highway (Hwy. 11) heads west to Nordegg. The road, which was officially opened in August 1975, winds through some of the most spectacular scenery in the province, eventually connecting with Hwy. 93, and the Banff/Jasper corridor. The highway was named after the famous explorer David Thompson, who actually followed this route on a trip he took in 1807, when he crossed the Great Divide at Howse Pass, but the route was well used by First Nations people long before the coming of the white man. Even if you're not stopping at one of the

Cowboy Trail partners along the way, try to plan a day trip to enjoy the scenery. Stop for a hike and pack a picnic. Locals recommend the Shunda Viewpoint (60 kilometres from Rocky) or Crescent Falls (20 kilometres west of Nordegg), but there are an incredible number of options to choose from. Be sure to stop at the Information Centre before you head out. They have an excellent collection of handouts and maps with detailed descriptions of the trails and stops along the way. There are also two Cowboy Trail partners located on your way to Nordegg.

DAVID THOMPSON DIED IN OBSCURITY

In his 28 years in the fur trade, Thompson travelled an estimated 88,000 kilometres. In the process, he filled in what had been an empty map of Western Canada. His map covered an area of 3.9 million square kilometres. It was so accurate that parts of it were still in use into the twentieth century. Despite his legacy, he died destitute and in virtual obscurity near Montreal in 1857.

Voyageur and Klondike Ventures   www.voyageurventures.ca
Jill Bennett and Jeff Wilson
P.O. Box 278, Rocky Mountain House, AB, T4T 1A2
T: 1-877-846-7878
E: info@voyageurventures.ca
ACCEPTS V, MC
Open all year

WHAT THEY OFFER: All-season cabin rental west of Rocky has wood stove, full kitchen (no running water); camping available. As well, half- and full-day options combine exploration of the North Saskatchewan River by canoe with a walk at the Rocky Mountain House National Historic Site; both include full hot lunch plus breakfast with full-day option. Overnight stays include extended river travel, candlelight dinners, sauna, and accommodations in double-tarped tents at private river camp; customized vacations offer multi-day canoeing, hiking, and rock climbing in wilderness areas around Nordegg. And winter options include one-day or weekend cross-country skiing or Skijoring (Husky dogs help pull you on your skis); multi-day trips can add dog sledding, backcountry travel, snowshoeing, or ice climbing; meals, lodging, and transportation included.

GETTING THERE: Trips begin and end in Rocky Mountain House.

Camp 'n' Fun Adventures   www.travelnordegg.com/campnfun

Christie Clark

Site 147, Comp 2, R.R. 4, Rocky Mountain House, AB, T4T 2A4

T: 403-721-3975

E: camping@telus.net

ACCEPTS PC

Open May 1 to Canadian Thanksgiving in October

> WHAT THEY OFFER: Five group (require reservations) and 12 public campgrounds (use self-registration); accessible via Hwy. 11 west of Rocky Mountain House or Hwy. 734 west of Nordegg. Firewood included in the fee at most campgrounds. The group camps are at Chambers Creek, Jackfish Lake North Shore, North Ram River, Shunda Viewpoint, and Snow Creek. Public campgrounds include Aylmer, Beaverdam, Chambers Creek, Crescent Falls, Dry Haven, Fish Lake, Goldeye Lake, Harlech, Horburg, Jackfish Lake South Shore, North Ram River, and Saunders. Check the website for specific directions and details.

As you drive west on Hwy. 11, you will pass the access road to the hamlet of Nordegg. The Stoney name is *watanozah*, meaning "where we saw loons." The town is named after its German founder, Martin Nordegg, who actually changed his name from Cohn to Nordegg in 1909. He had come to Canada in 1906 and began investigating potential coal fields on behalf of the German Development Company. In 1909 he joined forces with William Mackenzie and Donald Mann of the Canadian Northern Railway to form Brazeau Collieries Ltd. They wanted to develop a number of coal leases that Nordegg had staked out along the eastern slopes of the Rockies, extending from Grand Cache to Kananaskis. Initially, the South Brazeau field was selected for development, but when coal was found at the Nordegg site, it was chosen since its accessibility for a railway line would save millions in construction costs. By the time the line arrived, Nordegg had almost 100,000 tons ready for shipment.

Nordegg designed a model town that eventually became one of the most modern mining towns in

DID YOU KNOW?

When the North West Company established their fort at Rocky Mountain House in 1799, they hoped to establish trade with the Kootenays but hostilities between them and the Peigans had pushed the Kootenays west across the mountains. Since they couldn't come to the fort, it became Thompson's job to find a route for the traders to go to the Kootenays. During his explorations of the area, Thompson actually made two trips in 1800, the first to the Red Deer River and the second to the Bow River, in which he criss-crossed the present-day route of the Cowboy Trail from Rocky to Cochrane. The path he travelled in 1807 would eventually become the basis for the David Thompson Highway.

North America. It boasted 300 homes, churches, a hotel, and a number of stores and services. It even had a library, curling rink, golf course, and the largest, most modern hospital outside of Edmonton and Calgary. With the outbreak of World War I, Nordegg was asked to leave the country, but the company continued operations because it had Canadian investors. Although it became a major producer of coal and coal briquettes, oil eventually became the preferred fuel, and the Collieries and the town shut down in 1955. From 1963 to 1994, a minimum-security prison operated in Nordegg, but the original townsite is now a ghost town that you can tour on foot or by car — a free guide is available at the Nordegg Heritage Centre. The hamlet of 70 now serves as a stopping-off point for travellers driving the scenic David Thompson Highway, and is the home of two Cowboy Trail partners.

Nordegg Resort Lodge   www.nordegglodge.com

Jim Nelson

 Main Street, Box 36, Nordegg, AB, T0M 2H0

T: 403-721-3757

 E: nrl@telusplanet.net

ACCEPTS V, MC, AMEX

Open all year

WHAT THEY OFFER: 38-unit motel offers single, double, and triple bed units and kitchenettes; a three-bedroom modular home complete with full kitchen, Jacuzzi, and stone fireplace is ideal for families. Restaurant serves breakfast, lunch, and dinner. Dining room features large collection of archival photos. The store sells gas, food, snacks, fishing supplies, and licenses; on-site laundry, games room, and mini-golf course; Ice Cream Hut open in summer.

Shintangle — a bush growing in clumps

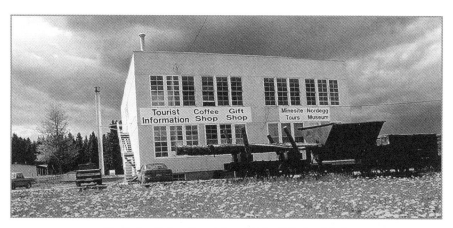

The Nordegg Heritage Centre is located in the old Nordegg School.
NORDEGG HISTORICAL SOCIETY

Nordegg Heritage Centre and Brazeau Collieries Industrial Museum

www.nordegghistoricalsociety.8m.com
Operated by the Nordegg Historical Society
Main Street, Nordegg
T: 403-721-COAL (2625)
ACCEPTS TC

Open from mid-May to early October from 9:00 AM to 5:00 PM daily; special group tours by appointment.

WHAT THEY OFFER: Tours of the Brazeau Collieries Industrial Minesite, designated as an Alberta Historic Resource in 1993 and a National Historic Site of Canada in 2002. The Technical Tour takes visitors to the mine portals (but not underground) and through the briquette processing plant buildings; the Overview Tour follows the same route but does not include the processing buildings; both include commentary on the history of the industry and community.

The centre is located in the old Nordegg School and houses a museum (by donation), tourist information centre, Coliseum Gift Shop, and Coalminer's Café. The museum has a good collection of photos and information about the lively history of Nordegg when it was a thriving mining town in the early 1900s. The café provides full service to tourists and locals from 8:00 AM to 8:00 PM, with a buffet from noon to 3:00 PM every Sunday. A Ghost Town Trails walking or driving tour guide is also available free of charge.

From Nordegg you can continue your journey west, where there are several Cowboy Trail partners and plenty more magnificent scenery.

Cheechako Cabins

www.cheechakocabins.com

Bonnie and Lowell Summers
P.O. Box 47, Nordegg, AB, T0M 2H0
T: 403-721-2230
E: info@cheechakocabins.com
ACCEPTS V, MC
Open all year

When the Summers came to the area back in 1997, they were newcomers, so they chose the native word *cheechako* meaning "tenderfoot" for their new business. The cabins have been built to reflect Nordegg's historical mining background, using an architectural style reminiscent of the early miners' cabins.

The cabins reflect architechture from the early mining days.
CHEECHAKO CABINS

WHAT THEY OFFER: Four self-contained cabins with bathrooms, fully equipped kitchens, private decks, barbecues, wood stoves, and satellite TV. The Chickadee sleeps four, the two-bedroom Owl sleeps six, and the Raven sleeps four, while the more secluded Rosy Finch is ideal for a romantic getaway. Guests have access to an outdoor common area with a large firepit and picnic tables. Good spot for bird and wildlife watching from your deck.

GETTING THERE: From Rocky Mountain House, take Hwy. 11 west towards Nordegg. Just past the Nordegg turnoff, turn right (north) at the sign and go 1.9 kilometres, then turn left (west). The cabins are on the left side of the road.

Chungo Creek Outfitters

www.chungocreekoutfitters.com

Diane and Greg Kristoff
P.O. Box 32, Nordegg, AB, T0M 2H0
T: 780-786-4790 or 403-844-3368
E: krisfarm@telusplanet.net
ACCEPTS MC, PC
Open all year

WHAT THEY OFFER: All-season rental of rustic cabins with beds, cooking facilities, and coal oil lamps (no power or running water). From June to August, hourly and full-day horseback riding excursions (with cowboy lunch and barbecue) can be extended to six-, 12-, and 14-day trips into the wilderness using tent camp with foam mattresses, cots, wood stoves, and showers. Custom trips can be tailored to groups, couples, and singles; the area boasts some of the finest backcountry stream and lake fishing in North America. Also available are customized hunting trips, which run September to end of November from tent camps or cabins using horses, ATVs, or on foot.

GETTING THERE: From Nordegg, head west on Hwy. 11 for 2 KM to the Forestry Trunk Road, Secondary Hwy. 734. Turn right (north) and go 10 KM to Chungo Road, then turn left (west) and go 15 KM.

56 **Wild Horse Mountain Outfitters**   www.wildhorsecamp.com
Bear and Diane Baker
P.O. Box 45, Nordegg, AB, T0M 2H0
T: 403-990-5576 or 780-720-0607
E: info@wildhorsecamp.com
ACCEPTS PC, TC, MO IN ADVANCE
Open year round

WHAT THEY OFFER: The retreat centre is focused on healing, wellness, and renewal; facilities include multi-purpose hall, kitchen, and dining hall, rustic cabins, eight authentic tipis, wall tents, dome tents, and rustic showers and outhouses; ideal for reunions, getaways, and gatherings. Activities include hourly riding, plus breakfast, lunch, or steak supper rides; hiking, fishing, mountain biking, horseshoes, volleyball, snowshoeing, and cross-country skiing; a riding weekend offers lots of time in the saddle with meals and accommodations; also riding weekends for families, vison quest hikes, Reiki, reality

Hear the silence.
WILD HORSE MOUNTAIN OUTFITTERS

counseling, healing retreats, and Sweat Lodge Experience, with options for a weekender to a one-month stay.

GETTING THERE: From Nordegg, drive 18 KM west on Hwy. 11. Turn right (north) at the sign just before the Bighorn Store and go 0.5 KM.

Aurum Lodge and Cottages   www.aurumlodge.com

Alan and Madeleine Ernst
P.O. Box 76, Nordegg, AB, T0M 2H0
T: 403-721-2117
E: info@aurumlodge.com
ACCEPTS V, MC, TC, MO
Open all year; minimum stays may apply depending on the season.
German and French spoken.

Alan and Madeleine Ernst opened the lodge in 2000 with the objective of becoming an environmentally sound operation. The name *Aurum* is derived from the Latin word for "gold." It reflects their philosophy that "there are values in life which cannot be measured in monetary terms but are equally precious; among them are a healthy, unpolluted, and intact environment and peace of mind!" The lodge practices what it preaches. It is the only property that currently holds the Five Green Leaf Eco-rating by the Hotel Association of Canada.

The Aurum Lodge boasts a Five-Green-Leaf Eco-rating.
AURUM LODGE

WHAT THEY OFFER: Six different rooms in the lodge with private baths and a choice of B&B or half-board; three self-contained units, including a two-bedroom apartment and two cottages with full kitchens, private baths, wood stoves, and a patio. The facility is geared to adults, but children can be accommodated in the apartment and one of the cottages. Packages can include just accommodation and meals, or add in some guided activities; can be customized to suit your needs; fall and winter photography trips often feature well-known Canadian photographer.

GETTING THERE: From Nordegg, take Hwy. 11 west for 44 KM. Turn left at the sign and drive 0.5 KM to the lodge.

HOME OF THE SASQUATCH?

On August 23, 1969, five workers at the site of the Bighorn Dam reported seeing a giant "creature" that fit the general description of a Sasquatch (often called a Bigfoot in the US) – standing between 2.5 to 3.5 metres tall, with an apelike head, short, thick neck and wide shoulders. Once they reported the sighting several other people came forward with similar stories; fear of ridicule had kept them quiet. You can take the Sasquatch Track along the ridge. The trail is located at the Bighorn Damsite Information Centre, 5.6 kilometres south of Hwy. 11, 23 kilometres west of Nordegg.

Icefield Helicopter Tours   www.icefieldhelicoptertours.com

Ralph and Susan Sliger

Box 146, Lake Louise, AB, T0L 1E0

T: 1-888-844-3514 (Toll-free in Canada and the US)

E: info@icefieldheli.com

ACCEPTS D, V, MC, TC

Open April 1 to October 31, seven days a week, 8:00 AM to 8:00 PM. French spoken.

WHAT THEY OFFER: Family-oriented tours good for any age, from small children "all the way up to granny." Their location on the Kootenay Plains (with one of the lowest amounts of annual precipitation in the Rockies) means visitors have a better chance of good weather; tours include Cline Glacier, Wilson Icefield, and the Columbia Icefield; extraordinary add-ons include a one-hour stop at an alpine lake, meadow, or ridgeline with the pilot as guide, and can be added to any of the tours; gourmet picnics can be arranged or bring your own; guided and unguided fishing adventures, full-day heli-hiking, heli-caving, and heli-skiing options available.

GETTING THERE: Head west on Hwy. 11 from Nordegg for 45 KM to the Cline River Road. The entrance is well-signed.

Recommended Reading

Martin Nordegg: An Uncommon Immigrant by John Koch
Rocky Mountain House National Historic Park by Fred Stenson
Small Moments in Time: The Story of Alberta's Big West Country by Anne (McMullen) Belliveau
The David Thompson Highway: A Hiking Guide by Jane Ross and Daniel Kyba
The Trade by Fred Stenson
To the Town That Bears Your Name by Martin Nordegg
Where the River Brought Them by Pat McDonald

WHAT'S IN A NAME?

Both Abraham Lake and Abraham Flats (located along the David Thompson Highway) are named after Stoney Indian Silas Abraham and his family, who had lived along the valley since the nineteenth century. The lake was formed in 1972 with the construction of the Bighorn Dam. In the process, it buried several features associated with the family, including Abraham Flats at the mouth of the Cline River. Abraham had helped a number of famous non-Natives during their travels in the region including Tom Wilson, Elliott Barnes, and Martin Nordegg (see page 219).

DID YOU KNOW?

Tom Wilson was a former North West Mounted Police constable and a well-known guide and outfitter in the Banff area. He is credited with "discovering" Lake Louise. For eight years, beginning in 1902, he operated a ranch on the Whiterabbit Creek in the Kootenay Plains; it was called the Kootenay Plains Ranch or the Powderhorn Ranch. Wilson wintered his horses on the Plains and traded with the local Stoney Indians. In the summer, he worked the tourist trade in Banff.

Tom Wilson's trading post on the Kootenay Plains ca. 1903–11.
GLENBOW ARCHIVES NA-696-1

WHAT'S A BUZZARD-WING ANYWAYS?

The word "chaps" (pronounced shaps) is an Americanized short-form of the Spanish *chaparejos* meaning leather breeches or overalls – it seems the Spanish word proved to be too much of a mouthful for the American cowboy. Chaps are worn to protect a cowboy working with cattle in heavy bush or riding a horse that likes to push him up against a fence or another horse.

Over the years, they have been adapted to suit the needs of the particular area and job at hand. Mexican cowboys used a shortened version that extended just below the knee and were cooler to wear. They were called *chigaderos*, which became anglicized to "chinks." In the northern climates, heavier chaps made of bull hide, bearskin ("grizzles" had the hair left on), or angora goatskin were warmer when rounding up strays in a snowstorm. Bat-wings (the chaps resemble bat wings when they are laid flat) or buzzard-wings became popular in the late 1800s. They snapped on and did not require the cowboy to pull off his spurs every time he shed them. Because, despite what we see in the movies, a real cowboy doesn't wear his chaps to town. They're too hot and they're too hard to walk in.

WINDY PLAINS

The Kootenay Plains are the warmest, driest region in the Rocky Mountains and one of the largest intact montane regions in Alberta. Frequent chinooks (see sidebar page 31) keep the area relatively snow-free in the winter, making it a mecca for wildlife, birds, and plants not commonly found in other areas of the province. The Kootenays hunted the abundant wildlife here but were forced out by the warring Peigans and replaced by the Mountain Cree and Stoney. The Stoney name, *Kadoona Tinda*, means "windy plains," for the prevailing west wind.

The Kootenay Plains 1908.
GLENBOW ARCHIVES NA-1263-24

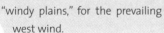

Tapaderos – a leather covering over a stirrup for protecting the rider's feet

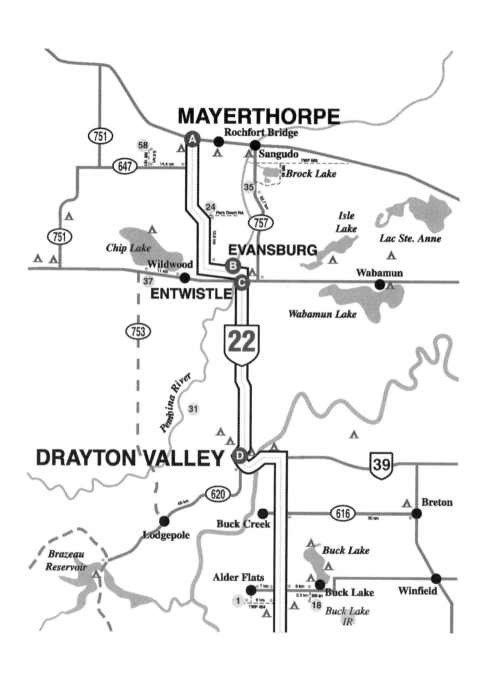

9 : NORTH OF ROCKY MOUNTAIN HOUSE TO DRAYTON VALLEY AND MAYERTHORPE

"Big talk ain't worth much on a bull ride."

—Ted Stone, *Cowboy Logic*

Communities

(D) Drayton Valley

(C) Entwistle

(B) Evansburg

(A) Mayerthorpe

Accommodations

(18) Kramer Pond Lodge

(1) Em-Te-Town

(D) Super 8 Motel Drayton Valley

(37) Lone Pine Ranch Bed and
    Breakfast and Bale

(24) Rustic Ridge Ranch and Lodge

Attractions & Events

(1) Em-Te-Town

Farm & Ranch Vacations

(31) Bent River Ranch Adventures

(35) Lakeview Guest Ranch

Outfitters

(58) Hog Wild Specialties

Bring Your Own Horse

(18) Kramer Pond Lodge

(1) Em-Te-Town

(37) Lone Pine Ranch Bed and
    Breakfast and Bale

(24) Rustic Ridge Ranch and Lodge

(35) Lakeview Guest Ranch

Camping

(1) Em-Te-Town

(37) Lone Pine Ranch Bed and
    Breakfast and Bale

Restaurant

(1) Em-Te-Town

(D) Super 8 Motel Drayton
    Valley/River Rock Grill
    Restaurant and Lounge

Shopping, Antiques & Artisans

(1) Em-Te-Town

MAJOR EVENTS ALONG THE TRAIL

(check www.thecowboytrail.com for a complete listing)

May
Drayton Valley Rodeo, Drayton Valley
Wild Rose Rodeo, Mayerthorpe

June
Bronc Bustin', Wildwood
Bull Bash and Fair, Drayton Valley
Guns of the Golden West Western Show and Gun Draw, Em-Te-Town
Horse and Livestock Show, Drayton Valley
Rangeton Festival, Mayerthorpe/Evansburg
World Class Horse Show, Drayton Valley

July
Entwistle Rodeo, Entwistle

August
Mayerthorpe Agricultural Fair, Mayerthorpe
Pembina Valley Daze, Entwistle/Evansburg
Wildwood Agricultural Fair, Wildwood

Yahoo — a coarse, brutish or uncivilized person

9: NORTH OF ROCKY MOUNTAIN HOUSE TO DRAYTON VALLEY AND MAYERTHORPE

As you travel north from Rocky Mountain House towards Drayton Valley, the history of the area is actually unfolding along the road as you pass through heavily forested areas that open up into rolling cropland and pastures dotted with cattle, elk, and bison. The first settlers in the area arrived in the early 1900s. They were lumbermen attracted by the large trees and the presence of the North Saskatchewan River, which was used to float logs downriver to sawmills at Edmonton. By the 1940s the cleared timber areas brought the next wave of settlers, who established the mixed farms you see along the highway. Finally, the presence of bobbing pumpjacks signals the next chapter in the area's history. In June 1953, the sleepy little community of Drayton Valley was catapulted onto the world stage with the discovery of the giant Pembina oil field right on its doorstep. The field is Canada's most productive and one of the largest in the world. Although oil and gas remains the dominant industry in the area, forestry and agriculture continue to thrive. The area boasts some of the best forage and pasture producing land in the province, and is home to a number of well-known purebred livestock breeders.

There are two Cowboy Trail partners located south of Drayton Valley, close to Hwy. 13.

WHAT DO CAN OPENERS AND RIB WRENCHES HAVE IN COMMON?

Can openers, rib wrenches, hooks, diggers, hell rousers, petmakers – they're all just cowboy slang for a pair of spurs. A cowboy uses his spurs to control his horse, never to punish, and when used by a competent rider, they will require only a slight nudge to get the desired result. Most cowboys will file the points of the rowels (the rotating parts of the spur) until they are blunt in order to avoid injuring their horse. As Will James explained in *All in a Day's Riding*, cowboys did not buy big spurs out of vanity, but "because the big one is less cruel. The bigger the rowel and the more points it has, the less damage it does. It is the little spur with few points that sinks in."

Many cowboys attached jinglebobs or danglers to their spurs to make a pleasing noise out on the range and to relieve some of the loneliness. But they made a bit of noise in town too. In 1881 journalist W.H. Williams walked into a Fort Macleod restaurant full of cowboys. He noted, "Nearly all wore heavy Mexican spurs, which clanked and jingled as they walked about in a manner that would have made a blind man think he was in the company of a lot of convicts in transit." These days the jangling of a cowboy's spurs probably has much more to do with the attention it attracts than with lonely nights spent out on the range.

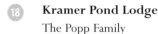

Kramer Pond Lodge

www.kramerpondlodge.com

The Popp Family

P.O. Box 521, Buck Lake, AB, T0C 0T0

T: 780-388-2209

E: kpond@telusplanet.net

ACCEPTS PC (BOOKINGS ARE USUALLY PREPAID)

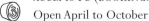

Open April to October

WHAT THEY OFFER: There are three rustic lodges, equipped with modern conveniences and fully self-contained, with private kitchens, washrooms, and outdoor hot tubs. The Pine Lodge features a cathedral ceiling, two bedrooms, fireplace, and piano. The Creek Cottage has four bedrooms, fireplace, piano, and glass-enclosed addition with seating capacity for 50 people. The Cedars contains four two-bedroom units with fridges, microwaves, washrooms, and cookware. An all-seasons gazebo with a fully equipped kitchen and table setting for 20 or more adjoins these units; ideal for family or corporate getaways. As well, there is canoeing and fishing on the pond, with a wide variety of bird life. Llama treks can be arranged; horseback riding, hiking close by; corral available if you bring your own horse.

GETTING THERE: From Hwy. 22, head east on Hwy. 13 for 8 KM to Balsam Road (RR61). Turn right (south) and drive 2.3 KM. Look for the sign on the left (east) side of the road.

Em-Te-Town

www.emtetown.com

Ed and Jackie Buziak

P.O. Box 103, Alder Flats, AB, T0C 0A0

T: 780-388-2166

E: emte@emtetown.com

ACCEPTS V, MC

Open all year

The logo reads, "We are the Old West," and it isn't too far from the truth. The town is an authentic recreation of the old west, complete with saloon, jailhouse, sheriff's office, livery stable, church, granary, tack shed, morgue, and two-storey outhouse (to name a few). Located in a large meadow on the banks of Rose Creek, the town was the brainchild of Len Mohr, a retired building contractor from Spruce Grove. The Melin family opened the gates to the public in July 1989 after they purchased the property from Mohr earlier that year. Both the church and the school were built with a community "raising," where 60 or 70 of the locals showed up with their hammers, handsaws, and log peelers and were rewarded for their efforts with food, drink, and a dance in the evening. The country church has hosted over 80 weddings since it was built.

WHAT THEY OFFER: Two 15-foot tipis with cots; camping facilities; cabins complete with bedding, towels, and cookware; and a modern eight-unit motel equipped with private bathrooms and TV. Activities include hourly or day trail rides with lunch, a steak supper ride, fishing, hunting, golf, skiing, and snowmobiling. Annual events feature the Guns of the Golden West live western show and gun draw contest in June, a Halloween party in October, a Thanksgiving supper, and a Ukrainian New Year's party. Meals are available in the saloon year-round; caters to weddings and family or corporate functions.

GETTING THERE: From Hwy. 22, take TWP 454 west (there is a big sign on the west side of the road) for 9 KM to the end of the road.

The town is an authentic recreation of the Old West.
EM-TE-TOWN

Drayton Valley   www.brazeautourism.ca

T: 780-542-7529 or 1-800-633-0899

The town was originally called Power House (for a proposed hydro project that was abandoned at the start of World War I). When Bill and Dora Drake opened up the post office in 1915, Mrs. Drake decided to name it after her hometown in England. There is one Cowboy Trail partner located in town.

Derricks at the entrance to Drayton Valley symbolize a major industry in the area.
TOWN OF DRAYTON VALLEY

Super 8 Motel Drayton Valley / River Rock Grill Restaurant and Lounge

www.super8draytonvalley.com

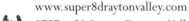

3727 – 50 Street, Drayton Valley, AB, T7A 1S4

T: 780-542-9122 or 1-888-561-7666

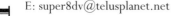

E: super8dv@telusplanet.net

ACCEPTS ALL MAJOR CREDIT CARDS

Open all year

> WHAT THEY OFFER: 60 newly renovated rooms, from standard to Jacuzzi suites (handicapped and non-smoking rooms available), free parking, 24-hour coffee, high-speed Internet, free local telephone calls, in-room mini-fridges, free con-

tinental breakfast, laundromat, treadmill, and a hot tub. The nearby five-kilometre walkway system features winding paths and a pond. The River Rock Grill Restaurant and Lounge is open daily, 8:30 AM to 11:00 PM.

Other Points of Interest in Drayton Valley

Drayton Valley Tourist Information Centre   www.brazeautourism.ca
6009 – 44 Street
T: 780-542-7529 or 1-800-633-0899
E: info@brazeautourism.ca
Open daily May long weekend to September long weekend, 10:00 AM to 6:00 PM; Monday to Friday 10:00 AM to 3:00 PM the rest of the year.

> The information centre is located in the Rocky Rapids General Store Museum at the Drayton Valley Historical Society site near the Omniplex. Guided tours of the Store Museum and the old Anglican Church are available every Wednesday and Saturday from 1:00 PM to 4:00 PM year-round.

Grub Stop

A&W Restaurant, 5821 – 50 Avenue, 780-542-4333; B&W Dairy King Drive-in, 5216 – 50 Avenue, 780-542-4231; Bad Ass Jacks, 5505 – 50 Street, 780-514-2732; Best Western Black Gold Inn, 4320 – 50 Street, 780-542-3200; Boston Pizza, 5645 – 50 Street, 780-514-5000; Burger Baron Drive-in, 5303 – 50 Avenue, 780-542-4565; Cake and Coffee House, #9, 5150 – 50 Street, 780-542-7040; Caesar's Restaurant, 5208 Industrial Road, 780-542-4255; Dairy Queen Grill and Chill, 5501 – 50 Street, 780-514-5800; Drayton's Restaurant, 5119 – 51 Avenue, 780-542-2286; Drayton Valley Bakery & Café, 5029 – 51 Avenue, 780-542-5940; Goldie's Chicken Plus Pizza and Pasta, 4912 – 50 Avenue, 780-542-2272; Kentucky Fried Chicken, 5716 – 50 Avenue, 780-542-3302; Mae's Garden, 4905 – 50 Street, 780-542-7879; McDonald's, 7901 – 50 Avenue, 780-621-1522; Panago Pizza, #10, 5105 – 50 Street, 780-310-0001; Pembina Perk, 5147 – 50 Avenue, 780-514-7375; Rusty's, 5403 – 59 Street, 780-542-4451; Skyro's Restaurant and Pizzeria, #2, 4341 – 50 Street, 780-542-7525; Sub Station, 5048 – 50 Avenue, 780-542-5090; Subway, 5817 – 50 Avenue, 780-542-3949; The Gallery Coffee House, 5137 – 51 Avenue, 780-621-1440; Three Knights Steak and Pizza House, 5211 – 50 Street, 780-542-5222; Twin Dragon Dining Lounge, 5112 – 52 Avenue, 780-542-3737; Westwinds Restaurant, 4225 – 50 Street, 780-542-5375; White Bull Restaurant, 5140 – 51 Street, 780-542-5695.

Wrangler – a cowboy or a person who herds cattle on the range

Evansburg
Entwistle

www.ev-entchamber.ab.ca

Evansburg and Entwistle are both located on the Pembina River, just a stone's throw apart. They share the Pembina River Provincial Park, where visitors can camp, swim, fish, and enjoy a large variety of birds and animals that call the area home. Many of the walking trails provide excellent views of the valley, which was once the site of a thriving coal industry and a stone quarry.

Entwistle started as a railway town. It is named after James Entwistle, who built a general store in 1908 in anticipation of the boom from railway construction and homesteaders coming to the area. His wife, Mary, secretly submitted his name after two other suggestions had been rejected due to duplication. She was confident the name was unusual enough that it had not been used anywhere in Canada, and she was right. Entwistle became a thriving business centre, described in the *Alberta Homestead* newspaper as a place with "the most progressive class of people in the Province," boasting a long list of businesses and services. A 1909 issue of the *Edmonton Journal* gave a different perspective, calling it the "toughest town on the northwestern frontier," harbouring a number of houses of ill repute, gambling joints, and moonshine stills. Growth was fuelled by the opening of coal mines in nearby Evansburg, named after Harry Evans, who found rich coal deposits in the area in 1907. Once the railroad builders left and coal was no longer a viable industry, the communities gradually declined. Both have recently reverted to hamlet status.

Point of Interest in Evansburg

Evansburg Tourist Information Centre
Located in the old train station on Hwy. 16A
Open daily, July 1 to August 31, noon to 7:00 PM

Grub Stop in Entwistle

Journeyman Restaurant, 5011 – 47 Avenue , 780-727-4000; Lighthouse Restaurant, 503 – 47 Avenue, 780-727-4014; Riverside Diner, Hwy. 16, 780-727-3630

Grub Stop in Evansburg

Coffee Rose, 5115 – 50 Street, 780-727-4600; Evansburg Bakery, 4918 – 49 Street, 780-727-4636; Evansburg Deli, 49 Street and 50 Avenue, 780-727-6633; Jack and Judy's Restaurant, 50 Street, 780-727-3909; Royal Canadian Legion, 4823 – 50 Street, 780-727-3879; Ruby's Café , 5112 – 50 Street, 780-727-3787.

#10 FROWNING STREET, OFFICIAL RESIDENCE OF TOWN GROUCH

Evansburg has a Grouch of the Year Award. The grouch is responsible for maintaining the image of a grumpy coal miner, reminiscent of the town's mining history. Look for "grouch zones" around town, complete with "beware of grouch" signs. Each year's new winner gets a sign for his or her lawn, with an official address of #10 Frowning Street, and is presented with a license to "criticize, complain, harass, grumble, and antagonize."

CRITTER WATCH: MOOSE

This Canadian icon almost looks like it is still in the process of evolving – with its long legs, short neck, long ears, and distinctive bulbous nose, it doesn't seem quite "finished." Moose are actually superbly adapted to their habitat. Their long legs allow them to wade in boggy marshes and feed on aquatic vegetation in the summer. In the winter, that extra length helps them walk through deep snow, step over fallen timber, and browse the needles from trees. They can actually navigate through metre-deep snow quite easily by lifting their legs straight up and down with minimal snowdrag. The short neck allows them to nip off the twigs that are a big part of their winter food source, while the big nose and lips are used to hold the twigs in place to allow them to be ripped off by the lower incisors. The long ears help them detect noises when they are feeding in shallow water. Waterton Lakes National Park and Kananaskis country offer some of the best

The Canadian moose is superbly adapted to its habitat.
JANET NASH

moose viewing, but you have a good chance of spotting one on any backroad in the boreal forest on the northern section of the Cowboy Trail. Keep that in mind when you are driving, especially at night. Because of their long legs, they are just the right height to come through your windshield, which is precisely why many moose collisions are fatal encounters for both sides.

Further west on Hwy. 16, you will also find another Cowboy Trail partner.

Lone Pine Ranch Bed and Breakfast and Bale   www.lonepineranch.ca

Sylvia Martinetz

P.O. Box 88, Wildwood, AB, T0E 2M0

T: 780-325-3817

E: lprsylva@telusplanet.net

ACCEPTS TC

Open all year. German spoken.

Two of the ranch's residents.
LONE PINE RANCH

Sylvia runs cattle and sheep on her 139-acre ranch west of Wildwood. Families and groups are welcome, as well as cowboys (and cowgirls too) with their horses.

WHAT THEY OFFER: Six spacious log cabins (one is wheelchair accessible), each equipped with two queen-size beds, sitting area, and private bath. Sylvia serves a hearty breakfast in the main ranch house and will accommodate special dietary needs with advance notice. Ideal spot for weddings, retreats, and workshops. Travellers with horses have access to the barn, with five box stalls, or one of the paddocks. Eleven camping sites with water, firewood, and two bathrooms are also available on site.

GETTING THERE: From Wildwood, drive 11 KM west to RR102. Turn left (south) for 0.5 KM.

Once you have finished your explorations west of Evansburg, you can follow the Cowboy Trail as it continues its final leg north on Hwy. 22 from Evansburg to Mayerthorpe, the official end of the trail. As you head north from Evansburg, watch for the sign to Rangeton Park on the right (east) side of the road. It's a short 12 kilometre drive east to the end of the road, where the park sits on the banks of the Pembina River. Every June it is the site of the Rangeton Farmers' Day Festival, where musicians and bands from across the province come together for three days of non-stop entertainment. There is even a covered stage and dance floor. The park is open year-round and is a beautiful spot if you are camping or just stopping for a picnic. There are two Cowboy Trail partners located along Hwy. 22 on your way to Mayerthorpe.

Rustic Ridge Ranch and Lodge

www.rusticridgeranch.com

Ted and Ria Braaksma
P.O. Box 389, Evansburg, AB, T0E 0T0
T: 780-727-2042
E: tedria@rusticridgeranch.com
ACCEPTS V, MC, AMEX
Open all year. Dutch and German spoken.

This working cattle ranch sits on top of a ridge that offers views of over 200 kilometres on a clear day. Part of the cedar-lined lodge was originally built in 1894. In 1987 it was completely rebuilt, and renovated with large picture windows, open-air verandahs, and a western décor.

WHAT THEY OFFER: Seven rooms, most with an ensuite bathroom; a new fully self-contained two-bedroom log cabin sits in a secluded spot on the side of the ridge with sweeping views; B&B or country vacations, reunions, and retreats, including all meals, snacks, and use of the hot tub. Meals can be booked for groups of ten or more. Ideal for weddings and private functions. Activities include hiking, horseback riding (bring your own horse), and cross-country skiing on the ranch or adjacent Crown land.

GETTING THERE: From the junction of Hwy. 22 and Hwy. 16, head north on Hwy. 22 for 12.5 KM to Park Court Road and follow the sign. The ranch is on the right (east) side of the highway.

Waddy — a young greenhorn or untried cowboy

Hog Wild Specialties

Deb and Earl Hagman
Box 1209, Mayerthorpe, AB, T0E 1N0
T: 780-786-4627 or 1-888-668-9453
E: dhagman@hogwild.ab.ca
ACCEPTS PC

www.hogwild.ab.ca

Open all year

Deb and Earl Hagman have been raising beef on their Lily Creek Ranch for 23 years, but in 1991 they added European wild boars to the mix. They consistently have between 300 and 700 animals at various stages of maturity. You can sample their wild boar meat at some of the best white-tablecloth restaurants in Canada and the US, including Teatro's and the River Café in Calgary. While you're at the ranch, you can choose from a variety of meat products to take home.

WHAT THEY OFFER: One-day wild-boar bow-hunting adventure complete with guide, crossbows and lunch. Processing available at nearby abattoir. Hunters can camp or rent a rustic cabin with wood heat, sauna, and hot tub (meals on request). As well, whole animal barbecues for private parties and sporting events.

GETTING THERE: From the junction of Hwy. 22 and Hwy. 16, head north on Hwy. 22 for 40 KM (or south from Mayerthorpe for 7 KM) to Secondary Hwy. 647. Go west on Secondary Hwy. 647 for 14.4 KM. Turn right (north) at RR101 and go 5.6 KM.

European wild boars.
HOG WILD SPECIALTIES

Mayerthorpe

T: 780-786-2416

www.townofmayerthorpe.ab.ca

Mayerthorpe took its name from "Mayer," the name of an engineer who homesteaded along the Little Paddle River in 1908, and "thorpe," a north England word meaning "little village." The region was settled by European homesteaders in the early 1900s. Settlers used three major trails – called the Three Trails Home – to come into the area. The Junkins Trail came north from Wildwood and lies east of the present-day Cowboy Trail; the Lac St. Anne Trail came west from the area close to the Catholic Mission on Lac St. Anne, established by the famous Father Lacombe; and the Belvedere Trail followed the general direction of the never-built Grand Trunk Pacific railway from Edmonton, northwest through Fort Assiniboine. Once the rail line between Edmonton and Edson was completed, settlement accelerated northward from Evansburg, with a considerable influx of immigrants during the 1930s, mainly from the dried-out prairies. Agriculture remains the mainstay of the entire area, with mixed farms producing grain,

THE END OF THE TRAIL

Although it actually ends about six kilometres north of town, for all intents and purposes, the Cowboy Trail ends in Mayerthorpe. So it's probably fitting that the town has renamed a portion of 52 Street (which is Hwy. 22 as it travels through town) to Denny Hay Drive. Denny Hay is one of the famous Hay brothers who ranch nearby – living proof that cowboys are alive and well in Mayerthorpe. Since turning professional in 1989, the brothers have won a string of championships in saddle bronc competition. Besides winning the $50,000 at the Calgary Stampede, Denny was the gold medallist at the 2002 Olympics, 1989 Rookie of the Year for Canada, and three times Canadian champion. Rod was the 1989 Rookie of the Year for the World, eight times Canadian Champion, and a five-time winner of the big $50,000. You'll notice that the

The end of the Cowboy Trail.
TOWN OF MAYERTHORPE

town sign also mentions Daryn Knapp. He's another local cowboy who competed as a team roper in the 2002 Olympics and was the 2002 Canadian Champion.

hay, and a wide variety of livestock, including bison, elk, and wild boar. The County of Lac St. Anne is one of the major beef producing areas of the province. It claims to have more cattle than any other county in Alberta.

Points of Interest in Mayerthorpe

Mayerthorpe Tourist Information Centre
4406 Crockett Street, next to the Fas Gas
T: 780-786-4497
Open mid-May to August 31, Wednesday to Sunday, 11:00 AM to 7:00 PM

Last of the Prairie Sentinels Still Standing

In 1999 the last remaining elevator in town was in danger of demolition. Concerned citizens formed the Country Elevator Society and were successful in raising over $25,000 needed to save it from the wrecking ball. Since then the society has worked to establish a museum and tribute to the prairie grain elevator. These landmarks once dominated the skyline of practically every small town across the prairies – in Alberta there were over 1700 of these giants built to serve the province's expanding grain industry. In most communities they have been reduced to heaps of rubble, as concrete regional terminals gradually replaced them. Summer tours of the Mayerthorpe elevator can be arranged by calling 780-786-2348 or 780-785-3289.

The last Mayerthorpe elevator escaped the wrecking ball.
COUNTRY ELEVATOR SOCIETY

Grub Stop

Bentley's Family Restaurant, 5014 – 50 Street, 780-786-4870; Burger Baron, 5004 – 45 Avenue, 780-786-2411; Curiosities Tea House, 4809 – 51 Street, 780-786-2910; Lariat, 4905 – 50 Street, 780-786-2177; Mayerthorpe Golf Course, Hwy. 22 south of town, 780-786-4737; Pizza Napoli, 4918 – 50 Street, 780-786-2336; Shorty's Kitchen, 5015 – 50 Avenue, 780-786-4111.

OFF THE BEATEN PATH FROM MAYERTHORPE

Rochfort Bridge: Take Hwy. 43 southeast of Mayerthorpe to the hamlet of Rochfort Bridge and follow the signs. This route will take you to a back road viewing spot where you can stop your car and have a good look at the bridge. It is 33.5 metres (110 feet) high in the centre, and is the longest all-wooden trestle in Canada. If you're hungry, the nearby Rochfort Bridge Trading Post sells a Bridge Burger that claims to be the biggest on Hwy. 43 – if you can eat it in 20 minutes, it's free.

Ol' Pembina River Ferry Crossing RV Park and Antique Museum: Take Hwy. 43 southeast of Mayerthorpe, past Rochfort Bridge. Watch for the sign just past the Shell service station on the right (south) side of the road. The park is at the end of the road. The ferry provided service for car and truck traffic across the Pembina until 1954 and was a major crossing in the area. The museum houses a wonderful collection of restored and operational tractors as well as pioneer artifacts. The Coca-Cola room is straight out of the fifties, with plenty of memorabilia and, of course, ice cream and snacks.

Sangudo Sundial Elevator: Take Hwy. 43 southeast of Mayerthorpe for 17 kilometres to the village of Sangudo. This unique landmark is the only known sundial to take its shape from the country grain elevator. At a height of 6.4 metres (21 feet) and a total weight of 40 tons, it is one of the biggest sundials in existence. It can tell you local solar time, true north, and geographical information including latitude, longitude, and elevation.

Sangudo Sundial Elevator.
L. ANDREWS

Prefontaine/Brock Lakes Provincial Natural Area: Take Secondary Hwy. 757 south from Sangudo to TWP562. Turn left (east) and go to RR63. Turn right (south) and follow the road as it skirts Brock and Prefontaine Lakes, then heads west back to Secondary Hwy. 757. The lakes are great spots for viewing pelicans and cormorants.

One Cowboy Trail partner is located along Secondary Hwy. 757. You can reach it by driving south on Secondary Hwy. 757 from Sangudo, or by going east on Hwy. 16 from Hwy. 22 and then north on Secondary Hwy. 757.

Lakeview Guest Ranch   www.lakeviewguestranch.com
Eckhard and Diana Krah
Box 133, Sangudo, AB, T0E 2A0
T: 780-785-3270
E: dekrah@telusplanet.net
ACCEPTS V, MC, AMEX, TC, US CASH
Open all year. German spoken.

WHAT THEY OFFER: Comfortable country-style guest rooms with private or shared bathrooms, large sitting room and verandah in a new addition to the ranch house. Options include B&B; hourly horseback riding and ATV tours; one-day guided fishing trips with lunch and boat included; three-, five- and seven-day Country Living packages, including meals, ranch activities, and access to mountain bikes and canoes (the ranch overlooks its own private lake); three-, five- and seven-day Ranch Action Packages add trail riding and ATV adventures; a two-week all-inclusive package combines all of these activities with a sightseeing day-trip to Edmonton and area tours to local rodeos and attractions; all-inclusive 14-day Ranch and Rocky Mountain Adventure adds horseback riding from high mountain camp near Nordegg; the 10-day Parkland Big Game Package provides hunting in the wilderness of Parkland County while enjoying ranch accommodations in the evening; the one- to three-month Ranch Experience Stay caters to young adults, 18 to 35, who want a more in-depth ranch experience and to learn about the tourism business; ideal for international visitors looking to improve their English and learn about the country; will also customize packages to meet your specific needs.

The ranch overlooks its own private lake.
LAKEVIEW GUEST RANCH

GETTING THERE: From Hwy. 22, head east on Hwy. 16 to Secondary Hwy. 757. Turn left (north) for 22.7 KM and watch for the sign. The ranch is on the left (west) side of the road. From Sangudo, the ranch is 12.5 KM south on Secondary Hwy. 757.

The Cowboy's Prayer – For the End of the Trail

This prayer often appears on the tombstones of cowboys, marking the end of the trail:

> Heavenly father, we pause, mindful of the many blessings you have bestowed on us. We ask that you be with us at this rodeo and we pray that you will guide us in the arena of life. Help us Lord to live our lives in such a manner that when we make the last inevitable ride to the country up there, where the grass grows lush green and stirrup-high, and the water runs cool, clear and deep, that you, as our last judge, will tell us that our entry fees are paid.

Cowboy Trail partner for this area added just prior to press time:

Bent River Ranch Vacations

P.O. Box 6361, Drayton Valley, AB, T7A 1R5
T: 780-727-4564
E: lawood2@telus.net

Recommended Reading

Birds of Alberta by Chris Fisher and John Acorn
Boondoggles and Bonanzas by Brian Brennan
Cowboy's Dictionary by Carl Huff
Cowboy Logic: The Wit and Wisdom of the West by Ted Stone
Men of the Saddle: Working Cowboys of Canada by Ted Grant
Scoundrels and Scallywags: Characters From Alberta's Past by Brian Brennan
Story Behind Alberta Names by Harry Sanders
Trees and Shrubs of Alberta by Kathleen Wilkinson
Wildlife Watching by Michael Kerr

Index: Cowboy Trail References by Category

Recipes

Acknowledgements

No undertaking of this size gets done without a great deal of help from many sources. Without the co-operation of the Cowboy Trail Association, who allowed us to use their name, maps and logo, and who gave us access to their members, the project could not have proceeded. I would like to thank all the partners along the Cowboy Trail who welcomed me into their homes and businesses and who gave me a number of interesting story leads and suggestions. Several went out of their way to spend time answering my questions and to provide me with photographs and original sources of information that I hope have made the book more interesting.

Thank you particularly to Ginny Donahue for sharing her beautiful photographs and to Debbie and Tony Webster for taking an afternoon out of their busy day to tell me about Barbed-Wire Johnny and Sleepy Cat, and for giving me access to Betty Webster's wonderful tale of her first year spent out West as a new war bride. Thanks to Farley Wuth, the Curator at the Kootenai Brown Pioneer Village in Pincher Creek, for taking the time to help even though he really didn't have it to spare; to Barb Proudler of the Caroline Historical Society, for tracking down a picture of George Bugbee and his record breaking grizzly bear; to Marilyn MacKay-Waddell of the Sundre & District Historical Society for setting up the interview with long time rancher Reuben Olson; to Margie Moore for her many story leads; to the Cochrane Historical & Archival Preservation Society for their information on Cochrane; and of course, to the ladies at the High River Centennial Library who cheerfully managed to find everything on my list from sources all over the province. Thank you also to Ted Stone for allowing me to quote from his gem of western humour *Cowboy Logic: The Wit and Wisdom of the West*. Several books were also particularly useful as references, including Harry Sander's *The Story Behind Alberta Names: How Cities, Towns, Villages and Hamlets Got Their Names;* Hugh Dempsey's *Indian Names for Alberta Communities;* and Carl A. Huff's *The Cowboy's Dictionary: A Dictionary for Cowboy Poets and Their Fans*. Finally, a special thank you to Barbara Dacks of *Legacy Magazine*. Without your vote of confidence none of this would have ever happened.

L A R R A I N E   A N D R E W S   is a freelance writer who makes her home in High River, Alberta, a short distance from the Cowboy Trail. She grew up on a farm near Vulcan, Alberta where her lifelong addiction to the history of the Wild West began with her dad's collection of Zane Grey novels.

J·A N E T   N A S H , a resident of High River, Alberta, has been drawing with pen and ink and pencil for over 25 years. She also does oils, pastels and coloured pencil. Check out some of her work on www.artincanada.com and www.hockeyartinternational.com.